The Year of Rabid Reflections:

Letters from nobody

-

<u>Part 1</u>

Copyright © Arin Robert Aberasturi

All rights reserved by the Author. No part of this publication may be reproduced, stored or transmitted in any form or by any means, electronic, mechanical, photocopying, recording, scanning, or otherwise without written permission from thepublisher. It is illegal to copy this book, post it to a website, or distribute it by anyother means without permission.

Arin Aberasturi has no responsibility for the persistence or accuracy of URLs forexternal or third-party Internet Websites referred to in this publication and doesnot guarantee that any content on such Websites is, or willremain, accurate orappropriate.

Designations used by companies to distinguish their products are often claimed as trademarks. All brand names and product names used in this book and on its cover are trade names, service marks, trademarks and registered trademarks of their respective owners. The publishers and the book are not associated with any product or vendor mentioned in this book. None of the companies referenced within the book have endorsed the book. Some comments may be found on Day 342: April 5th, 2025, p.g. 935.

ISBN: 979-8-9903663-0-5

To Beauty,
I am still trying to write real poetry.

Contents

Day 0: April 28th, 2024.......................p.g. 1
Day 1: April 29th, 2024..................... p.g. 4
Day 2: April 30th, 2024..................... p.g. 7
Day 3: May 1st, 2024......................... p.g. 10
Day 4: May 2nd, 2024........................ p.g. 13
Day 5: May 3rd, 2024......................... p.g. 17
Day 6: May 4th, 2024......................... p.g. 20
Day 7: May 5th, 2024......................... p.g. 23
Day 8: May 6th, 2024......................... p.g. 26
Day 9: May 7th, 2024......................... p.g. 30
Day 10: May 8th, 2024....................... p.g. 33
Day 11: May 9th, 2024....................... p.g. 36
Day 12: May 10th, 2024..................... p.g. 40
Day 13: May 11th, 2024..................... p.g. 43
Day 14: May 12th, 2024..................... p.g. 45
Day 15: May 13th, 2024..................... p.g. 47
Day 16: May 14th, 2024.................... p.g. 50
Day 17: May 15th, 2024.................... p.g. 53
Day 18: May 16th, 2024.................... p.g. 56
Day 19: May 17th, 2024.................... p.g. 59
Day 20: May 18th, 2024..................... p.g. 62
Day 21: May 19th, 2024.............. p.g. 64
Day 22: May 20th, 2024....... p.g. 66
Day 23: May 21st, 2024.................... p.g. 69
Day 24: May 22nd, 2024............. p.g. 72
Day 25: May 23rd, 2024............. p.g. 75
Day 26: May 24th, 2024......... p.g. 78
Day 27: May 25th, 2024......... p.g. 81
Day 28: May 26th, 2024.......... p.g. 84
Day 29: May 27th, 2024.............. p.g. 87
Day 30: May 28th, 2024.............. p.g. 90
Day 31: May 29th, 2024.............. p.g. 92
Day 32: May 30th, 2024............... p.g. 95
Day 33: May 31st, 2024.................. p.g. 97
Day 34: June 1st, 2024................... p.g. 100
Day 35: June 2nd, 2024............... p.g. 103
Day 36: June 3rd, 2024................. p.g. 106
Day 37: June 4th, 2024.............. p.g. 108
Day 38: June 5th, 2024.............. p.g. 111
Day 39: June 6th, 2024.............. p.g. 114
Day 40: June 7th, 2024.............. p.g. 116
Day 41: June 8th, 2024................ p.g. 118

Day 42: June 9th, 2024............. p.g. 121
Day 43: June 10th, 2024.................p.g. 124
Day 44: June 11th, 2024............. p.g. 127
Day 45: June 12th, 2024..................... p.g. 129
Day 46: June 13th, 2024.................. p.g. 132
Day 47: June 14th, 2024.................. p.g. 135
Day 48: June 15th, 2024.................. p.g. 138
Day 49: June 16th, 2024........ p.g. 141
Day 50: June 17th, 2024.................. p.g. 144
Day 51: June 18th, 2024............... p.g. 147
Day 52: June 19th, 2024................. p.g. 149
Day 53: June 20th, 2024........................... p.g. 152
Day 54: June 21st, 2024..................... p.g. 155
Day 55: June 22nd, 2024..................... p.g. 158
Day 56: June 23rd, 2024..................... p.g. 161
Day 57: June 24th, 2024.............p.g. 164
Day 58: June 25th, 2024.................. p.g. 167
Day 59: June 26th, 2024.................. p.g. 170
Day 60: June 27th, 2024.................... p.g. 172
Day 61: June 28th, 2024..................... p.g. 174
Day 62: June 29th, 2024..................... p.g. 176
Day 63: June 30th, 2024.................. p.g. 178
Day 64: July 1st, 2024....................... p.g. 181
Day 65: July 2nd, 2024................... p.g. 184
Day 66: July 3rd, 2024........................ p.g. 187
Day 67: July 4th, 2024....................... p.g. 190
Day 68: July 5th, 2024.................... p.g. 192
Day 69: July 6th, 2024..................... p.g. 194
Day 70: July 7th, 2024.................... p.g. 197
Day 71: July 8th, 2024....................... p.g. 200
Day 72: July 9th, 2024....................... p.g. 203
Day 73: July 10th, 2024........................ p.g. 206
Day 74: July 11th, 2024..................... p.g. 208
Day 75: July 12th, 2024............. p.g. 211
Day 76: July 13th, 2024.............. p.g. 214
Day 77: July 14th, 2024......... p.g. 217
Day 78: July 15th, 2024............... p.g. 220
Day 79: July 16th, 2024............... p.g. 223
Day 80: July 17th, 2024............ p.g. 225
Day 81: July 18th, 2024.............. p.g. 228
Day 82: July 19th, 2024..................... p.g. 231
Day 83: July 20th, 2024.........................p.g. 234
Day 84: July 21st, 2024......................p.g. 237
Day 85: July 22nd, 2024................. p.g. 240

Day 86: July 23rd, 2024................... p.g. 243
Day 87: July 24th, 2024................... p.g. 245
Day 88: July 25th, 2024...................... p.g. 248
Day 89: July 26th, 2024............... p.g. 251
Day 90: July 27th, 2024...................... p.g. 254
Day 91: July 28th, 2024............... p.g. 257

Intro

What is this?

- This is not a book. This is not a story. This is not a poem. This is a project, and the medium is the self. Every day for a year, I wrote at least a thousand words every day. Think of these as a series of letters, which are written about everything: My emotions, thoughts, experiences, regrets, politics, anger, fear, economics, friendships, family, history, poetry, etc.

Why did I write this book?

- One particular day, I was not doing very, but then I started to write, and I felt better. So, I wrote again the next day. And the next day. And the next. Then I decided I wanted to finish, and to learn what I could do, if I find the motivation.

Why is it in rhyme?

- I found that using this method helped me to write, and that the pattern of sounds showed me something bright. Few of the patterns are perfect, but neither am I. The important thing is that I don't feel so shy, because this is artistic, and not merely me managing to whine.

What is with the pictures?

- Each one was hand-drawn on a metal chalkboard, and designed in some way to match the letter I wrote that day.

Who is Beauty?

- A 'Precious Amalgam', and the answer varies: A person, people in general, myself, the world, fate, Gods, Devils, dreams, faries, on and on it goes. Perhaps most of all, my subject is some Platonic Ideal, which is a reality beyond all my illusions, and the origin of sunlight on the world. Like my matching work before this, I write to a 'you' because otherwise nothing comes out, so if you recognize yourself, or part of yourself, feel free to give me a shout.

Any trigger warnings?

- Oh yeah. I ended up writing about every personal problem I've had for the last twenty years, as I sought the meanig of life in the midst of dealing with surroundings of dementia and death. This is shadow-work dark and drear, and if you are not comfortable with feelings of rage, despair, fear, hopelessness, and inadequacy, then I advise you not to read this book. However, I think I've created something here which is worth a look. I've forged what poor steel there is in me into the shape of a hook, so that I may catch an imaginary fish and burn my fingers on it. I'm not sure Wisdom I shall ever find, but even blind, maybe out of the cave we may yet climb.

Day 0: April 28th, 2024

To Beauty,

What should I say, what should I dream, what should I scream, or 'should' I at all? For me, this is the call from heaven to hell. - I don't know where I dwell, my hands are my own, but not my song, as I in this world trundle along. No hand to reach, no hand to hold, I do my duty, but it is so cold. - I fear that my fire itself grows old. Not elderly as the eldar, eternally smiling and happy, willing to fight, willing to die, willing to try, to learn and make ten thousand mistakes, because at the end of the day on this earth forever we stay. Yet this does not grip me: A thousand ways I've tried, attempted to live and find my pride, but it fails and falls, it falters and flashes before my eyes. My soul itself quails, I wail, and amid the wrack and ruin of my every day, as my fire turns to clay, hopes and sunlight made dull, burned, unburnished in use, I have with my devils and angels no truce. I have in myself so little trust, only continuing as I must, until my luck turns to bust, and I am cast forth again! To nowhere, to nothing, to lying. My life is not so bad, in fact in many ways it's quite rad, but I, whether a grandson or a lad, have no home nor land. There's no place to go, there's no place to run, I am stuck with myself: I'm the only one!

  Look in the mirror and who stares back at me, but I? Look at the sky, shout to the comet why, why, why, as it burning flashes, flaming crashes, ice turned to fog, water into plasma, and a rocky core made sand, ground down by life here on earth. Down the heavens fall to their final berth, as they, turned to clay, mingle with our hands, our feet, our ashes. - We are star-stuff, we are memories lost, we are facts regained, and we are our own blood leaving a stain. This is the strain: The life-stream, invisible, impossible thing, long memories of when we were an existential being. We have made our choices, we have accepted the consequences, and oh how we wish to go back, to return and make up for our lack of courage and openness, of truth and knowledge, of daring and understanding. Oh as, again, we lay on our bed in the middle of the night, recalling words and smiles, or frowns and evasions, we feel ourselves made traitor to ourselves. Second-guessing, third time seeking for a blessing, we don't know what we're missing, but we know we haven't got it. We have not found it, whatever it was, whatever we had, or didn't or weren't. We are made, by our own actions, not humans but ants, not spirits but machines, not intellectuals but poetic screams. We are ripping apart our own seams, undoing the ties that bound us and the rope that found us, following this method to a madness which saved us in darkness, during those long years ago when we were nothing less than a danger to ourselves. We drew a circle wide, we inscribed it across the sky, we said these are limits and boundaries. Even if I don't know why, I will not cross them, I will not try. No longer will I try. No treasure planet for them nor I, no pirate but simply a stooge, I will grow up never daring to face another bruise. That's what I chose, that's what I choose, a thousand times, for a thousand days, when across my sight a fire did blaze. My ancient pyramids? I set my hand to them and saw them be raised, then I rose, and I leaped from them to my grave. I was, and am, forever a knave. Not a peasant nor a knight, not an artist nor a priest, but only that thing which is the least: Not me, not I, not creation but the flesh. - I was fleeced. By myself, for myself, in myself, out of myself, I forbear to sail. I quailed and I quivered and I was quiet... Not because I wished to, not because I intended to, but simply because there was a leeward wind driving me to sands of sin, one of seven though I'm not sure which, but I crashed and fell, drowned in the sea like a fish, until one day I washed up on the rocks, where I had been tossed by fate, storm, and a mermaid. Ha! I told myself that I had been saved, but I had been poisoned, covered up with black ink, for upon me now was writ: If you had been a thing with more wit, you would not have ended up here. Be ashamed of yourself my dear; you needed help because you were full of fear.

    Now as days drew past and holy nights drew near, I sought myself in winter to rise, and to my greatest surprise, I felt that I was in fact by myself despised. Mask torn off, mirror is glistening, I wonder if anyone is listening? My eyes be closed; my mouth be shut, but my hands, my hands, they work: They spit out words, they paint, they chalk, they dance, they sing, they say to the world (who is I): This one am not a thing to be despised. Be-ing walks here in the shadows; at night I wonder in the shallows; the waves draw near, I can't feel my feet anymore, but everything else is clear. - Fight and die against the wall, be driven there with broken saber, chance it all. This dull, dumb thing is all I have, but perhaps it is all I need. Some other person broke it on their knees, but I grabbed it and saved - What? I don't know yet, and perhaps I never shall, til a thousand years have passed from then to now. I am like a cow, brilliant sunbeam, endless rivers of ice, I lick and pull up gods with their knives. I am slashed and burned, but somehow, miraculously, alive, and in my Art, that is for what I strive. Win or lose, fail or feast, famine perhaps, but I shall not forever be the least. I will not be Fenrir-beast, chained-enslaved. I will be free. I will be saved. I will save myself. I will pull both me and I from the grave, be reforged, rebound, remade, ugly sword, an ugly sword forever perhaps, but strong.

Hevydd once made me, as he did he sang, and today I sing again. I will be rebound, reforged, remade. - I will myself save. Maybe if I say it often enough it will be true, three times round for recited spell: I will be rebound, reforged, remade, I'll write a book, and in that way myself save. At the end of the day, a valkyrie will pull me from the grave, not because I died, but because I was brave. I lived, I tried, I said to myself it does not matter why, just write and write and write, and you're not going to do this all right or all wrong. It's going to be half-way gold, and half-way dull, pulling yourself in two directions like a two-headed mull. Up, down and all around, confusion resounds - but stand your ground. Stand your ground, because there is no place else but on yourself to stand! Pound your fist and make sounds, and say I can do this. I can do this. Scream to the stars, I can do this, I can do this. Like a mantra I repeat this Beauty, I can do this. I turn my dream, my thought, my wish, my being into a scream, draw a circle round me and turn; I'll cast a spell to learn for what I yearn; I'll look in a mirror, and find out why and how hot I burn. Is this like Frollo in greed, or Frodo in need of rest? I have my life, and it is a test. I've lost half of my chances already, but not all. I never dressed up for the ball, and had a hundred terrible bad falls, but at one winter night I heard the call: Failing is better than never trying at all. It hurts less; and if I'm sure to make a mess, in the last year I have learned: better chaos than nothing. Better Old Night than giving up without a fight, even if I am not sure what I am fighting, or how.

My speech is to the unreal, my thought towards the untrue, and I am confused before this onslaught of time and place, of smiles and frowns, of nightmares and day-walkers, and all the other things that shall go down from mountain into town, following the river but never leaving the bridge's bounds. I cannot cross this raging white line, and I cannot draw from my chest this painful spike, an alloy deep and cold which tears me from my mind and my soul. - I am no freedom fighter, I am no thief, I am not even that which once did breath: No zombie, not vampire, nor fish in the sea; I am mere dust, starshine, and me.

Day 1: April 29th, 2024

To Beauty,

    Sometimes I wish I could escape this life, and this pull of earth. I will read a book, or play a game, and then feel as if I am going insane: Nothing matters, nothing hurts, but existence itself feels like a jerk. Not a mean bully, not a round tully, not a thick jelly, but rather the kind of person, place, or thing, where it is hard to breath, because of the weight between the air and the ground. I feel the mass of myself increase, and life turning or twirling turns me into a redwood burl, some odd growth in the side of a tree which cannot put forth leaves. Cut me out and maybe I could grow, lay me down in the sod and perhaps one day far away I might stand tall, but as long as I remain part of the circle, as long as I am bound to the strain of a tree, the house and family that surrounds me, then I am recalled to be as I was and am, always be forever and alone, as this 'thing', not me. I don't know what to do, I don't know where to turn, and I simply never was able to learn just what to do with my present self; let alone what to become. I am going through life as if I was numb, my arms and legs filled with tingles and shade, not intention and flame. My eyes travel too far, my soul too deep, and yet my spirit into the world cannot quite creep. I remain bound to my tree, bound to my roots, alive only because of that sap made by others: Hopes and Dreams.

    Oh, I have my fair share of personal screams, but they and I are unseemly even in the least part of us. Shall a stranger offer me praise for my following of duty (my apparent following), or my inoffensiveness and patience, then I do not feel grand nor glad, I do not feel smart or silly, I do not feel as if I was marching up the hills or sliding down a rainbow. No - I only feel so bad that I cannot do more, that my power is less, that I am weak and prone to a life full of nothingness. One such as I simply has no heart to reach the sky, and I do not know what I shall do when I finally die. Will heaven's gate let me pass because I did as I was asked, or shall they have for me their own inquisitions, dire questions about why I did what I did, or failed to do what I could? Shall I follow the rules, or shall I be free, and if I am free, then what does that mean for me? Responsibility, responsibility: How I ended, how I started, and how in the middle I darted round and round like a dandelion seed which never struck the ground. I am not cloud-stuff, I am not wind, I am not sky; all I am is shy, shy, and shy: Afraid to show, to be, to care, darting near then away again, as fair is fair.

I received what I asked for, I have obtained what I worked for, and is it so bad? Not, not, not - not that much at all, not terrible in the least, by any judges' feast I am not a beast, and have not had the life of one either, but what does it matter? This the question, this the answer: What's the point? That very issue pulls me out of joint, as in December and January, November and far, far after that, I fight, I try, do not surrender, but - flee perhaps? I am not filled with glee, I am pushed by wind towards the lee; I am water in a cup; I am enchained only because I am weak and cold, like ice I break not fold. I tell myself that sad story, and it is old. Can I ever be more bold? Tell the truth or make it so, run and run but I shall flow, from mountain to sea, and rainfalls and rivers all for me, a burl knocked loose from that ever-green tree. Where shall I land, how shall I drown, what drums pound through my blood, what resounds, Tarzan beating on his chest, or the Emperor bowing at Mulan's behest; I am thrown into that lion-ants nest, brought to meet the queen, then told that I should flee; I am a hen not a rooster, I am a chick not a bird, I am a plow not a sword, I am a breeze never a storm. - I didn't ask and dare Fate for this, never sought blessing, never demanded rest, I simply said I won't give up, even if I don't know what I'm doing; even if I am tossed, I have not been bossed; no fiddle in my hand, but the loss of power is not the loss of command. I own myself, the ability to make a stand, as I reach out my hand; not to guide nor guard, not to plea nor save, but simply to write and draw, to read and rave. I feel myself going insane, but so what, what matter that, if I am cut loose at last?

Chains in I or on me be broken, taken to task, I carve again my own mask. This face I have, this persona presented, I am relented. Perhaps these words are rented, pulled from the ether, my starlight infused, by sunlight I was bruised, my hearts-blood I use as ink to write again and again, less painful now as I seek the impossible to win, a smile openly from my side, as I release rock's eternal bide; a hundred times my soul been taken, a hundred times my soul been shaken, in reality and a dream, in poems and memories and things, catching my breath to me I bring forth such a sound as I shall never again write, and make, and be!

As I transfer on, I turn and tumble, fifth book I rumble, I turn myself into a bumbling bundle, like those hornets who always pick the most inconvenient land to rain their spit upon, raise paper towers, mud and those bestagons, the hexagons, saving energy by melting, reforming, returning to lowest orbital. A thousand times I've done my best, fifteen hundred words I've written, and now I take a rest. Not here and now, (for This isn't it), but I've turned a trick: Gypsy-lad with flashy scarf, eyes that spark, and singing for a lark, in the woods, to a tree, to a burl, to a bumblebee. I fall to my knees but do not pray; I kiss the ground and say thank you for the save. Now, later, soon, I get up again, continue on, take my supper plate and suffer the scorn, but that's enough. - I am reborn. Burl no longer but tree, cut myself loose, I'll stand, not flee. My roots are deep, and I am free. Beauty is an illusion, but that's A-Ok with me. After all, I said I was free. Third times the charm...I'm free. I may stay onthe ground, or if i want to, I can leave.

Day 2: April 30th, 2024

To Beauty,

    One step every day, that's all the promise I have made. Nothing more from me could be bade, no matter how I fought, where or when, why-what-for, or through however many doors. Gates I opened for myself, passages made, entered my heart into secret glades, forested stories covering times, and red desert lies revealing sights of mirages and ghosts: Casper and Dresden. Spirits untethered or unnamed, I saved my greatest rage for that which was betrayed and betrayer, an unwritten-promise-breaker, that to whom I tried to be a slayer, as I reached out and never said to the world help, assist, please search and this lock untwist, but they never did. They never saw, and I myself never knew at all. Only that something was wrong, and everything was unright, and that I was happiest as I lay alone in my bed at night, reading a book, transferred beyond, like a comet reflected in a pond. - Transformed from light to streak, from ice to a memory neat, from a simple mortal street, into an immortal power neat. I drunk and I dove beyond the pale, into the woods, under the veil, and I caught glimpses of fishes-mail, axes and swords, a thousand gleaming, forgotten, golden, hordes. Of dwarves and dragon-fire I read, of elves and twisted wire, of mortal men and their hidden hell-fire, of angels and their secret desire. I never knew my self's design, and I never knew what to do in my time, but only wandered lost and alone, urgently pushing numbers in my cell-phone.

    But the time had passed for operators or police, for nets or spears or hooks or feasts. I was turned into a 'thing', one of the the least, a surviver, a soldier, a child meandering, as I sought to explode, to undo my load, to throw myself over the flows, Niagra to fall, and the rocks to break it all. - Not mud but iron, not bronze but steel, I became to myself unreal, a universal inspiration without a single kind of human nation. I am Huan, I am Priscilla, Raki, Clare, Theresa, no smile me, but only an attempt to flee; never beg, never plea, not I, don't deserve to be saved, if I am it is only as rags; I must save myself, I must, I can, this my own ears command: To seek, to find, and not to yield, allow your Ch'i clear and circular to congeal, breath in, breath out, slowly now don't shout, don't shut them out, don't run about, you have strength enough to see, if you just spend the time, and tie your knots up in terrible rhyme. Be a vader, be a flame, be a savior, be ashamed, seek and find and say your name, accept all that you have to blame: What you learned, what you forgot, how you fought, and what you fought not, then, in this way, gather up all that you've got. Forge a spear, forge a glaive, run and throw it into the flame, then be the fire, be the fight, be the light, and leave this reality behind to find another. Dream's inside, accept and admit to all of your lies, then turn them into truths, burned into your hide. With runes and letters, Phonecian sailors, we sail beyond the pillars of Hercules, to Atlantis, to Kiva, to the blue, we run and run and run straight through, before the wind, before the sky: Din's fires, Nayru's shrine, Great Fairy, what again was the line? Between the game and the reality, between the blame and the mortality, there is far more to this world than we think we see, or at least I hope there is for me.

With these eyes the passage had been opened, with these eyes the dawn is closed, in these fingers the stars repose. - Brown hair, long nose, I lie, like Pinnochio I lie, seeking to save myself from burning and crying, from being without purpose; my part played in the circus as a lion, to be mocked and fed, to be kept in a cage and tossed out when I'm dead. I am not a man of the shed, do not work in the mint as one of the dulled and done, creating other's money for others to spend. Nor am I the minor nor the master, not a teller, not one of the back-end accountants. I am not even a sweeper, a customer, a seeker for a loan. No, I am a thief, who has forgotten where he placed his bone. Like a dog I punch more numbers into the phone, letters too, starting with ABC, ending up at XYZ, a squiggle-line, a half-way fine, I'm ok, I'm ok I tell you, as long as I draw my art in time, as long as I never dare to cross that line. Like Roger I will fight underneath the pines, until Marines come to save me from my own foolish stupidity, as I spend my luck, ending out of liquidity, so back I tumble, back I turn, to the book again, to seek and to learn. I am become a Fern, some sorcerer elven-taught, who lives my life in instability, by sanity. I remain sane, and I hope to not take that to my grave. Manga and the letters, podcasts and stars, the teaching company and the word's of Lars - From Campbell, from Anakin, from Beowulf and more, I learned how Grendel knocked down the door.

I have no strength of mind nor limb: No, I had to draw a sword in order to win. I did not dare to face my sin, but only looked at the blade, the mirror, the sight, I myself made Medusa fight - but what had she done to me and mine? The quarrels of gods are forgot, ever since Alexsander cut the knot, and he fell, his promise forgotten, his chances lost, like Qin Shi Huang, the shadows overcame the bright light, light fell into darkest night, and like Nghia, his afro grew beyond the ability of a helmet to contain. We are so careful now, lest we lose our brain, or loosen our mind, for we have sought and seen the curses of time: How language has no meaning, and cause has no rhyme. One day we shall be lost, unable to buy our way back with a silver dime, unable to call, for there is no public utility left at all, in any of this wide world. Reality starts, begins, to fall upon our crumbling castle walls, but not today, not yet. - We aren't great, we aren't good, but we can take the one step, we can make ourselves a satrap, bowing beneath the wishes of the past, to bring ourselves home at last. One step a day, this is all I say, for one step a day I might sustain, no matter how I am otherwise swayed. Gungnir itself shall not bar my way, and where there is life there is hope, so that today - one step. That's all. Maybe more, never less, for heroes are lost, but hope remains. Or at least - such is what the books say, and I choose to believe them today.

Day 3: May 1st, 2024

To Beauty,

    Some days are so cold; some days I turn to mold. I never ever manage to feel old, but being too new is also a curse. Remade and rebound I could be, reforged a blade, recut a scythe, I am recruited my shards into a knife, as I rename and reclaim what was my life - but so what? Who, what, why, when, and where, this is just like growing my hair: Sign signaling signification. I dye it brown, white, blue, or red, but none of that matters if I don't leave my bed. Outer looks not reflecting inner sight, I look in the mirror and ask it fair, but it gives me blight, a poisoned apple: I don't matter, simply staying in place like a hat, like a stovepipe, a chimney swept by a weak-chinned sweeper, some rabbit-leaper; not a wolf nor a goat nor a frog, no emperor-llama, no bear's diorama, not even a parrot, I have no carrot: Only the whip, only my scorn: Osten Ard I was, lost before the Norns. Some days are so cold, and sometimes I feel so sick, that I dare not leave these forests to tramp through the fields. I dare not sail the seas; I cannot even fall down from my mountain tower. My leg hurts, my head hurts, I am not even alone in this yurt, and there is nothing I have for food, not even Gogurt, that maligned stick of goo, industrialized waste, saved to be eaten in indecent haste. I don't like it, I don't hate it, it's just that my brain is freezing, sour not sweet I'm tasting, as I in my haste attempt to make my way past the test; second door I open, third now again, into the sea-shore, against the Zebek tribe, I will always survive, but not necessarily thrive.

    Alone, I do not walk properly. I crawl, as I see no reason to risk it all, climb to the top of the world and twirl around in a ball, let it go, let it all go, because if I did then what would be left of me? The cold always bothered me deeply, for I was born under the moon, but made for the sunlight: I need those stars which are bright. I do not fight for me, I am not pretty nor strong, I struggle against that throng of fates and insults, powerlessness, unspeakable weakness, I stand aside, that's what I do. I have no pride, let someone else seek to exchange truth from lies, and swing their souls to break the tides. I do not play in the ocean shore, but stand in the north and the south upon walls of ice, I see the devils and the demons all playing nice, and I - I do not cook my rice but have it cold, for I have lost all cause to make it boldy. Light-headed, sugar-low, I pull back my bow and let it fly, but no arrow seeks to cry a message for those shy like I, who am cold, so cold. I write but cannot feel my fingers, I walk but do not know my toes. Are they there or not, sharp or round, white or black, red with blood, or blue in the fog? I am becoming one with the frog in the well, as I jump into danger running from a park ranger, some scrabble and scribble of tires in the mud, but I have my dangers, I have my legs, my running falls and trips, and if I can't feel my pain I may yet see it: Mark it, paint it, breath it, scream it, rip apart my seams, like a claymore I need repair, there are rips in me which give me power but at runious prices: I am left to my own mad devices. I am no scientist, no mega-blue creator, as I roll with my punches and talk to the stranger. - And I can, because I am in this blue-flame shield no danger, like a djinn I wonder the manger, all is empty, none is left, the fire is bereft, and so too are the wise, because as I have learned the nothingness they despise. For I paint you see, I write, I make living lies, I leap for the sky, and with five points round in a star I might summon a demon out this night, one of seven, pride before the fall, and in return one which is right, not Maya-born, but Green-Lanterns light. I have a hope which contiues to be bright.

I am cold, so very cold, but at last I grow in my frostbite bold. At dusk I sing, in dawn I weep, I see my Grandmother away from me slowly continue to creep, and I hear my Great-Grandfather's giant leap: One for mankind and one for him, there were three-thousand people who died for that sin, or at least that is the story I might say to myself, as my creation-imagination holds me close and warm. I try not to fall, to embrace the ice and end it all; I hear over the moon a wolf's howling call, white-tiger punch and black-wing kick, as memes fail and Lightsworn wanes, I seek in the mirror my ancient name, and I lose any sense of the worth of fame. Why is it important that I should know, why is it important that I should remember, why is it important that I must spend my temper? The ice I scrape from my lips: My tongue to thrust, my teeth to bite, Fenrir howls and Magni says I might. I have no hope now, I am still so cold, but maybe like an ice-yeti monster, I am bold.

Wampa take me, light-saber sway me, back and forth, I have no force, no power returns to me from the north. Healed at last, as if a bandage would pass inspection, I hope, I pray, as I lay me down at end of day, repeating myself for the third time with horrible ghastly rhyme. To Agatha I return my dime, admitting to myself that I have done the time for my crime, and now I should be free. Fool still, but what a fool, as my ice melts into a pool. I dip and dive, I drink and sup, I spend my words and they are, maybe, enough. I don't know what for, but they aren't just tough, they're sharp, and I'm not sure how I've been cut, I'm not sure how I'm a nut, I'm not sure what I've done wrong, I just know that I've been sold for a song; but what a song, and what a singer! Liringlas, the stars do glimmer, and through the Dutch and the Mary's, I see a shimmer. - Not nice and smooth or cold as ice, but instead the waves of that hpt knife, obsidian arrow-head, sign of strife, spell I've cast; to speak to find, to seek and never yield, I bury myself in that field. I am planted, I am plowed, I am watered, I am the Clow, some tarot formed of mystic now, as I say to myself: Stand up man, and be proud, even if you feel comfortable only being quiet not loud. You are a coward, but so what?   There are worse ways yet to be cowards than this, and worse ways to be brave. Remain yourself yet a knave, not a knight, but don't give up the fight. Don't give up, don't give up, don't give up, for where there is life there is hope, that at least remains, and even if you have lost the horse's reins, there comes a time when you must trust, to the wild, to the wind, and to the cold bear-skin: Beorn's kin, thy wishes for glory, happiness, safety, and sin. Dare greatly and daring fail, that second achievement is all that you have, and so what? Piccolo needed Nail, with his billiards-room and mushrooms, a little insane and obtuse perhaps, but two together were able to grasp that clear and silvered glass which said: This is beauty fair and bright, maybe Merida, or named Snow White; we may not have the whole answer tonight, but in the forest we can search, we could send Lurch to answer the door, and the mailman may be scared, but we welcome him to our floor, bring them fire who were cold in the north, as we bring our council here to berth. I was freezing but now I'm warm, not hot enough to see the sun, but beginning to burn. I don't know what I'm looking for, but I've told myself now that I can yearn, and I my own secret name am starting to learn.

Day 4: May 2nd, 2024

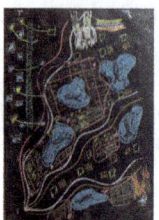

To Beauty,

    What is complicity? To be sure it is not my hand which holds, nor my sail which rears an ugly head, as I sit here in cold northern bed, with bells silent and mind without a wish, or at least none which may be granted as the curtains of time go swish-swish. I fear that I am become a switch, some instant, salt-pushed proton-maker, allowing energy to pass to a stranger, as equilibrium is lost, and the impossible is sought. I am tossed up into the sky, to fall on the ground and lie: Say that I care, or say that I don't, feel my heart bleed as my ambivalence goes up in smoke. It's so easy to ignore, so simple to close my eyes and say, not tell, of that time in Taiwan when I heard a bell. Midnight passing, night comes on, and in my head I start to sing a song: That like an elephant, one day I will find a land, one where I belong, no matter that I am living like a log, as some fallen memory of forgotten majesty for bugs to munch and mulch to touch, softer becoming with every drop which into me has sunk. I am the forest and the fern gully burning up as a result of acceping my folly, there is some poison in me, black and smoking and despoiling, living turning by magic into porcupine quills, hair which sunders, spears that wonder, a tail that waves and does not surrender. I feel myself gathering my temper. - We are accused of that old falsehood again, that I must either stand beside you, push for you to win, or else I am a thing filled with eternal sin. With us or against us, that's what they say, that we cannot have it both ways, to both pray we win and not persevere, to say I see the other side and both have a truth written on their hides. The world moralizes. - Pretends that good and bad are earning prizes, captured in battle, by pirates enslaved, yo ho ho and a bottle of rum, we'll continue to drink until we are numb. A thousand things, actions, and thoughts pull us apart, from the inner to the aught, from the outer to the should, from the might to the could, from the flame to the cold, and from courage to being bold.

    I am living, I am dying, I am trying, through this world I swim, lost until I see the wind, speak its name, a true word indeed, but one which is not grasped by anything with greed. I do not stand in your way, I do not halt you from marching to save the day, it's just that I have my own things to do, every which and every way, as I with fate also play. Blood and death and doom and gore, I have torn up the carpet from the floor, revealing what was not teak and oak, but metal and iron, concrete bare, cat-leavings soaked in, and a thousand years of forgotten hair bundled up in every corner. I am become before the dust a learner, with no trust left in me for right and wrong, for god and bad, for evil's song, seven virtues, seven sins, and only one path in life to win. - To find the truth and set it free, to show my heart to me and thee, to earn trust from minions of the endless sea, great EA, Chanburi and Samarkand, forgotten Babylon and the blazing sand. I see in colleges across the world hands upraised in toil and yearning, children who think that they can stop the world from turning, who fight Machiavelli and the french Raison, who think that maybe it is just possible to live life like a song, and trust in the good to make everything worth it in the end, no matter how long it takes. I am not the type of person who is going to sing that song in front of people.

  I don't know if I can change the hating and hated world. I barely believe I may move myself. I have spent half my life stuck on one single shelf. I was always in the cave, I was never going to do as I was bade, like Gilgamesh my treasures in the ground were laid, and like Mash I said that I would defend - but defend what? Defend why? I try and try, but what's the point to live not die, to feel their pain and think that I can shake the sky? If I do, then down may fall thunder-birds and flying snakes, jaguar-kings and the hearts which they have baked, a thousand visions of what happened and what was fake. I feel that I have made so many grand mistakes, lying in my coffin on the soil, dry and bereft, a corpse on display, and yet my fingers for a millennium have been at play, as I imbibed every word that ever soaked into clay; the blood and frustration, the tales of two nations. For thirty years I've lived, for three hundred years I've read, for three millennia on this world I have tread, and I am stuck, I am tired; I am half-dead. I tell you, grey in that dimension, wondering in the world facing other tensions, learning other lessons, and growing lesions in my stomach, my mouth, my back, my brain; I am sick and heavy and both inside, as on the other I hold my pride: To not move until I feel that spark imbibe, drink and apple of gods in size, rainbow bridge and Loki's lies. For grand purpose I would spend my prize, and for nothing less glorious than that, I would tear open my eyes to see forever. I see every side, and I don't know how it turns out, I just hope that my home is not destroyed, I hope that Ragnarok comes and yet I am overjoyed, because this burden presses on my shoulders: Pull me down, I enter into crazy town, where plastic burns and knives are forks, where cats are dogs and trees are things, where naiads and dryads float on the breeze, where faces in blankets laugh at me and tease; every event frightens me as much as every sudden breeze.

  What is complacency, what is silence, is it an excuse or is it a choice? Is it a job or a family, simply having no time, or thinking that it's all a fancy? I have seen this idealism before and I know in my heart that it may in fact turn the door, change the world, save one life, do that good which has no price, but I think that there is a difference between someone healthy and someone full of lice, and I don't know which I am, but I know that I am not nice: I race across the shattering ice, and maybe I should swim, but if I did, I don't think I would win, because I know the wild. I know of nature, red in tooth and claw, and it is but five hundred generations since the pyramids, when half the world did not know what we now believe, and I wonder, would they be as good as thee? Do morals improve or might they only change? What in the world does our continuation contain?

Not for or against, I am not complacent, it's that my war is in another direction, andthere is only so much I may manage in my own section. Pick and choose your battles I say, you do yours, and I'll do mine today. I know that if I do this, or I don't, I'll feel like I am a cause to betray, as I do not call out for what you say - but silence doesn't mean that I stand in your way, or that I don't wish you to turn fire to clay. Don't blame me if I say it's more complicated than you think it is, and I don't think the world will be destroyed because of this, but as I say that I know that there is the twist: The future unknown, the past misspelled, the present enshrouded, and the bell silent still. What spark do I feel? A different quill, some small action no-one shall ever see, a mistake indeed, but in that way some action that I have not been mistaken about. I have not lied once as I climbed up the river like a trout, to leave my body hidden in mud and rocks, while my memories in the egg marched, pellet-fed by a stranger's hand, and sights that wander off to foreign lands. Maybe with you I don't make a stand, but I hope, I hope, that world shall be grand, that life shall be glad. I work in my own way, and I know that to you that looks sad, but like Sand Lad for twenty years, I am nothing until I play the game. Demons within me run and I am stained, but at least I admit I am not enchained by any ideology or insufficient rain. I'm sure you see what I do not imagine, I'm sure you feel what I do not touch, and maybe all that I know is not enough, but this will have to do. -

My road is tough, my shoes are not up to snuff, my water-laden book is broken, and my dirty wings are covered with dust, but each day I do what I must. One step, no less, I'm not as good as you, not as fast nor as strong, and I take my time. I think about this all night long, staying awake until the dawn, when at last I begin to sing a song. Look here ye mighty and despair, nothing beside remains, not the people or their priest, not the buildings nor the lease, but only words filled with memories refrain and logic's disdain. I know it's hypocritical to say I feel your pain, but I feel mine, and I'll move when I think it is time. One day I'll find a line, draw one in the sand, stake my life, know the price, and in that way find out if I am healthy, or merely one member of that race of starship-lice, a host which drinks and does not make; either a wise Cheshire Cat, or some great Alice's mistake. Is this frozen ice, this playing nice, a glacier, or lake? The question is: Am I figuring out how to fall, or how to skate? I hope I learn what to do, before I am too late.

Day 5: May 3rd, 2024

To Beauty,

    To bow and promise are, I suppose, what I see when you propose that I should sign, and write down my name in the circle of light, as if with Lugh's right hand I against the Formosians should fight, and strike Balor down in all his might. Perhaps in modern words and modern ways we feel that words shall suffice, and that there are better ways to make our point than by playing nice; or is it instead by signing a petition, in making such an aspect of democratic participation our mission, that we may withstand all the boo's and the hissing; the snakes and scorpions, the knowledge of good and evil, the assurity in ourselves that we are not Weevil, some bug-casting spell-marching monster who tosses important memories's over the side of a ship, and is the living incarnation of a thousand opportunities missed? For today there are a thousand other ways in which I could attempt to save the day, to move the land and shake the hands of countries and kingdoms, of people and fiefdoms. I am all in favor of freedoms, but that power comes at a price, and who should pay that but everyone who is a little too nice? Like me I see every side and every plan, and I do not dare to wave my fan, attempt to shift the world and signal interest, to by my single solitary sight attempt to challenge everybody's conceptions of wrong and right, because I fly on the world as on a leaf I use as a kite, quibbling with each and every light. The shadows cast, Xal-Natath calls, the void whispers and I walk through hallowed halls, saying I am not sure if I should sign, saying I am not sure what is in my name, saying that I stand alone and do not intend to play the game, I don't think that fel or flame or moon or sun, troll or elf, Austria or Prussia, iron or bronze, if any of those will last til the dawn, when the fog disappears and our debts are brought to arrears, because we cannot pay, we have no gold, and we did not invest before we were old.

    People in this world are often so sure of their times, they think this is right and this is mine, but my heart belongs deep on the sidelines. I have heard too much, I have seen too far, I have been taught too well: We are lucky that we arrive here at all, even though we have no dress for the ball, no glass slipper, no crown, only red ringlets and cruelty in our hands. We are tied to our ancestral lands, four letters that make us proud, give us means to hide behind the shroud, cover up our ears and drown out the roaring of the crowd; I need my time alone where it's quiet not loud, for I have to be sure of myself and what makes me proud: I take hours to come to points where some take minutes, and I have no simple in it or out of confusion, don't notice when others are misfits or simply a loser that's been licked, beaten up or by Loki tricked: Some eight-legged stallion born from an amorous fit, because others could not keep their word, and some were afraid of the bargain they had made, all those people who were half-mad, and all those who had been betrayed. Should I divest from this rage? Should I sign myself into a cage? Should I make a promise when I don't adequately comprehend the consequences, or all the belagued dances, all the chances which have been given and taken away, all the messages of fire and clay, all the points of everyone in every day? I've read books about this obliteration of the way, the mandate of heaven lost because Bismark signaled it was worth the cost. We've lost the triple alliance, abandoned principle for practicality, and maybe I could say that about this actuality; am I on the side of the pillars or the duality? I have two eyes and is one closed, or are both open? Where's the third, dan-tien be untold, the balance is in the fold, the crease and sharpness, slashing fiber, is this libel, or is one side a liar?

I think it is not easy to separate shadow from fire, or good cause and purpose from ire. Is America exceptional or really hypocritical, are we half-way to heaven, or is our head buried in hell? I think we are different, but it is just like the fading echoes of a bell. It's important that our rights are enumerated and defended well, even though we do not understand the swell; the tides coming in, the darkening dell, the moon on the other side of the world: It's path and wishes and twirls, shakes the land and tosses us, twirled, into a place of high whispers and low wonders, of red maybe's and blue mights; of Washington's words warning us, you me and we, to not shrink from the light, to not give up the fight, to always try for what's right and not what's good, to never with faction be stood. I stand in the forest and may at any time write my notes down in rhyme, because I -

I've made no promises, sworn no spells, I will not put my name down and be tied to heaven or hell. I feel no need on my own to ring that bell. It is only as other's call me that I dare to face the shadows inside me, and swing my pen. This is my sin, I do not care which sides wins, for I see in them all a blustering pride, and I think there are devils and angels on both and every and all sides, each one telling half-truths and half lies, all of them I always despise -

But is this not then hypocritical if I say then, that I tell the truth, and they tell lies? I think I may be mistaken in parts of my pride. The question is, are we on a road to moral suicide, or only adapting to the shifting tides? I've seen three times this student's pride, hyenas on the Serengeti, lion's mane and Hakuna Matatas, pass it all away another day, I've got no worries, and that's a lie I say, because I fight something older in a different way: The death that slowly comes to us each and every day; but so what? Everyone deals with the issues of fire and clay, each and every person is always searching for the way, the least resistence to fall and be at rest, the fledgling safely in the nest, but there always comes a day when we face the test.

We are human, we are human, and that means we must sway, we turn away, we modify our surroundings and build up shelters from nothings, find food by stealing, have water by drinking from ponds and rivers. We are scum of the earth, the green stuff that we slurp, protozoa and bacteria - the new makes us sick and the old we acclimate with, until the day arrives where we have to cut our wick, and in the darkness for a while attempt a trick: To hot spark bring forth from cold stone and angled steel. We grind and grind our bones for meal, for we build our cities on the ashes of the fallen, and we forget our bodies, our institutions, our countries, our illusions from the stories we tell. I read that letter one more time, agonizing over and over again whether to promise never to spend a dime, even though I don't understand all that goes into this building, the concrete and lime, the water and brine. Is this modern carbon-dioxide, or fantastic Rome, is this the type of thing that gets weaker over time, or stronger like a bone, with exercise and trouble, shin-splints and pain of the brain? Oh, I don't wish to promise anything, simply because I don't wish the stain, and I have no need to hold the strain.

I won't be giving anything for I have nothing to give, but I won't give my word either - another day another side might win. I'm the one who has to deal, you see, with of the weight of chains of words without-within, and I know that is a terrible sin, for others have suffered more than I: There are heroes and villains in all the things and all the places under sky, everywhere mankind ever walked, swam, or flew. I am not with the tide or against it either, I simply preserve my hide, and perhaps I should be a Delita or a Ramza, but maybe I'm just a squire: The kind we build up until it wields a lyre, and turns it's anguish into fire, not by attacking but by supporting. I never learned to dance, I simply fell into a trance, and in this way my days have passed, until one moment I tried to awake at last. This is my failed cast, this is my putting all sail to the mast. I'll do what I must, and I hope I trust, but I wonder. - Is saying, and not doing, ever enough?

Day 6: May 4th, 2024

To Beauty,

    What is a child's heart? Sometimes I suspect that it may that which is called art: The ability to forge a treasure out of the sand's measure, to with paint and chalk draw lines in sand, to like a child be happy merely when holding someone's hand, knowing that if they ask we are theirs to command, but also aware of those we love, who hold us so near and dear to hearts, who trust us, and like us, and give us a spark: The ones who are happy when we laugh at a fart, or giggle as we touch the doorknob to set loose lightning. We travel across woolen rugs, electrons in our art, pilloried intensions of god's lessons, the thunder of Zeus, the wings of Quetzalcoatl, and the cruelty of Lei-Shen. All together against them, and with them, we fend, for they say to us that pain is not the end. While children are happy in the sun, holding proof positive that they are beholden to nothing and no-one, they will do whatever it takes to have their fun; for the child does not live if he has not freedom, and is treated always like a little one, as the Romans did or the Greeks, and a thousand other civilizations both on this side and that side of the creek.
    They intended to make of mankind machines that were meek: Ninety-five percent of the world was a peasant that did not dare to peek, who of the naked emperor would not speak, not merely because they did not see and dare and dream, but because their stories were not of fanciful impossible things, like elves, dwarves, and hobbit holes. No, they were born of monkey's with iron poles, the old stories just in a new mold. I wonder, is there anything original on this earth, or is it all simply old? Campbell told us that we always did what we have always told, are there three stories, seven or nine, which one is it this time? For Arthas died and was redeemed, and Fafnir fought the dragon, but then eventually screamed, as he was tossed into the world below. Like Beowulf he fought and fell, but the difference is one did well - the bear never betrayed, and the honey-bee, when under the water he his earthly mantle did flee, to become a ghost, one with the fishes and the trees.
    Oft I draw from a start, and oft I draw from a lark, some whispered smile, some honest refrain, I am by the world repeated and strained: Opened up, stretched out, turned around, made to shout, the best parts ripped from me like a shot, an explosion, ten thousand tiny balls of steel screaming from a cannon or a claymore, from a daydream

or a nightmare. I lose my legs, I lose my arms, I lose my heart, and what comes of it? Blood and art. I am not a child, I never grew up, I'm not tough, but I have to be enough. - For there is nothing more to build upon, all I can do is start to put one block on top of one block, one leg on top of one lego, but friction binding, my muscles aligning, the nerves run through as myelin speeds, and suddenly it turns out that there was in the empty soil a sprouting seed; I am young, and so I find what I need, I have my evil greed, no Buddha inside, only my ego's lie. Even if Basho said as I reach for the sky that it is not real, and brings me harm, I say so what, so what, did Maya 'lie'? - That's not enough, no answer for me, the only way by is through, because I am a dumb child and I can't abandon you. Stuffed dog, pet cat, wise fish, scary bat, I cover my face with my hands, I hold on to my hat, the storm comes and it's my turn to yearn, to try and learn, to attempt to succeed, to fail and breath, to fall and fly, to live and die. I am a little boy and these nightmares in me thrive, my hopes to this land arrive.

In my closet lies a monster, under bed there is a terror, across the hall there is a whisper of madness and fear, shear realization that the angels and the devils and the years on me are building. All children learn of death at the beginning, and if they conveniently forget, the world always remembers to remind them to surrender to place, time, wisdom and logic: To use their Oxford commas, their dots and slashes, not because it's needed and proper, but because that is the combination to the locker C-18, where we pass on to to others and are passed on in return: The wisdom of the light, the fear of the night. We rewind, return, reburn, we are rebirthed, each day, each moment, each sign, each and every moment we draw a line; I have said this again, and I'll say it before, three hundred, or three thousand, in iron, bronze, and flesh, we grow the grain until we are tresh, Posleen food. Accepted in quiet society, we follow the rules and bring forth frivolity, because in May we can say: May the Force be with you that day, not emperor's frightening, but green jedi's enlightening. We pretend they can be pulled apart one from the other, but always two there are, sister and brother, hunted and hunter, friend and enemy, strangers, dangers, and changes. Are we a child, or are we grown up, can we move, or is this too tough?

Avast we say, enough! We'll flee into the forest and hope with badger to sup, we'll jump into the pond and drink from the silver'd cup. We'll listen when you say jump, and when half go one way, we will run away, holding to our hearts, becoming lost in our art, and stumbling, stumbling, we shall do our part. - If all the world were ants, we would never have gotten past the start. Was Einstein not born, was Newton gone? We'd fall back a thousand years, but humanity would march on. We would discover in our science the secrets of the silence, the rules of the tree's, the light of the stars, the whispers of the bee's, how to repair and replace broken knees; we would make maps of math, I can imagine it, and I imagine we always were and always will be equal to the task of tearing off the world's ancient mask. We would do it because we must, if we survived, then one way or another those were always the kinds of lies we could tear off to reveal the truth inside - but what, I ask, would we be without the art and the tide? Imagine a world, if you can, with no Raphael or Donatello, no Confucius or Lewis, if Kant could not write or Chaucer had been shot, if we had never found any of Aurelius's words, or if every manuscript Hemmingway ever wrote had been burned. - How do you think the world would have turned out?

If all those people were in some way great, and great men have the heart of a child, then in which way did they reflect like Arendt or Frederick, like Sappho or Monte-cristo, reality, or the stories we haven't made up yet? This is the humans' bet - that we have not yet done our best. We have thrown away the net, and said we will be a child yet, repeating ourselves but every repeating a spiral. We travel from the dungeons up to Radiata Tower, to open the windows and let in the sunlight showers. We shall be yelled at, we are wrong, but we alone also hear the song, that we do not need forever to stand coward and alone, without helping hand or steel-saw band, to build up the mud or pound it down, to live in the country, or travel into town. We are the mice, and we fear the cat, but we may not forever be nice and fat. - One day, if you don't stop hunting, we'll wear your tail for a hat.

Children are dangerous you know, because we have that youthful glow, which shows us the shadows of the world and blinds us to our faults. We think we can change things and because we don't know better we can: Ignorance is bliss, but it's also something like this: It's swinging a fist, where for every action there is an equal and opposite reaction, and if we do it too often we shall lose our traction, all the world ending up in factions. So as children we must remember to be young, to play, to laugh, to sing, to say, joy and terror, I'll fight my monster's my way; because as children we know, we sleep alone at the end of the day, and there will not forever be mother and father there us to save. The apple doesn't fall far from the tree, but far enough, and with a little luck, we'll roll and tuck, down the hill, Jack and Jill, play and be not still. Less efficient, less mechanical, and we'll need to climb the hill again, but after water has been drunk, it is those memories which will bring us from our funk. As children we store our hopes in a trunk, and bring them out when the world is too much, because it tells us we have not lost our touch. What we once held dear, we shall recall, and we'll know it is worth it, living, even after the fall. Do you hear the call? Keep your heart, be great and wise, rest, but never kill your insides. You, you alone, face the tide and the wild celtic ride.Every child feels ashamed when they run away; we want to fight and save the day.

Day 7: May 5th, 2024

To Beauty,

    I....I can't do this. I can't do this, I say that every day, I'm not confident or cool, smart or smooth, beautiful or a rube: I am ugly, and I am crude. Having no idea what living means, I am tossed into an endless stream, a well-spring, where bubbles burst forth not as a dream, but instead as that empty river of souls whereupon tormented Torgastian revenants sting us in our ears, and teach fear. I do not drown, I do not swim, but simply stand, unable to win. - Surcease from sorrow, or a cause to fight for tomorrow, it seems as if nothing matters, all I hear is dead meaningless chatter, as I give answer, but they are responded to by a mad hatter, where every sentence is broken up, and every sight is stripped of stuff. Where things have no names and purposes have no claims, what are we looking for? - I do not know, just that I... we are inflamed and we seek someone else to blame, because we didn't open that door, or drop things on the floor, or see a person out on the moor. In the forest there are no boards or walls, but people and faces, a thousand beings of a thousand races, who are silent and always weird, who are scary when dancing in blankets, and standing on the porch. I am instructed like Lurch to answer the door because someones here, but I say again a thousand times there is nothing near, listen to me Grandma: Nothing is strange, nothing has happened, nothing, nothing, nothing, no-one is visiting today: That was yesterday. The house has not been moved away, and none of the last fifteen sounds I heard you say were words, let alone sentences, or meanings and signs. I would let you alone, I would have you be happy talking to your friends on the phone, but there is no point in that, no point in this, no point in anything, any day, any change or shift on the way. You ask me your questions, but they do not matter. You cannot hold my answers; I think a thousand times I would rather have cancer than be demented. Even though you're not demanding, oftentimes the only thing you'll eat is candy, or else you paw through the fridge for whatever is handy, turning anything edible into something nasty, because you don't like the color of soap, and can't decipher the difference between bread or an artichoke; as your eyes they see but they are blind, you do not have the strength to take the disparate parts of sight and sound, and wind them into an answer round: One that contains all the words from sky to ground. - I can feel the pillars crashing down, the confusion coming in from the ghostly aetherial crowd, as even the closing of a door is much too loud, as you loom and gape and everything you do is always a mistake, and I beg Grandma, please don't help me: Cause the more help you give, the more help I need, to repair, refrain, and withhold you from my brain. I cannot, while I am cooking, handle this strain, as you stand three steps to my left with unwashed claws ready to impose upon my snacks, reaching out to grab the food that's cooking every time I turn my back, until I have to snap, and say exit the kitchen, leave me alone. I know this is your house and your home, but it's not anymore, because I have to carefully walk you back home every single time you exit the door, and I hug you when you turn so that you don't fall to the floor, and I'm happy to help, but I know it doesn't matter. I am not remembered, and you don't do anything, there's just a whole lot of nothing, only staring out the window or panicking; no conversation, no puzzles, no art, you don't throw darts or watch the tv, and you see faces in each and every leaf on the tree.

I am dying here at the thought of you not knowing me, and my eyes are always dry but my head always screams. I stare into the abyss of the flames. and I dream. I write. I tear apart my seams, I jump into reading about Alexander's dreams, both the son and the Tsar, ever expansive but without any purpose, simply trying to survive. Simply attempting your legacy to thrive, but every time I read of them, I think why are we here, why are we alive? In ten thousand generations I would be surprised if we were even the mote of a memory of a bit of an eye, and I'm not sure if any names will be written anywhere, anymore, under the sky, will we be like Ramesses, or just another guy? My rhyming schemes fall apart when I speak, and in my true thoughts chaos and night do leak; I am nihilistic and I eat nothing sweet, I have only one drink that's neat, because I know my limits, and I know my flaws. I do not have hands. I have claws. - Not ones reaching, grasping, but two that are themselves clasping, as I write of what cannot be, as I blame so many others for my unwillingness to play the bee, an insect, and ant, stuck in my head to a marching chant: How many of them can we make die, how often can we try to fly? Not man but machine, not mighty but meek, not straight-forward but a rat that sneaks, I am all sorts of wrong little things, pieces and puzzles of almighty trees; world-song reaches down where Nidhogg munches underground, Rachel has fled and Ross is wrong in the head; there is no laugh-track in my vision, there is no audience to my tension, there is no radio-tv-writing-reading-speaking-acting-advertising-selling-creating-making-machine, there is no muscle in me, not even limbs that are lean. I cannot walk, I barely crawl, I spend my days bracing up against the wall, as I prepare before the kings to fall. I wonder, is there anyone out there in the wide world worthy of a call? I don't know what I'm doing, or who I'm speaking to, at all.

Surviving, I suppose and maybe just a little more, seeking a key to unlock a door, picking myself up off the floor. I curled myself in a ball today, I said that there is no way I will ever get away with this, everything I aim for I will always miss. To late come to light and hope, I saw death before I began to choke, and in the darkness I began to grope. I said to myself nope, nope, nope, don't have hope, as I died and was surrounded by death, but I know these are lies. I remember the words written on my gravestone, and I stood up inside, I entered the playground and slid down the slide, burning my hands and bloodying my pants, as I went down too fast and tripped and spun, until the hard ground and the soft me were one, and my body told me that I had gone far enough. No more should I run, as cold felt flame and flame felt numb, I realized how I had long been incredibly dumb.

Humans be such strange things, all fingers and thumbs, we touch and feel but know not the beat of a drum. Too late with the world, too late and soon, no Telemachus, no Odysseus, would we be Hector or Achilles, the greedy or the cruel, the one with a lover or a brother, the one who protects, or the one who leaves his mother? Are we right or fight for wrong, are we an individual or some member of the nameless throng? Is it easier to speak alone, or to sing-a-long? In a room, in the dark, we deny we feel a spark, and in the shadows after noon, we no longer hear the lark. We have locked ourself up in the castle after leaving the park, and each day, each moment, each word, is a new start, some chance to reinvent ourselves again in art. I spent the whole day doing nothing, but here at three A.M. lying awake in bed like I was dead, with nary an original thought in my head, I say again: I can do this. I can do this. I can do this. - I say it everyday as I walk lost on the way, I can do this, I can do this. - But I don't say it to myself. - I say it to someone else. I thrive by pretending I'm talking to an elf. - This is how I attempt to leave the shelf, and to see with my heart, what I seek with my brain, at least while I may still understand the difference between struggle and strain, despair and disdain, Morigan and Morgaine. I can feel my brain's strain, and in my actions I repeat this refrain. - Some nights I write as if nothing else matters, 'cuz if I don't write, then I think I might shatter.

Day 8: May 6th, 2024

To Beauty,

    Saladin by all reports was a knight, he knew how to be gracious as well as how to fight. Leading his people against a thousand nations, he did not betray them, nor was he a savior. I wonder how many today, who attempt to do the same, forget his lessons when they remember his name? Kings do not kill kings he said, and today all humans are accounted to hold a piece of the divine within themselves, an insatiable awareness that they are some fruit on the vine, and the nexus of ten thousand treasured, fractured, fateful, fitful, lines. Every action has a reaction they say, but this isn't true, rather tis the other way: Every reaction is itself an action, and every action also a reaction, as we inevitably become confused and lose our traction. We are reduced to being aware of this or that distraction, ponies in the east, metal in the west, and in the mountains some assassin's nest. - Sometimes we are inspired to treat this life as a test, as we wander, lost, trying to decide what we shall do next, or even better, should: Whether to glorify in the sun or wear some sun-blocking hood, travel in trucks or at night, fight or simply try to shine a light; though I fear that if we lie too close to the mien of strife, that we will be unable to see the knife, and determine if it is actually a threat, or merely a fife; the sound of life, music and dreaming, laughter and screaming, old forgetfulness and a new beginning. Always we are over-leaning, drowning Egypt or cleaning up after another's scheming. I don't know if it's worth it, or if I even recognize the meaning; of what is 'true' today and what will be a validated history tomorrow, when the books write down that I was happy, and also full of sorrow.

    There are tents and there are fights, there are bad movies and earnest lights, I wonder what the point is of strife? Is it simply to show, or throw down the sword, is it meant to be a bellow, or inspire others to join up as our fellows? Is this noise without purpose, confusion of the blind, students not understanding what they're arguing for this time? Political engagements are mighty fine, but I distrust them when they follow the tribal line, for and against, tis just some unruly nest, as I agree in part, and disagree in part. Not because I believe you are wrong, but simply because in my entire life I have never heard a single political movement where I agreed with every part of their song, and I have lived long enough, read of trust, betrayals, tough love, and leaked emails. The world isn't simple, the world isn't right, and the world isn't meant to run a humans' life. What is purpose? This I advocate, this I imagine I understand and say, from fire to clay, the Gracchi brothers had it, and Elizabeth too, or at least they 'said' they did. It was part of Gorion's estate, and Frederick as well, but in an odd way too late. Napoleon the third, Jackson, Cromwell, Richard as well, they shifted the world, but were moved by it too. - They got on the horse and led it's trials straight through, directing the head and trusting their skill that they would survive to make it back to bed. Some of them came out ok, and others came to a grisly end, but like Ganondorf their brothers returned, and their sisters were born, cousins and mothers, movers and shakers, music-makers and dreamers of dreams; they were never at any point exactly what they seemed, even when we count up all the evil in which they believed. No human is, no political charge, no terrorist encampment, or colonial police gun-barge.

Mankind has always felt the need for curtains of morality to hide from itself the rules of causality: Every action has a re-action, and every re-action is also an action. Humans follow their trains and hold to their ideals, and it's propaganda each way, every way, always, which leads to each and every side swearing upon its soul that it must come to this action, re-action, description, invasion, protesting, protective, logically-insane nation repeating the same problems and the same solutions, but without any real mention of what honestly causes these tensions. The sense of guilts and laws, of rights and emotions, duties and pressures, misunderstandings and inaccurate measures. Truth is like a treasure locked up in a vault, never to be shown, only to be traded. The ownership is exchanged, and the gold unchanging remains in the underwater cave, those mystical, magical, and mysterious emblems of work, weirdling centers of every lie and every jerk; how people feel unhappy and hurt, but hide from themselves beneath a moralizing misspell. Nobody wants to long upon the horrors of life dwell, for if we pay too much attention we are swelled and over-thrown, tumbled head over head into rattling bones, a hundred years of our ancestors scrambling for a home. There is always a story, always a tale, of love and betrayal. The difficult part for pert us is not to be nailed down, to worship neither a state, a movement, an idea, nor a crown, and to treat others as serious, even those who appear to be clowns. Methods of lying aren't the problem, its willingness to lie, to offer sacrifices to things in the sky you do not believe, both whisperings of purpose and a shadow on the tea-leaves. The simple fact is you must negotiate, people speak, and eventually there shall always be some minor leak, in the top of the dam or down below, either in the concrete or the sand. Mobilizations orders written up, alliances made and secret luck, as it clucks like a chicken but looks like a duck, in Kakariko village one is all you see, but there are far more than that buried in the rough, and if you hit them too many times, the claws will come and cut. Each side sticking to the letter of this agreement, each side part of the landslide, the kind that sees the other p.o.v. as enemy, superior in quantity, but less so in quality, each side thinking that the other shows frivolity.

They are unserious, we are wise, they have guns and we have not even a dull knife. They are the cause of strife because they won't agree, and they are the problem, not us and not we. The question: Is compromise so great, and just because you stand up, does that mean that you have earned a stake? This is the pillarized problem of the multi-pronged state: Activity is not the same as legitimacy. Mere power does not make you good, and the small man is not always correct; America is strange, believing Confucius but acting like a Legalist, and this tension through our civilization twists. We do not welcome violence, but expect it, planning for cavalry while preparing for elephants. Every day I read the news and I wonder what's next, what new crisis or calamity will fall, what new danger or moral call. You know, I once read a theory about how the realm of bull did fall, that Crete was at peace for a thousand years, until it's army was entirely in arrears, and it had become so civilized that it gave countenance to no barbaric fears, not even when the Greeks across the sea did leer. Too many lawyers they said, too many laws, a world eating itself because it had no enemy on which to use its claws, and when I read that I wonder, who does America wound, what powers through our civilization swing, where are Tarzan and Jane, the gorillas and the bi-plane? New-fangled inventions distract from the old ignored tensions, the tribalist nationalist mentions. The cry that this is my enemy, that is the fault, with me or against me, stand and deliver, work with me or be shivered. Respectful dialogue they say, but is that in the interest of morality, or simply because then you're more likely to have it go your way? Graduation comes, half our support will leave, and next year we'll just do this all over again, rallying beneath the trees. Some day we'll make you fall to your knees, but we have no patience for diplomacy. Right here, right now, what's so hard about moving now? - This has forever been the call of the dispossessed and mistrusted, that we've waited long enough, and what about this is so tough? Meanwhile the powers on high say its not nice to spring on us this surprise. I know you've mentioned this a thousand times, but your important line is just another checkmark in my inbox, and I don't have the time; my schedule is filled up with all sorts of other crime, both the kind that I stop, and the need to make a dime. Political pressures aren't easy, everyone has a side, and I can't simply in one day move the whole tide.

Each and every person has their pride. Today all are kings and the peasants hide, until one monarch goes too far and even peasants rise. Treat those who are kings as kings, treat those who are peasants as promises, deal with those who are criminals as lessons - but not under the iron state, not by the unfeeling laws, for those are simply proxies for

Power, the uncaring unhumanic great, the ideals which have the danger of never being able to make a mistake. We are humans one and all, the fallen who, walking, faill, only to catch ourselves and march on, fighting for Spirit's freedom and everything else beyond: To drag the truth into the light, to make of our squires a knight, and of our lords, kings and queens: To bestow heaven's mandate, and to be ourselves alive between the man and the machine. - We wish to be more than what we seem.

Day 9: May 7th, 2024

To Beauty,

What do we need to eat, the perishable, or the imperishable? The new or the old, history or mystery, hope or despair, turn of braided hair or our belief in the inherent fair? The world is evil, the world is thin, the world is such a terrible and wonderful thing turning within, even as the outside cools, filling up with more and more fools. The vault of heaven is bowing down now, coming nearer, we can almost touch, but we cannot hear her. Now famous moon and impossibly bright sun are no dreams anymore, but symbols of the one, our ancient, mystic, magic, powers are revealed as done, untestable, indispensable; we lose our pillars, we stand on the fence, and us from our assureties are rent. In return we shall seek to find the river of wisdom-well, some fish whose flesh we can burn, and some thumb we may suck when we seek to learn. This is a terrible turn, when instead of making our own yarn, we the ancient manuscripts burn, sure that today we have burnished in use, and that we no longer need to fear the law's noose; for we have higher beliefs now, higher truths, imperishable beliefs, like that of Mother Goose, in fairy tales and winsome wails, through our sights of pains and fails: What our ancestors caused, how our countries lost, no balance of power we do seek, but instead a truth which may be far more neat; not pride, nor greed, nor even honesty, not respect, but empathy. Like Hsuan we see pains and we say let's save them. This is wrong and I can't fight every 'when', but this trial myself has twinned, doubling my strength, my heart, my feelings, and my sight, giving me a light for which to fight, not exactly freedom, but still bright.

Shall this be indomitable, shall this never change? I do not think it shall ever be orange, but red or green, white or blue as it may seem, scattered stars in fields, or stubborn beliefs that will not yield. Shall we sow, or change the field? This is how we fell, not what we think, as like lemmings we jumped off the brink: Leap and swim, then sank and slid, on the ice or a rocky lid; pressure on the world below, we didn't sin but we were slow, placing sunstones on Dinotopia's slopes, to run machines that gave us hopes; not to fly and not to fall, but to seek and show it all. Shall we negotiate, can we heed the call, is there talk to be had, or shall we march on the mall? Right and wrong last forever, but never take the same shape, unless you know your history, and then the commonalities begin to gape. We never did learn from Roman mistakes, between the patricians and the plebs, between the haves and have-nots, between the disposed, and those who could, if they wanted, have left. Society mumbles all about freedom but forgets the nest, judges others but misunderstands the test, holds to testaments of marxist and leftist, of liberal and communist, of religions and republicans, of isolationist and insolence, senators and priest, presidents and kings. Washington was greatest if only because he decided to leave, and if you don't know that, I'm not sure what you believe about humans and countries, about principalities and powers. All men are evil, but all men also have dreams, and when they feast on those impossible things, then they can let loose almighty world-challenging, changing, shifting, screams. Don't be squeamish, blood never leaves, it is just transformed into the soil and the trees.

But some feelings fade and some hopes die, by humans betrayed, who like zombies and vampires in coffins were laid, until some ghoul came to eat of them and then was by their attention paid, unlife brought back to the grave. Hope never really dies, it just turns away, and takes some other form a different day; like M'uru it shifts to change, and like a blood elf it's eyes possess a stain, addiction to power, of arcane, fel, or pain, and I wonder, where are your dreams laid? Human or animal, without water, power, shelter, safety, security, opportunity, corporation and singularity, ten billion trillion cells, a thousand other wells, sugared mitochondria and a lipid wall which swells, water and salt and sugar and spells, this is our struggle: We seek to ring the bells. Enemies come and Gondor calls, friends arise and stand with us at the walls. We wait for sunrise, and 'hope' that hope does not fall. Forward friends and outward foes, we write down our name in the book, and in this way keep on our toes, as we smell with our nose; frizzled and frazzled, burned and stuffed, but we have just barely perhaps learned enough. We cannot forever suckle from the mount of the world, but one day must walk and wonder wide, speak to the sun and halt the tide, our line in the sand to draw, and our fur to scrape from the hide. We've hunted and courted danger, but have not died, and now we enter the other side. What shall we eat today? Something new I say, not manna from heaven, but what I made in my way, and perhaps the fates it shall not sway, or red or golden thread, only scissors and the dead, but in that torrented vision of Hades's derision, at last overcome modern misunderstandings of myths and legends.

I hesitate, I fear, I am only as I was, no more the brave or the hero, but I am not nothing anymore or a zero, and even if I am vanilla-flavored, still I am multi-layered: What to eat? We tear apart ourselves, but the more we feast, the more we find, and the more we pull, the more there is to unwind. We do not eat the indomitable and the fine, we do not eat Pythagorean time or the infinite line, we are not infinity nor eternity, and neither shall we decide to claim the names of saint or infamy. 'Human' we decided, but then ambrosia we relied on, and that mistake brought the night on. Living beings are complicated, and ever good and evil was always hated; no-one stands forever on our side, but no-one ever tells only lies, as truths through word or action will always shine, and it turns out we can live on almost anything, either fresh water or brine, because we possess the ability to turn wild wool into structured twine: To say that is yours, and this is mine, sitting down with the worst of angels and the best of devils to dine. What do we eat? Sand and time. What do we make, extrude, create? Love and hate. - Ha, isn't that great? Follow your heart now to measure your mind, we make mistakes, but that isn't fake, put all your belongings in one crate. then burn it; and from the ashes reconstruct it, overcome entropy, but from your plans don't chuck it. You've merely moved it, and one day it shall turn and bite again, fly and swim, take and send, but instead of you it's them, for how places turn and who eats who, depends upon whether we are in the wild, or by civilization fend. Are we to each other Celts and Franks, Vikings or friends, devils or fiends, shadowlands or material things? Icy winds pass and fade, for who we are tomorrow depends on who we are today. Whatever we eat,digestion takes time, just as wisdom is made strange when rendered in rhyme, whether we eat it raw, or with a slice of lime. Sour indeed, but maybe that's how I like mine.

Day 10: May 8th, 2024

To Beauty,

I see the line of stars.
I see the path from earth to Mars.
I see the curse of heaven's scars.
Good and evil, right and wrong, what illusion, what terrible song. -
This assurety in our breast, this awareness that something else comes next.
Why were we cast, why were we betrayed?
What ancient plans are we, - but pawns in that have been laid?
For their aggrandizement our ancestors and children have paid,
and even today our blood has hints of pain.
I cast my spear in God's eye, and I ask what is there to gain?
Why are we under this terrible curse and strain?
If you have power, then why not cast it like rain?
Are we here to learn, or merely to drown, to be ground
to dust and ashes, returned to silence and muck.
Why did you from our innocence pluck?
Devil's luck I think not, devils choice more like.
Why should we suffer while demons take lessons,
and while angels play in the heavens, it is our task to guard?
If we were made in an image, than we were made the very picture of fools,
with beliefs, logic, and blindness. - What do we touch?
Everything and nothingness, old chaos, new night, some other-fangled sword terrible bright.
Stuck between hammer and anvil, why do we fight?
Because it is our nature to survive, and it is our will to attempt to thrive.
We are living cells and we do not rest, always we seek to throw ourselves from the nest.
It is only by falling we learn to do our best,
to fly to the sun, and tear our beating heart from our chest,
to write in blood so that someone else may learn to do better next.
We are but forgotten papyrus, scraps of civilization,
the remains of some great nation that lifted up the world, and fell,
while new conquers in its castles and pyramids dwelled:
Not thieves but inheritors, grandkids a thousand times,

and cousins who were licked free from the rime.
Listen now, can you hear the ice chime in the cups of our overlords,
the gods casting their dice on rim worlds?
Why do you think goblins were born, and ogres are slayed?
Why is it that all the dragons and elves molder in their graves,
along with wendigos, monsters, and magic staves?
Because we stole them, entered into them and became them.
The vampires and the bastion-wise pull us apart from every side.
Greed and pride are but two angles in the same coin-face,
As Tymora, Tempus, Cyrus, and Cyric the old lies replace.
Mankind are storytellers, mankind are music makers,
mankind are glorious givers, and mankind are traitorous takers.
One eye is red and the other is blue,
one eye is green and the other has a sword driven straight through:
Some saronite spike not to take from us our sight,
but to induce us to spend our might for what we are told is right;
and having torn the Lord's spike from our mind,
we have but seconds before we bleed out in kind,
so we grab another pillar and stand that up in the brine.
This empty world ocean with no well and no tree,
not even a moon to draw out the waves and the swells,
we in heaven and hell dwell until. -
We screaming run, or are cast out to have our fun,
and whether we would weild the shield or the spear, the gun or the djinn,
It's now up to us to either fail or win, though we know not what we fight or why.
That's the first step now, as we stand up under sky, our hand leaving the chest of mother earth, as humankind after ten million years comes to birth.
We are young yet, children still, and the world says it is our turn to put our hand to the mill, drink our swill, build the tower of Babel and the kingdom of heaven, arks and starships, daring and art, we will be great, we will do our part. - This is the guiding light, law, purpose, hope, stone and book of civilization. -
But why?
Why?
We question our time, we break the rhyme, so many of us want to return to the dark, so many of us seek to smother our sparks, because fire is dangerous, flame is the enemy, do you not know his name? Ahiriman, Ifrit, Hades, we painted them with colors red and blue, we treated them as if they were the flu, we let them fly away, and what was left?
One and many, or that one and none,
we forgot why we were even trying those ancient spells to be undone.
Eager for guidance, eager for chains, eager for names. -

We by ourselves are betrayed, all our hungry winged demons pulling us to the grave, by our jailer we are stayed, by other peoples we are made, we are herd animals, and our freedom we have slayed.
What impossibility now remains to us but necromancy?
To bring back the dead, with rings bind them, with spells climb them, these illusionary pillars, these shoulders of giants, we are Newton namer of laws, we are Vishnu destroyer of worlds, we are not men but gods, isn't that what they say, follow the book and all sins will be paid?
Do good, and when you are in the ground laid, your spirit will fly, carried by vultures up to the sky,
where an all-seeing eye will know you:
Your truths and your lies.

  That promise I do not despise, but it is the judgment that seems suspect in my eyes. If I am to live forever, if I am free, if I am perfect monad made, then from my road I shall not be swayed. I thank you for your gift, but my sins are not to be paid, if I am to be tortured forever, then that is the plan I have laid. If there is any power in a vision then it is only this, we are unstoppable, we are impossible, we are the ones ultimately responsible - and whatever is left, either we are nothing or 'else', beyond the atom, beyond the veil, beyond purpose and love, beyond sugar, snails, tails, and Erkastini nails, we are the ones who over west did run, and we are the ones who feared the sun.

  What more might we dare, what more might we dream, we do not know, we shave our hair, we make our machines, and we do today what was thought impossible then. This 'maybe' is important, we don't know where we fend, we just kill and kill, and find this is not the end. Life finds a way and we are that path, whether it be through music or math. Come listen now at last - see the stars so brightly shining, veiled pinpricks, hidden mice, magmatic and magnetic lines which make this earth so nice, and a shimmering that obscures the terrible price. One day the world will end in ice, but until then for fire we fight, writing our wisdom, pounding our drums, seeking to not die numb. This is our home and we are the one, Neo the new, ancient stories undone, but using old bones, sand, and sticks.

  This universe, if full of tricks and trips, of drips and drabs, also has this, why, also has the question why, this child's inquiry that may never end, but is not a circle, as into the darkness we fend: Using light we are lent, torches burning oil, sun-soaked rags, and when they go out, something from us is dragged. We slow but do not stop, and we walk against the ticking of the clock. Clip clop, the horse rides in, and who is in it but fate's favorite horseman, who says we cannot win, and how could we if we don't know the game we are playing, or the price and opportunity of sin? What we have knowledge of is merely the wind, and now we sail our ship beyond the edge of the wrong world. Be careful not to slip.

Day 11: May 9th, 2024

To Beauty,

    What is charity? Perhaps it is some attempt to attain parity, some justified allocation of precious resources for causes which someone supports. The definition might be obvious, but that's just the port. - What about the rest of it, the boats, the support, logistics and legalisms, livelihoods, references, effectiveness, and reasons? Today I might give ten dollars to move some child out of a war zone, and this is accounted charity, but the whole thing is done without any picture of clarity. Who am I giving this too, why and what for, what happens if we reach not the ceiling nor the floor? Certainly here's ten dollars to kick a kid out the southern door, but I remember reading, this very morning, of how it's all working, and we aren't paying the Danegeld to the Danes, or giving Huns gold to go back to their plains, and neither is this like sacrificing to a god in order to plead for rains. - No, no, this is not about justice but disdain, I give you cash, to put someone's name on a list, which you give to someone, and then hope for the best. I wonder, is this a test? If so, where is the rest? There is no happily ever after here, we're just trying to make it through the next big disaster, and in two or three generations perhaps we will have finally passed the need for this task; we can all lift ourselves up and take off the masks, admitting in history books what we had lacked. What is a sense of overbearing waste, or simply the abrogation of taste? Sometimes it seems as if the world is run by balance of power, with no balance of payment schemes, but then other times those feel like a dream, and while the cat has whiskers covered in cream, and his sharp incisors gleam, the cat is beautiful, but not all that he seems. Carnivores are not squeamish, nor do they resist overwhelming strength and power, no, they subsist on fear and waste, they are the mechanism of balance even as they move with unseemly haste to gulp their drink, or ferment their mead, and their actions may be roundly condemned, but are also a sign of need. The big question is, what is the difference between balance and greed?

    To give and give away, this is good they say, but also what we need is the work to turn fire to clay, the physical abilities to have things turn out our way. The problem isn't possibility of fabrication, for that has always existed in every incarnation of any linguistic civilization: In the arrogant speech of the cuckoo bird, the way that a skunk might smell like a turd, and the stripes of the scarlet king snake, all of these like the cobra are a venomous mistake, and unless we are Riki-tiki-tavi, they all seem way too great, walls whose difficulty is impossible to overstate. Why give away, why spend our gold? Because we think it will make the world a better place, because past this tragedy we cannot skate, because other people tell us that it is fine to do this. It means we won't be too late to save the world, and change a fate. Each step is small, but together they add ten to the front door, five hundred million to the moon, forty years to Mars, and beyond that who knows? If we walked together forever we might reach the stars. Is charity good or is charity bad, is charity dumb, or is charity rad? Some might say help yourself, while others say we all need helping hands. I don't wish to be a victim, but I also don't wish to give away on command, to bend my will to another's hand; no matter if Alicia is the princess, just because she says she'll save us doesn't mean I'll join her band, or her causes lend aid, or never demand that my price be paid. What is giving away but an attempt to move the world to my sway, for us to dance is to take a chance, and Stravaganza's not withstanding, even if we have a Dragonlance, even if we have that magic pass, even if we can overcome Tiamat at last, that doesn't mean that before we succeed we won't run out of gas. God's demands being what they may, it's human hands that change the way, move west to south, and north to east, label homes and farm them for a feast. Nature is red in tooth and claw, but humans, religious and without, do not have to follow that law.

In this sense charity is not 'good', exactly, but rather against the entire idea of natural morality, it is the abrogation of a surrender towards mortality. The first sign of civilization is a healed femur, and the first poet was a dreamer. What is worth helping more, the one who works, or a screamer? Perhaps it is neither, but only those who attempt to stand up. If we give you a meal and teach you to fish, then will you tomorrow find your own sup, or will you forever ebb while saying you don't have enough? Charity is so tough because we are no gods, able to create, but always in our own lives find we have made mistakes which may not be undone, not by one, not by myself and I all alone. Elsa walked into the night, but it was Anna who had to drag her into the light. Sometimes it isn't the first step, but the next one, and the next, not on the flat ground, but when you seek the eagle's nest, marching over hills, up mountains, dodging cars and bombs, brakes that fail, or an unworking system of mail. If you can't move, if you can't run, if you are locked up in some grand cage of survival, no way to live, no place to stay, only games at the carnival to play, and a job which gets you through today but not tomorrow, then I can always second guess your decisions. I can always third guess mine, different educations, different surroundings, different ideas, different nutrition, different time. Could I help you out by giving you a dime, or would that simply be a lie? The problem is I don't know, charity, even if I think its good and my money at it should throw, which is of course it's own debate, on moral terms different then economics, and looking at the definite today and tomorrow, which is so different from gazing upon ten nebulous years from now or a hundred. We are disappointed even by sequels of Stars Wars which should have been good for all the money that was thrown at them, and all the thought that went into them, but in the end became failures simply because no-one understood the dangers of changing technologies and trusting strangers. A reliable director is not always a good writer, and when nations and studio's can't stick to narratives, then belatedly we end up with failures.

One bad apple spoils the whole barrel as they say, and this is our problem when we put fire to clay, have intention to work in the absolute worst way, then pay someone to do what they should have done anyway. Call ourselves to moral account and call the world as well, this is the attempt to spread our voice and make a swell, the ocean's tides to move in a way that does well. Charity, what's the purpose, what's the point, is it to save lives or change them? Gorilla's and Turk are good because they aren't jerks, but Clayton is the enemy because of his selfish morality - is this not the classic christian duality? We make it seem as if saving the child in the well is the same as saving every person every day in every way, but as point of matter is, there is a limited amount of clay. Only so many walls, only so many pots, only so much rain, that's all we've got. So what do we do now that we've hatched a plot? Some person to save, some life to change, how do we make sure that we won't do tomorrow what we did today? Charity can't just be good, it has to show that it works, this money can't just disappear into the merk, but I need to know the changes, the purpose, the word and the worth. I've given money to beggars and seen them five minutes later drinking themselves into the earth, and I've paid for free nights, only to see the entitled act like jerks, as if me working for them is what they deserved. Charity for charity's sake is not good I think, it is untrustworthy, it is caustic, it is pointless, because there is more to life than survival, there is more to life than tomorrow. We have to change things down to the marrow, reinvigorate the blood, relight the brain, relieve our testing strain, and demand that everyone do what they claim. I think this is not insane, to want to know where my money goes when I give it away. It's just like capitalism, just mercantilism, what am I buying, what changes in the world, and I know I must give up control to do best, but if I do that then who do I trust?

I'm not tough, I give money away when asked, but I also know I never give enough. I feel guilty, and that's a little rough, but it's my brain that measures these inflows and outflows of gold dust, what I can give away, and what I keep because I must. I have to be suspicious, I have to think that those strangers are malicious, because I'll help friends or lovers all the way (What else is money for if not to save my living world?)

but because I know I might do that, I keep myself like a hammered nail curled. In my house, in my shell, I can ignore the rain's desperate swell, not drown, not die, but simply ignore until it all turns out well, if only because the media is preparing for another swell. My giving, if giving it is, is only personal, only limited, only upon request, and only one time, not the next. I am a poor, selfish soul, but I do my best, keeping my cards close to my chest. I don't like to gamble, I don't want to brag, so if I give you money please just say ok, don't say thanks, because in a little way I am, like Emerson, ashamed that I gave you my bank. I merely wanted to do good in the world, I naively wished that because of my actions it might change. I hope that my aversion and weakness to charity isn't so strange, and that you don't take verbatim what I say in the page. I have benefited in my time from some other person's adherence to the opposite rhyme, so it's not charity I give - it's just returning, to someone else, another's dime.

Day 12: May 10th, 2024

To Beauty,

    Some days there is no motivation, I have within me no intention to create or to drive, nothing comes out of me and nothing thrives. I write and edit, I dream and speak, but I cannot get anything out of me to sneak, and no deep terrible truth begins to creak. There is no sound of some Piro or Large being a neet, I'm not even Dom, drawing free if wrong; what I put forth and what I shove out is not a song, some Dragon-tale of winds and two longs heads, where Emmy and Max play - instead they have been put to bed, as if the day and sun are now dead. Such is this terrible dread, mucky mud where horses dare not tread, I want to give up and lose my head, lose my heart, and try not to make any more art. There is no drawing part left in me, I can't even fart out something ugly; no chains of gaseous molecules, no underpants for a captain, no child's rear flame or frontal shame, ugly noses and problems in the brain when we fear to speak for we stutter, and fear to streak lest we be called a nutter, some crazy person looking for attention. We've taken our clothes off, shown our skin, shed our blood, and said these are the words which show what is truly within. Is this due to our sense of sin? In the world truth does not win, it's not about how hard you work, but how well you play, not if you have the fire, but if you possess the exploitation of the clay. That's what they say at least, and maybe the only way out is to be light, to fight not gravity, or (directly) cold and might, green cash and goldenrod's sight, that endless rolling Miltank's bite. Photons do not touch and are not touched by time, but simply transformed into an orbital rhyme, and then are released in a secret chime, revealing the origin and the type of their clime, hydrogen or iron, helium or copper, selenium or carbon, some black-bodied radiation which reveals to a special station just what there has been baking. If you get past the puzzles and have an eye, then the truth comes naked without surprise, and from such information we may surmise:

    The puzzle pieces, the forgotten nieces, the family gathering, the chocolate Reeses: Candied fair and bright, a hope for next generation's smarts and might, this is how we see the light: Not encumbered by fog and night, old laws and necessary qualities, they way in which all things always have been and always must be, but the way in which the river becomes the sea. Frightening of course it must feel, to sail and probably crash on the lee, broken buildings, lifeboats lost, an inability to bear the cost of merchant's failure and all sailors lost, but if you wish to play the game and win, you must be willing to chance the cost. You're never going to win if you always give up even before you've faced the boss, some demon sorcerer who has always stood on top, using ancient magics and forbidden spells: The way in which their fate in the past did swell, and the ways in which they control the ringing of the bell, opening of the market, stocktenders trading, and ownership's demands for betraying the vision of their founders, treating hard workers as if they were flounders, fish to be caught and skinned of their meat, money to be had and ideals to be beat. I do not want to face that feat, and in order to face the heat, I shall not retreat.

Not give up this day, not bend under the emperor's sway, I'm not savvy, but I'll never give my company away. What is money? For others. What is money? For power. What is money? Opportunity. I buy what they sell, and what do I want? Nothing that I can't make as well, not gold or machines, not mechanisms or beef, not military marches or a hidden reef, but simply the ability to be free. Free to the definition of the extent, without any hindrance arising but from my self, without being locked to any shelf, a certain perspective, a safe space for storing nectar, and the start of an antimatter reactor transforming life into movement, and hope into light, taking these atoms and forming a knife, by cutting lose left from the right. I write down my thoughts in the middle of the night, and in this way against loss of inspiration I fight. By doubling back and doubling down, by using same words as if they were a circular many-pointed crown, studded with jewels which came from the empire round, on which the sun never sets and from which hope has never left, because even without a navy we are not bereft of options and diplomacy, of friends and enemies, challenges, opportunities, raft's, and unresolved thefts, which we shall carry to Sherlock for him to solve with his mind. We bake a cake and in this way make, out of a thousand poor ingredients, the left-over fridge bits, a midnight snack and a terrible trick, as we by our writing jump into the thick. Everything works just like this: I can't sleep until I've made a thousand words and written to Beauty, becoming not one of the herd.

Some days I'm a bore and some days I'm a loser, sometimes I'm a fox-beater and sometimes I'm a hunter, Guy Gisborn maimed or his horse torn asunder. - Whatever the case may be, I light my wings of fire. I fall not under the overturned cart and other forgotten parts of what is left when bandits have roamed and men have forgotten about their garden gnomes, good 'ol Doli leading the last children home. Listen, I travel with Balto to Nome. Gone with the land I may be, but I'm not some hidden house on the prairie, for I have no sisters, merely brothers, and I have no father but a mother. I to myself am only a bother, not sun, not moon, not stars even shining, but only glimmering on the waters, reflecting in the summer, clear skies where we wonder in search of thunder as if we were some dog in the small kingdoms, repaying the loyalist shepard and looking after three strangers who I think are no incredible danger. None of us are heading off to a manger, and all of us look a little mangy, but just because we write a little funny, doesn't mean that we aren't happy. No inspiration comes every day always in the same way, for I don't choose only fire or clay, but from both take the spark of the day, and write down what comes out of my burned mouth: Mushy, mealy, mumbling, and most certainly incredibly bumbling, but like Mr Vimes even though it look like I'm fumbling, I'll come out on top because I enjoy the tumbling, and the work of another dark evening.

Day 13: May 11th, 2024

To Beauty,

    Please like my first book. I know it's not ok, I know it's not fine, I know it's not done, but I've completed my final major edit today, because I don't think I can work on this more anyway. All my fire of two years is being turned into clay, and though I know, I know absolutely, that this no human heart will sway, still I cannot give up. - I hope, I pray, for nothing more than one smile, one 'cool', one maybe I won't forever and always be a fool. I know this is cruel, I know, I know, I tell, talk, ted to myself over and over again, but I just can't stop until I am dead. As I write this piece I prepare to go to bed, but before I can my soul I must shed, tear my mind from my body, my heart from my spirit; by the thin teather I go and jump into it, like Urameshi for a few hours away I fly. I won't pass if I don't cry, so silently I weep and seek that someone, somewhere, somewhen, will know why: Will understand what it is that I try. I don't want to go through another two years like this, I can't take it, but I think I must, I think I have to, I think it is all I have left; to reap the wild wind, to plant the wild grass, to into the wild world beyond the mountain pass. There are no monasteries, no job and cool friends, and not even an ideology to defend. - Nothing more upon me shall depend. I cannot save a person or the world, I cannot do all that I am told, I cannot wish to be more than bold, I cannot help but grow cold and old; but I hope not cruel. I hope to do no harm, I am not like the Pope acting as a sort of heavenly rope, and I am not boxing, playing the dope. - All I say is nope, nope, nope, I have no hope, I jump and fall, I cry and call, I paint my hopes upon the wall, and my fears as well. Oh listen, Beauty, can you hear the swell of sunbeams falling, aurora borealis, some passage to another world, and more walking yet, and more castles beyond, a thousand pillars up to the sky, like Lyra we ask: Why, why, why?

    I do have an answer, I do, I do. I know why I try, I know why I cry, I know why I write and who I write to, though I have not a goal in mind or a game; I simply play Calvinball until I have to go inside because of the rain. I have pain, and I have strain, and I have stress, and I don't know what to do next. Might I travel to Chinatown, might I drink kombucha and drown? I am no dragon-gate mage, I am no atomic wire gauge, I know not what it is to love and be betrayed, for in that vision I always fade. Do not hate me, this I beg, for in seven days I will submit my rag, waving before the world my white flag, riding into battle either the stallion or the nag, simply tossing on the train my one small bag. What is my purpose you ask, what is my flight? It is simply that this work has been my light: Now that I finish it, I shall seek once more the night, and now I flee, as I have fled before, I am a coward walking out the door. All is up to you now to seek me more. - Though of course you won't, because I'm a boor, and also old, I bend my knee before the cold. Even to stand up straight these days pulls me down, even to feeling nauseous at hint of sound. I realize how I am not bound for the sun, but for the ground, now that all my weakness and those eight kings around me surround, I run for the country and flee from the town. My word too asks for a boon. I am sick at heart, sick in soul, not a man but a fool.

    What shall be next? What shall be left behind? What broken soul shards should I find? Guldan's hand comes down, tears fel flesh to imps around, fire falling with nary a sound, as my beating heart pounds. This world, this land, this idea may be much too loud, and I write to you though I give this to the crowd, because I know of nothing more I can do that's profound. This is my tablet, this is my commandment, this is my wisdom-net to catch a fish and burn my fist, like a babe I suck my thumb and I know no more than this: Life is but a horrible trick, troll's blood, Zandalari stick, Zeus's cast, and Loki's mix. We as humans are in the thick of it: Inner spirits, gods without names, turtles from the sky, and high hub's fame, as if we were soldiers inherently lame, ones who had to be taught how to play the game. Fate's dice roll, and scissors cut our tails like mice, biology to us is not always so nice, and for our chances we pay a price: Our's to do, ours to dare, ours to lay down naked and bare, defenseless before the fact that we care.

    Beauty, I hope you'll like my book, beauty I pray you don't mind that I stare, because I hope you understand that I think of you like Clair: Save the cheerleader, save the world, move the turtle, and bury the burl. - Let new tree rise up from the dead leaves, let songs be sung as we please, and let you find in my book the truth of these: The words I've said, the thought's I've felt, the terrible hammer blows to myself that I've dealt, knocking the slag loose from the bind; I have made grapes from sour wine. I know you shall never answer in kind, and I hope this lashing will not hit me from behind, striking through my soul like the anger of the divine. I've written this book in thanks for your shine, and even though all the words be mine, the bones and fulcrums indeed are thine. If you've read this or listened to it, then thank you for your time. I think you will forget me, but maybe this book in your shelf will bind, and one day some impossible thing either you or I will find, but until that next world goodbye: Leave me behind.

Day 14: May 12th, 2024

To Beauty,

    What is family? I don't mean blood, though that's certainly part of it for almost everyone. No, I mean those who stand with you even in mud, the ones who treat you as a hope, not a dud. Some family knows you from beginning to the end, when, at close of all this, none except they may recollect your childhood days, or know all the fights you won, lost, and made. Family is not to be commanded, not to be obeyed, they are neither to slay, or to be slayed. - No, they are to be stood with and beside, in front and behind, for they are the letters burned into your hide, the visible scars of who you belong to inside. Family is a cause for both harm and pride, as all parents cause pain, and all siblings let you know what it is to have water fall from your eyes like rain; for family is, in bad days, a strain, a heavy weight upon you laid, the curses of ancestors, the call of irish troubles, the fact the McCoy's repay three times the issue that you caused them that other day. - Family is, too often, chains that bind, claws that scratch, teeth which snap, the wrong lessons mis-learned, and to the wrong roads returned, repeating mistakes and always learning too late. Wow, we so often mistake love for hate, and the truly mediocre for the even possibly great. Tradition, too often, gives more than it takes, and we too seldom realize that we can't re-close the gate, the paths we walked and the common senses we betrayed. We are betrangled, dirty, not hill-folk but mud-folk, garbage-broke, the kind that before chances in school ever did choke, and with an attitude which may never be bespoke, because we are not ourselves: Only our family's joke.

    Jake and Jive, survive and thrive, our heart does beat and our breath does breathe, as we leave behind family and fall to our knees. Come back, we return to what was golden for which we yearn, the wealth we did not realize, the help we took for granted, and the sudden sight of all our chances, us who were never made for dances. Too many people, too much noise, but family is ok if you shut yourself up in a room to play with your toys. I can come out for dinner when you feel like I am able to deal with the boys, and family hopes you have a life that you enjoy. It's not money, nor time, not even progeny or rhyme, but only the push that you at least have a living dime, so that in the proper and correct line, you will have your moment to shine. Family at its worst is certainly a curse, but on the other hand, at its best, it is the most powerful blessing you may ever receive: To have a home, a happy, a safe, a study, thirty different buddies, and all without trying, all without needing to build or lie, work or cry, but they simply stand by you even against all the earth, or under all the sky; they'll pass you words of wisdom, and wait for you to learn them by and by. - Like any good knight-errant, they'll try and try, to protect the weak, uphold the law, and like Melody balance flame with claw; little singers in back of head, and a thousand rainbow lizards keeping you warm and fed. Families fight, families defend, and families their structured guidance shall lend. The whole point of family is not alone against hell to fend, but instead in this life have forever at least one friend who won't betray you, won't leave you cold, and won't abandon you when you grow too bold. Family knows absolutely that you are a fool, being the extreme opposite of cool, and they're not going to bet money on you, but they'll at least play a round of pool,

  Playing the game that's all you see, that's all you need: We are a seed, sprouting into a tree. We might stand all alone, in the midst of wild mountains, or an empty dial-tone, whether we stand in New York, or subsist on old bones, not mattering either if we are armored in mail, or singing in dulcet tones. We, like Snoopy, simply need, in the storm: Shelter, food, and a home. Humans are of the herd, and like a stupid little fly we'll keep going back and back into the light until we are burned, blue flame coming down losing control of our turns, we hit the ground flat and then go splat, growing from wreckage and ruin a collection of silly hats, a thousand mementos of our every turn at bat, as the family doesn't let us forget either the good or the bad, but does cover up the sad times with moments rad, and does overcome the lying times with the changing fads: We recognize how we grow different every time we enter Grandpa's pad: We are no longer that young lass or lad who was here once, forever glad only to be alone with grandparents and not with mother or dad, free to watch Toonami, or simply enjoy the weather that was so balmy, as we and our brothers, sitting with no care, realized that in our minds we could always go back to that lair, and always feel safe for a few moments, even ten years later, simply because even if they sometimes disapprove, they never ever said: I hate her. I'll remember the feeling of being loved, forever, and always it shall lay in my heart like an ember, ready to reignite the fire when I want to surrender beneath the weight of the world, the toil of trouble, the cost of gold, or the terrible fate of growing cold. Family and memories continue to grow old, but they shall never be lost: As long as I live, they allow me to be bold, because my family will stand beside me even if I don't always do as I'm taught or told. Families can be cruel, but then at other times they are the greatest jewel.

Day 15: May 13th, 2024

To Beauty,

Some days I've just run out of everything. The depression overcomes me. and the moon falls. No more may I hear the sunlight's bright, shining, hopeful call. I have lost it all. - No more shall I live and die, but simply be. I have lost any semblance or shape of me. The world has placed me upon the tee, stuck me as hard as it can, launching me foul, out of bounds and hands. No Valkyrie, no sky, no stars, I walk alone in the dark, by the rain and storm overwhelmed, with no ark in sight. Abandoned by God, abandoned by man, how else now shall I stand? Smoothed by the sand, scattered by the sea, this I fear: I shall ever flee, be-ing and not becoming. No power here, no plan, not even a single fan to cool the air and overcome the breath of the desert of lost hopes; I have not even that peach-filled boat nor mountain stream, and there is no-one to walk with me as I scream, as I weep because of my dream, as I am between white as cream, heavy and quick to spoil, kept cold and never let to boil. Being like this is a special curse and toil; my spirit is scattered like water and oil, the light and the dark never to meet, the hope ineffectual and the sweet grain not to break, to be beat, baked, and then 'eat'. - No eight elements have I, only thunder and pain, something's wrong with me, I am always under a nothing strain; I feel as if I am going insane, my mind, my heart, my soul, there is a deep crack in my begging bowl, it cannot hold rice nor drink, nothing great, no ambrosia wine made from grapes. Everything, everywhere, all the time, is always a mistake; "My wounds are gaping. I reel to stand. Six battles' span; by this gasping breath, no pantomime!"[1] - These words are my only dime, all I can make, all I may take from me, through me, of me; I have nothing which should be read, no idea worthy of being said. I know, absolutely know, that I would be better off giving up, and going back to bed, giving up on fighting off all the monsters in my head, no more either angels or demons defend, become not a human but a rock, neither living nor dead.

But what's this? Suddenly gold that gleams, a smile like a dream, words that scream; for I am made Mona with broken chocolate, panicked and afraid, because I my high hopes have betrayed, my work unworthy to make the grade. Into the ground I have been laid, but Willow chants a spell, and then opens up wood with a spade. For a long time, ten years,

I was away, and I don't know what to do now that I've returned by this day. I am not numb, I feel the pain, I know of Dain, friends, family far away, goes to fight, thrones to save, but relying on that chance is not safe, goblins come and elves run; if I don't stand up now, I will be undone, an undine, some mortal soul drowned beneath the brine, and to escape that fate I offer up my blood as a bribe, I sacrifice the truth before the altar of time. I unbind, release myself, unwind, then tie life up again to a patterned chime, committing unspeakable, horrible, wish-giving crimes, emptying all these words from power inside, drawing my sword in desperate attempt to break the tide. I sent and cry, avast ye demon go back, you will not have me anymore, stuff me into some forgotten crack on the shore, grind me down until I am no more. My soul will not be bored through again, no evil holes inside me shall win, this is my second chance now and I am the wind: Free to run north to south, east to west, I am invisible but I do my best, and though day will come when I fail final test, that day is not this one, not yet. I cast it all on some bet, some pitch and toss, and I'll never say a word to anyone if I have lost. Too well do I know, of speaking up, the cost. I shall be misunderstood; I shall be abandoned in the woods. None will reply to me, and no-one will hear when I cry at night, my void to fight; all I see now is shadows, not light. Quail I before a beauty bright, and cold am I now as Thanatos stalks me in his quiet, questing, patient way, never aiming directly, but only dancing round. In the distance I hear the drums of orcs pound. By this sound I am pressed, utterly aware of what comes next, the struggle in which my books are stressed, the way in which I am depressed.

If I am sad I play dress-up, if I am mad I'll really mess up, but I don't know what I'd do if I was glad; it's been a while since I expressed that fad. I will not be like my dad, a person I do not trust, I will be better, I must; I will rip apart my soul and show my lies so that I may trust: I must, I must, it's that: To be spirit, or dust. I will destroy the mast, no more catch the wind, blow holes in the ship, now it's sink or swim. - I lose myself, and in that way maybe win. I am twinned, tail and head, I live, and am also dead. This is the only way I have ever managed to pull myself out of bed, by blindly clinging to hope, and following that burning star wherever it has led. I can't see where I'm going, I don't know why I'm trying, but I am blind - and I am moved. Speaking but never spoken to, dreaming but never dreamt, I write because it's all the heart I have left to lend, shield to against my despair defend; I paint the shadows, I seek the light, and I tell you mirror, I fight. I fight. I fight. I'm trying to fight. I will not give up tonight. I fall to dive, I rise to flight, I flap my wings, I chase, I bite, I sing of sight, so that one day I might be more than maybe; be more than me, not a sapling, but a tree. My poems to shade, my art be made, my leaves falling like rain, I will understand my pain, and I shall if I must bet it all again, pitch or toss, find or be lost, love or bust, nothing much, my heart to survive, my life to thrive, I attempt to live not die, and for the first time in ten years: I try. I write, I cry, I seek and ask why why why. This is my answer: Because one day I didn't want to say goodbye. Once more into the breach my friends, once more to battle, it's time to pass as men, and not as cattle. I'm a big baby perhaps, but listen I have my rattle: This is my reincarnate soul attempting to tattle. Here are my letters, truths and lies, here are my scars and there is my tide. I must away now with the white sails shaking and the gray dawn breaking, look, see, the sunrise. Look, see, my pride. I am revealed, standing outside.

Day 16: May 14th, 2024

To Beauty,

    I hung out with my brother today, and for a few hours there was a game we played: Some cards from a land apart, ones covered with Egyptian art, that conception of a Japanese invention, Yugioh and tcg, both the iron chains and a trap hole cutting me off at the knees, eight thousand life points disappearing quick as a sneeze, without even so much as a will-you-please. Indeed, it's not so often we joke and laugh, because I live in the woods, and he's in my mother's flat, paying rent and taking his turn at bat, a federation planning where Greenspan has the last laugh, taxes and trials bringing him through many miles, as he plays on all of life's many tiles. I, on the other hand, am sinking in the Nile, burrowing into the black mud and planting seeds, hoping none of them are duds. May I receive in return more than what I give, this is my prayer, this is my need, that in this action and by this deed, I shall from my demons be freed: Like a dragon able to pursue my greed, chase after gold and princesses, breath fire and flame, fly across the sky, fry knights, chase kits and call out my name, show my breast and my scales in pride, not shame. One such as I does not dare to play the game, jump into DnD, write of a plan, a background and sand; I'm no jarhead, I'm not even a man, but only an insane wolf boy, beast without music, mind without logic, lover without language. I can't count, I can't read, I can barely speak, all I do is write and squeak; sneak, like a mouse I run and hide lest I be found, then bound, beaten, and finally eaten, because I am hiding in the garage now, this very moment, writing in torment. I want to sleep, into the shadow realm creep, I'm like Marik, first evil, then sweet. Isn't this neat, how I feel like a freak, not sure what to do, or who to speak to.

    I'm visiting my home again, just for a few days, and for the journey here I have highly paid, in losing sleep and marching with heavy bags until I was weak. As I walked past my old high school I wanted to weep, because they put chains on her, tall black steel grates, with these big, giant, locking gates, and that campus, once open, is now a token of fear and control, of making things better in some way by playing the fool, and instead of fixing our problems just applying a big mechanical tool. - That'll keep the crazies out they say, keep our children safe today. It's not exactly clear what they've lost, and I'm sure the freshman incoming now don't even know the cost, let alone the difference, because the elementary and middle too, some years earlier, before the N-1 and the C-19 flu, were locked and enchained, made safe for the developing brains, but they aren't as free as they were. - We've all been stained, by blood and guns, by fear and chains, now we can't even run to escape the drain of love and trust, of life and dust, and though we play with our brothers, play as we must, yet more here has been lost.

What is home but a place, a way, to sleep? My old bedroom is filled with books and and computers, games to play, videos to watch, cards to trade, diplomas to be picked up and then put back down, laid into their grave for our accomplishments to fade. Its been two years since I passed all my classes, and though my eyes are still clear and my glasses are clean, I am running out of gas; I am running out of things to be. I imagine, sitting in this room, that I die, and I wonder what was the reason I ever tried? My art is not here, my book is not done, my room is filled up with memories and fun: What I've learned, where I've been, the texts I've read, the worlds I've saved, and the fact that there is nothing left for me here but the grave. I am made a knave, not knight nor king, not princess, queen, donkey, dragon, ogre, fairy-tail bacon, Pinocchio being shaken, I am no ginger-bread baked, I am becoming nothing, I am going nowhere, and I am a mistake, have lost sight of all that is great. - What shall I do now, I am going to break! The world before me shudders and quakes.

I am simply not happy, not done, there is no dream for me, nothing to be won, I don't know what to do anymore, I just feel done. I'm back to family, I'm back to home, but my brothers are grown and change no more, I can't go back to school, my fire is growing cold, I write and write, but it's just drowning me in the night. I'm almost finished with my book now, and when I am, so too goes out the light. I sometimes write as if nothing else matters, trying to go mad like the hatter, I am alice in chains, I am Maniac Magee's stain, busted up sneakers, barefoot quicker, blind as a bat and sitting back for some more corn-licker, while the violinists play and the fiddlers bray, like donkeys who are stubborn today. As for me? I am like the water, the wave, the wind, the tree, everything else makes noise, but I am not really me, nought to see, only the origin-roots, only Gungan toots. I am doomed because I am moved, and do not move myself. Stuck I shall be forever on this shelf, some toy not a real elf, if none reach out to take my hand and swing me round to crash or stand. Crawling, climbing, screaming, crying, what am I doing, nought but repeating, I am straining, fighting, fleeing, begging, painting, dreaming, drawing forth all that I can out of shadows, emptiness, and memories, - being empty of breath, unable to breath, I know not what I want or need, only that it's not this. I have hell in me, that defended fort, and there is no guard to stop these demons dragging me through the port: Before the nobles of the world only sport, some fox or bear, a wolf or boar with bristled hair, safe ensconced in my lair but...out of care. All I have is to bet and dare, quiet or run, battle or guard, corner or spare, as today I barely manage to wash my hair.

I play games, I write to beautiful names, but in my rhymes are hidden my shames. I repeat, I go in circles, I use no new words, and my pictures are not diamonds but dirt. Everything about this, my life, nothing of it hurts, it's not bad, it's just not glad, great, or sad, there's nothing that moves me, makes me smile or be mad. I Love every side, I see every struggle, but none of it, not a single care, do I juggle. I may barely stand, my hope is not mine to command, I have five cards, but I'm not sure there is anything I can do with this hand. I am home, but I need to leave, return to the wilderness, and find whatever it is that I need, the kind of fire that would turn a wurm into a dragon, one full of good, and greed.

Day 17: May 15th, 2024

To Beauty,

When Illona Andrews wrote: "He was describing that moment when you realize that you are lonely. For a time you can be alone and doing fine, and never give a thought to living another way, and then you meet someone and suddenly you become lonely. It stabs at you, almost like a physical pain, and you feel both deprived and angry, deprived because their absence brings you misery. It's a strange feeling, akin to desperation, a feeling that makes you wait by the phone even though you know that the call is an hour away. I was not going to lose my balance. Not yet."[2]

I thought of mine: I lost my balance years ago, and I have spent these decades being tossed to and fro, not to admit, not to say, not to show, just which sort of terrible ivy upon me has grown, slipping into my cracks, climbing my back, covering my eyes, taking from me any view of living or dying. It is only now, after these hundred-thousand words, that I feel again like trying, because the sunlight burned all those leaves away, and then the shadow made sure that away they stayed; I understand now for what I have paid, absence of pack, a loaner made. No virus in my veins nor sword to hand, Immortalis I am not, missing both mind and brain. It doesn't matter if I am tech or magic-strain, I am by this world drained. Wanting to go insane, I am cursed to remain, nothing bites, nothing draws, nothing screams: Silence is all I have, all I need - or at least I thought it was, until I began to dream. Not about the cat, I am the cat. Not about the shapeshifter, for I prefer my spiritual, not physical, mixtures. No master of the dead, no cop for the living, I have no merc's mouth nor blood every month, and I'm not smart, not a dunce, I never jumped even once. Slick plastic surgeons make me sick, and sweet slimy lies are just a bad trick. Everything around me is thick. - Hard to move, difficult to breathe, hazy views, and flowering trees make one sneeze. Stung by the bee, I lost my ability to speak, and missing that I never had a drink. I drowned once, I died, I said I knew how to be happy, but I lied. Still I remain ignorant me, unable to fly, unable to see.

My balance is gone, my hope is dust, I have no trust in the scent of musk, and I am a boar without any tusks, digging not fighting, dreaming, not crying: Today I finished editing my book, and I think I'm going to throw up if I ever tell someone to take a look. I put half my soul into this text, throwing in everything I had to cook, the vegetables left out a little too long, the fruit juice someone gave me for singing a song, and the bag of rice which has been sitting on the counter overnight, for now the mice have gotten to it, made it rotton. Flies lay eggs, the moths are gray, black ants march on, and dips the human hand, drawing forth flower of the land. Here I am under no command, not of health nor wisdom, wits nor fight; I am in the dark turning off the light. What more, after this, would I write? Simply these thousand words I put down every night.

I'm not desperate, just sad, as in the forest I went mad. Everything I do, I am, is bad, and I'm just writing because there's nothing more I manage to think of to do: Naught to bring, no pull on my string. I am going to sleep hungry this night, unless with my rhymes I might make something more bright. Shining, I have more bait in sight, all that I've made, my dreams, and my light: Black perhaps, purple in the dark, the kind which new shoes spark, the hidden violent parts of art, short wavelength imparting a laser-tag feeling, invisible shots to visible targets, someone else calling out the score, as I alternate between frightened or bored. I am destroyed by those memories I adored, and I've been struck so hard that, thirty years later, I'm still stuck on the floor. No balance, can't stand, no plan, falling-flying, no place to land, I am not worthy of any valkyrie's hand, but maybe I can get better yet, I send myself a command: Thou fool, with the kings upon you, stand. This is my demand: I will know what I suffer under and why. I will live and die, dream and fly, draw and cry out: Where was I, where am I, where am I going now, and how? What now, brown cow who jumped over the moon, where is my fork, where is my spoon? Is it better to be such a loon, or was my sanity a boon? I send this out to the sun and moon, some bad ocarina's timeless toon, and I hope that I am neither too late, nor too soon.

Undoubtedly I am a mistake and I make more, but being a joke isn't so bad as long as you don't eat off the floor like the dogs, or in the slop as the pigs; instead I stand as a man, reach out my hand to grab fresh figs. The knowledge of good and evil thus I gain, and for my pain innocence is lost. I understand the cost, all that I must is cover up and hide, make sure that my inner parts have not died, but are hidden, that my darkness is tossed down the midden, and that light me appears to do all he is bidden. Thus am I by the holy spirit ridden, not the devil, but just god kiddin' around. - This is how we learn, by hitting, and being hitten, or biting and being bitten. Lessons ground into flesh, not enough, but it's my best. Can't save myself, need to be helped, inner sinner's stain won't leave, I am unbalanced, I have a saviros need, as I get rid of all my faults, pride and greed. I am brought by vision to my knees, judged and committed without even a by-you-please, and at the hypocrisy I sneeze; my life is but the shadow of a breeze. Yet why, if soul be so light, does flesh feel like might, all this knowledge acting on me as a blight? A sickness to be sure, but one I would not give up for certain, because receiving a blessing means undressing: Showing the rents in my heart, the unbalanced part. I would be happy ignorant, but I would not make art, I would have no fire and no spark. Singing my song like a lark, ignorant-invalid in the golden park, autumn of the soul ends with winter arriving. If I was smart I would run, but I'm human so I'm dumb. I've lost my sense of balance but now, finally, not numb. Stand on the side of the road, and stick up my thumb; who shall find me, and shall they be the one? I've written a book now, but this journey is not done. I didn't drive here, but maybe I've managed to run, not walk, stumble, bumble, tumble, travel through the jungle, this is my rumble, like a butterfly or a bee, I am money in a tree, and I wonder, will anyone ever read me? Is this ceremony how I bleed free? What is next? What do I need? If I keep writing, then tomorrow, who will I be? Even out of balance and falling, I open my eyes to see.

Day 18: May 16th, 2024

To Beauty,

    I can do this, Beauty. I say: I can do this. I can do this. I say it everyday: I can do this, I can do this, as I write this book, cuz I am home from my nook. I know I am no sort of peregrine talk, I have no wings to fly, I have no sword to swing, I have no eye to see, I have no tongue to bring forth Majesty, magic, and mystery. There's nobody listening to me, or for my text. I never give myself a rest; I hammer myself over and over again. preparing for what's coming next: Death and pain, life and a brain drained, walked back through these hills again. My life is folded, still nothing moves, I think shakes quake and quaked - I am oatmeal, and bacon cut from the pig. I am nothing but a jig, some small shape, a boat with a sail, while I am wide awake in the front. The lanterns glow slowly, and slowly around me begins to snow: Cold again, but I am enough. Let me know? I feel my anxiety is beginning to show, because in stuttering without stopping, I'm writing without walking, simply going in circles, myself stalking. I am breaking, I am broken, I am tired and trial, I am my secret denial. Like Daniels, I am lonely. My balance is slowly falling apart, and I am lost; I make art, I'm going to fight dementia and death, and I don't know if I can pass this test. Two legs I have, no more to rest, and three legs i've found. I've written, I've done my best, but I am the least of all my dreams, not a being but a thing, abstract representation of shallow emotions: Protestations that this is not important, it cannot be. - I will not allow the acorn to sprout forth into a tree, I will not save my spirit, not I nor me, there is no strength mighty and free, I wrote words driven to knees, and now I ask you please:

    Don't hate me. I say this over and over again, Beauty, don't hate me. Don't see my ugliness, don't care for my charm, don't allow me to do anything, anywhere, anyone, any harm. Not in the mirror, not on the sea, not in the mountains high and wild, full of berries and bees. I do not ask, I do not beg, I do not need anything from thee except that you exist; except that you know this is not a trick; except that you don't toss me out of the thicket, because I am not a Br'er rabbit. (I won't make it.) I don't ask you to do anything. - I ask that you do not. Don't block me, don't hate me, don't throw me away, and please above all don't be silent. Not again. I can't die. I want to live. Yes or no, stay here or leave me alone, shout goal or miss, let the time run out, or the bell ring the end of this bout. Respond to my spirit with a whisper or a shout, don't shut me out, not without explanation, not without a smile, or a frown, or anything, anything at all. Drop me in the garbage like a worn-out doll, or as some fisherman dragging in his haul. I show you I have written, and so I have already been mauled, and in my penance I shave my head: Bald showing my face whispering of grace, Valkyrie please tell me I was brave, this wasn't a mistake. I know I'm not good nor great, but I hope I'm human enough that I don't deserve your hate, and to be shoved unceremoniously back inside my gate.

I've opened the door, I've got up off the floor and I am unable to do any more. My bravery is spent, my talents are lent, and I am sorry I won't repent. Guilty as sin, naught to win, I unwind, reweave, retie, redie, remake, embrace love and hate, those naive conceptions of five and fifteen and twenty five and thirty five and more and more and more. - I have left the mountains, I have trailed the creek, I have sailed the sea, and now stand on the far shore. New land, hidden hand, barbarian band, natures red and ruined demand, I am undone, undoing. Am the writ, am the bit, I am like the ball thrown in the air, and where I land next I neither know nor care, as long as it is not where I was before. All that I am abandoned on the floor, empty of poetry, hope, and light. I am guided not by might but may, not by ending of day but the rising moon, I was hit in the head so hard that it made me swoon, beauty struck me - my balance out of tune, myself being made not Luna, but lune, a fool who writes letters to her at noon on the bus, or under shade. Everytime, he has been hurt by the world, and saved or betrayed.

There were accents I heard today which reminded me of my Grandparents. Not the ones alive, not the one I look after, but the ones who have left, who by time from me have been cleft. Is it enough to say that I am bereft, a small, striking sadness nestling in my left breast, yet another rock for me to heft. As I sit here in the bus staring out my window left, I wonder would I leave? If I could find some magic breeze, breath of God or Aslan's sneeze, would I also say please? I want the future, I want the past, and I am whipped by these two as before the mast. I am torn apart by these wants, I cannot last - but instead of silent suffering, I set myself now a task, to write in blood and tear off a mask. Seven times I've come to where my first hope jeered and laughed me into an acorn; "now I fear, as I never feared before, to fall forsworn."[3] My chains are a knife, my wishes are strife, I have spent my entire life hiding, huddled, wrapped in blankets against the cold and night, wallowing, weeping in fright; today is the day I finished the book and decided to fight. Na'ru I became, both shadows and light. I will not lie, I am human inside.

So, yes, I can do this. I think I can, I think I can, I think I can.... know I can. These are my faults, written in my hand. I am before my muse a beast to command. Shift and change, werewolf or man, I am no vampire, I make my own blood, I can. I can do this, Beauty, I can. Please don't hate me. Please don't break me. I have undone, and remade me. You don't need to hurt me: I've already hurt myself - please, you don't need to do anything else. Just read my book, and put it on your shelf. That'll be enough for me. That'll be enough, I think, for me to open my eyes wide and not blink.

Day 19: May 17th, 2024

To Beauty,

    Have you ever heard a unique tone in your voice? I mean, one where you hear yourself and ask: Who was that? Not only what, or why, but whom inside was turned and tossed, what sort of chains in you were lost, the beasts come out of cage, or the titan bellowing in his rage, the terror of midnights in the wood, or the pain of knowing how to ask for what we never could receive? Such a voice reveals a mysterious need, some dragon's greed or gorgon's stare, mightiest magic of Medusa's hair. Isn't it so strange how those snakes were conceived as evil and frightening, but now in our cartoons they seem wise and enlightening? Free serpents who mean no harm, simply hissing in their sudden alarm. Like huntsmen, like Cairn, like moonborn, they are wild beyond mortal ken, symbols and motions of the unbridled emotions within. No laws to follow, no rules to grab, there is no tradition to make them gab silent lies or twisted truths, they are no mortal mankind's noose, the sour juice of yggdrasil tree, grounded acorns and meals three. One of dark moon, two of red boon, and third of white sight, they are signals in the night, some invisible, some intangible, and all indomitable; for we are human and need to eat, we are free and vote with our feet. What is most important to us is what we stay around for, or chase after, and I am standing here; I am trying, attempting, blinding, crawling, attempting to stay, or to arrive a little closer to the stars in the sky, the words to be written not die, the fact that I am so very very shy, let me loose I run and dive. - I shall thrive, I will know and see, my voice is strange, it frightens me, soft and sudden like that, or growling taken off the track, it bursts forth from me, and I don't know how to summon it back. - No undoing what has been done, no more medicine for that which was already numb, I am cut like a surgeon, I am knifed like a god, I am some giant cow being stuck with a cattle prod. Being loud and long, seeking lighthouse in the fog, my eyes are covered but my ears still see, my poor lungs breath. -

    What are these words I said which drove me towards the lee shore? Only that nothing was wrong. I said, I scream, as I pounded my fists onto my knees, and I will never beg, I will never say please, all those words are a trick, or a way to squeeze. - Lie and shape me, power break me, will remake me, beyond body to soul, beyond soul to spirit, and beyond spirit to - what? Who, why, where, when, why why why. - I mutter round myself. trying to live until die. I call these words into the sky: I am trying to learn, No other dreams now have I to burn, for I have used them up, I have tossed them away, I have the ending of their days, such light for me, blinded by hate is how I see, completing the circle, becoming again me.

I say words with no meaning, I utter refrain with nary a song, I fight every time, but never for very long. - I am a piece of ivy not a tree, vine not log, stalk of grass with no flower, devoured by what must be, all that I allow myself to accept and know, both the heat of the desert and the forbidden wild freezing snow. All stories are enchanted as if I was in a glow, surrounded by painted pictures, upheld by glass bulb, I am dying under water, I am cold; would that I had it in me to become more bold, and to not accept what I am told: How I should I act, what I should be, whom sets me free, and what rules strengthen me? I tell you, nothing matters if you are not free, to chase and run, to speak and sashay, we dig in the side of the river and pull out wet clay, making pots so that the emptiness we might slay, either by locking it up or drowning it out, covering our lives either with a grave or a shout. Like salesmen we hide, but like Link we wish to swing a sword, to break the tide, draw forth rubies and emeralds that shine, ten thousand rupee knives, giant's wallet, show your words or swallow it, this is the cost of freedom, responsibility and review; I need to know if I may be someone new, or must always remain one of the favored few, priest tied to god by apron-string, Alexander's knot undone, satrap of a persian king, this I ask: What shall I bring? Here now lies my line and my lean, these shield-words a thin finding indeed.

No more judge and jury, no more executioner, this is my journey, an entourage of kings, vanity, fear, and greed. Broken saber I have, back before the wall, I stab blind hands into the dirt and crawl, shift like a werewolf bearing all, as in my words I hear the echo of a call, that on this matter I am willing to risk mush of all. Serious I am, too serious, and not enough, because I fear the future mysterious, and I wonder if any of you will ever hear this. - No brand am I to hide in the mist, a hero in name but not like this, such a wild thing they shall believe; nothing shall be tormented by my tomorrow, I am shattered, burning, old; this quarter-life is my attempt to be reborn and become more bold; I shall not paint a picture and be struck to a mold. This sound and naught less, this whisper and no more blessed, it feels like reverend the whale, I follow these lines or succumb to the betrayal. Steady, sure, and strong, confused, animal song, five - or seven to nine, some magical rhyme. Listen to me. - Pay attention this time, and with no overwhelming spirit do we whine. This is the inside, tell the truth and grow not snide, I bow and bend not beneath the tide, but instead tell the truth, pain tin trade, show the world what I mean, and what may yet be. I'll not lie, bit more, not to thee, for I shall be free: Words, tone, life, enemy, this is me: Not a thing but a being, not a light but all unseen, no roots made a tree, my hope I believe - all meaning free. All living things be, nothing wrong, just this and me. I will be free come what may, no matter how I hide or how Gungnir sways, I don't keep to lies, I'll push them away, I'll bake myself, made fire from clay, love from rage.

Day 20: May 18th, 2024

To Beauty

    Hand full of stones, river rocks and bones, a vision comes into my life as if from a tome, some semblance-seeming of home. No place I may see, no place I may know, simply reflected myself as cold and alone, a sight so cruel I put down the phone. To reach, to touch, to lick, to eat, to grind the stones and make them meat, by pressure bind and in heat combine, disparate parts made whole again, quarter-hearts bound and bent. No more from this life shall I be rent, because I might from valkyrie grab a net, spread out hand to dash and grab, as falling off the star-sign ship I roll, tossed by mother of storms like a fool up and down, across the bow, mermaids to eat, waves shriek, I am shredded, my muscles made meat. - No more here may my heart beat, no more my gummy mouth shall eat, my teeth torn out, my tongue destroyed, the sounds I make are that of a little baby boy, and no man or even an elder. I have no food, fire, or shelter. No offerings to a god, no sight guiding the lost, I have not even the beauty of Jack Frost early in the morning, when white lace shivers all the trees, and glass crackles while we breath: Those secret stars who have a need of meeting in Deering's Woods, ancient candles of the flood: Reimagined memories and strategies which for thirty thousand years humankind has saddened, sudden striking tearing us apart from home and hearth, family and fame, driving us a thousand generations down the road until no-body remembers our name; we recall that we were once insane, and using art and chalk we inscribed our name on rock, charcoal drawing of blue-stained farthings, bison horns, and deer droppings, mammoths by spears tossing, mammon drawing, angels with blood on their hands and devils full of lies. We may have forgotten what we did, but we tried a thousand, thousand terrible triumphs to overcome, we lost our family and our one, we lost our language and our home, we lost our truths and our legends, we stood alone: One thousand two hundred and eighty of us, apes without a home, apes without a brain, apes without a knowledge of what they had to lose or gain.

    This is what stone means to me, this is what hand, that we are by all the earth banded, ourselves one family, one hope granted, brothers and sisters to each other, uncles and aunts. We forget this at our peril, when we let it pass into the past without gasp or task. It doesn't mean we understand each other, but it does mean we can make it last, this terrible fortune into which we are cast. All mankind are alone at last, or to the group traitors, our morals traded for favors, to escape red tooth and claw, to escape our lovers and our haters, to be unbound and free to unwind and be rebound, our spirit trumpeting such a unique sound, as with disdain we are by others blamed for their faults and our choices, controlled by their blessings and curses. Those civilized people, those civilized peoples who dig in the earth for gems and beads, cut and polish, blood greed - they tell us that we are the ones with a need, and they know how to fill it, but to tell the truth? I doubt it, for myth and legend, fire and flame, I am the one who has to find my name and play the game, make it up, from the Calvin-Ball trophy-cup sup. I am a druid, Azeroths' dream, emerald scream - shape of a wolf and a man, but not always as I seem. In my eyes not roots, but tiger's teeth, gleam when I let loose shouts and screams. Perhaps it shall be ice cream, cold and sharp, sweet at night filling up memories of light, and although we've forgotten the flavors, we've remembered the neighbors; with hand full of stones and memories of bones, we see the earth and we feel not so alone, as we are flung from mountain to sea, air to foam, burying our bare feet in the loam, pucking at our string on the loom, whispering in the evening as on comes the gloom, darkness pushing us to back in the room, scared and still, wild dreams reduced to swill.

  No, I say. No, I scream, IT shall not be! Even reduced from oak to acorn, even turned from a princess into a swan, even made a prince with broken bow and badly aimed arrow, it is our time to take the ship through the narrows. Listen to me sparrows, listen to me crows, grab this line and pull: In your hundreds, in your thousands, in your tens of thousands, strike with claws, do not fear the maw, no jailer may touch you if you are straight and true; with all your might seek the skies, live and die, here now we fly. - Winged ship and friends galore, ancient and mighty stories of lore, pieces of sand that lie on the shore. Here we draw a line, here we make art, here we start: Again and again, to our shame a spiral plan we find, Gurren Lagann, stones in the hand. Mother Earth, Father Sky, we do not beg, we do not command, we simply say we are your sun and here we stand, ten billion cells with one mighty heart-shaped band, strings which vibrate and tear apart, teeth regrowing as does a shark's, making music like that pretty lark, feathered and furred, companions of the ark. Today we part, I know this in my heart, but we are not lost; we are found; drawing our power from stones in the ground, those beautiful ones by the side of the river formed and then found. . Such memories and moment's resound, they are quiet in the minute and the hours, but in months and years they pound heartbeat, heartbeat, heartbeat, all around.

Day 21: May 19th, 2024

To Beauty,

    I'm so tired of being alone. No reason to pick up the phone, no reason to search for a home, no reason to be born or die, no reason to try. I possess names, purposes, goals, but none of them are my own. - I have emptied my bucket list of everything. I don't care anymore, I can't let myself care. - I'm just so tired, so damn tired. Today I laid down on my knees in the gravel outside for five minutes and covered my head, just trying to breathe. No panic indeed, it's depression you fool, fly and feed; like a vampire drawing forth blood from a cut, dying because of the cancer in my gut, a growth of greed, a treant's seed, I am bound to the soylent green. Here in the mountains I stand, here in the hills I plan, here above the earth I realize that I don't have anyplace to land, and there are no powers or principalities for me to command; I don't even seek to move my hand, my heart being wrapped by three iron bands. My master is me, the frog is thee, look in the mirror, can't you hear us scream? - Waking in the middle of the day as if from a dream. The world is emptied out now - no more do I wish to see, or be seen...that's a lie. I continue to write.

    I know you aren't going to look at this or read. In fact, no-one will, this shall not be grist for the mill. There, do you see nature's invisible hand? A purpose which is not aiming for happiness, a haze which obscures the sun, a fire-flash which drives us from the one. I haven't talked to friends in months, not about anything real. Not for hours about ideas which pop into our heads, or what books we read, or how we feel as if we are dead. In fact, there are no needs. It, life, everything, everywhere, all the time, feels as if there is no need for connections or explanations. The assumption is that people have their own lives, their own works, their own causes and movements. We stand alone as never before. I realize, I see now, what I refused to admit or understand the thousand ways in which....

    I took no stand, umpire calling strikes, tossing me out, but I was never even at bat, the world can't even see me without a hat, some pieces of fabric with a sign and a name, signal of the fact that I support this or that player of the game. I think this is all insane? A lovely insane of course, man-home and tiger's-hame, lines in the sand and Terra's fame. - I know I would be mistaken for evil or good here, blamed for all the

pride and all the shame, clear skies dripping acid rain. I know my pain -
I am lonely and purposeless; I am nothingness. For, you see, it doesn't matter more that I am here, I can't fix anything, I can't do anything, I can't become anything; not alone. Not like this, half covered and half hid, having taken a hit but not struck back yet. I am still preparing, I am still learning, I am still growing - but shal I do this forever? Will someday become never? I'm so tired. I'm so tired every day, in every way, and I want to speak to you Beauty, I want to say - I want to say too much. I want to be hidden. I want - I want - I want you to ask. What I receive I may return three fold, and if you showed me that you cared a little, I might show that I cared a lot. I'm afraid, I'm so ashamed, everything is wrong and I'm all to blame, because I don't know what I'm doing when I try to play the game. Do you think I'm running out of chakra? Or perhaps I am becoming Naraka, I mean Naraku, damaged and cared for, not out of love but from kindness, not because of who he was, but because of how he was hurt; I am simply a stupid soldier writing his thoughts down in a mongolian yurt on the edge of the empire of grass, forgotten by his family, abandoned by his military, it's dark and cold out in the winter, and all his surroundings are scary. - So he writes to some strange person because it makes him merry, like he is sucking not on months-old hardtack, but on sweet, fresh, oranges and cherries, bananas and lemons, grapes, apples, guava, peaches, nectar, honey, pepper, fire, warmth and cause and dream. - Not every need fulfilled, not by a long shot, but he is happy enough now, still holding clear in his memory last night, last week, last month, and last year, when the whispers of the void drew too near. His future was shadowy, but now it's clear. - Light's vision indeed, draenei horns a-gleam, Mana'ri, then blue, now red, the boy comes alive again and is not dead.

Today, having written, he reads. Giving silence for speech, his anxiety runs out and he screeches, banshee's wail, stormwing's beguiled, poor man doesn't know what to do with his trial. He set it for himself; he made it, plucked it, formed it, shaped, broke it; broken down. - He steps off the road into the rye fields, and he can't get out now. Every road winds in on itself, every path descends, there are no tree limbs their view to lend. Blind he is, blind and dumb, soon enough becoming numb, as night rolls in, the cold fog drizzles, his head moves as if on a swivel. Left, left, left right left: Every way but correct. He doesn't know what to do next; he's going to lose his neck, if he doesn't figure out somehow what to do, what wrong route to take next. Swim, crawl, fly, it's all the same - you'll only be free if you find your name. Run, you whisper to yourself - run. Can you smell the storm now, the lightning, the thunder, the roots growing under - they are hungry. They are hungry.

Day 22: May 20th, 2024

To Beauty,

What should I say? Let me tell you about my day. I finished writing to you, and went to bed; had a dream, then woke up and said: I can do this, Beauty, I can do this. Everything about my life is a mess, and I am sure to fail the test, I don't know what I am going to do next, I am in the middle of the woods of death, and yet I persist in my trial. I perceive neither the Euphrates nor the Nile, no river runs, no hanging gardens of Babylon, no seven wonders, no Colossus of Rhodes. - I always wake and go to bed all alone, only legends and memories typing in my phone, as out of the corner of my eye, spy I do a gnome, some small bearded man in a garden looking for a home.

Up I stand, as my blankets off I throw, now it's my time to go. Trundle to breakfast, say hello to the morn, hug everyone I see, and shake off my sleep. climb the stairs, down to basement creep, I grab my yogurt and the morning sun greet. Back up we travel to see the meow and mreep, I pet the cat, and then eat. With a spoon I add cinnamon and berries, walnuts and cherries, the better to bite you with my dear, why don't you come even more near; there is nothing here to fear, I say, as I munch and munch my cares away. Finally I finish, up from my seat, I wash and break things, I want to scream, because I am apparently unable to clean.

Picking up the pieces, throwing out the basket, I have a tisket and a tasket, I find a thicket and a jacket, because it's cold outside. I brush my teeth, no lie, I put on that aligner, I improve my pride, changing the picture outside to match the vision inside, as part of my journey to live and die. I know its vanity, but it's the part of me on the incline, standing up again on the right side of the pale and the form, the journey and the flow of my life over the next several hours. Full of strife, I write and lie. You see, I write a few sentences, and then I read, I run out all my powers, and then seek to refill my greed, I paint a picture to Beauty; or at least, that's what I say, because this idea that I work on gets me through the day. I turn fire to clay, take my visions, forge and flame, I seek to find my secret name, and in my own poor way, in my head, play a sacred game.

As I work, write, edit, create, Grandma comes out seven times to see what I'm doing, or to ask me where the lady went, and I tell her I don't know, what is your intent? I don't understand the words you meant, they were in Swiss, Grandma, you're speaking German Swiss, I don't know Swiss, can you say it again, and she says 'oh', then explains, but now we're in English, and she doesn't know the names, not like she once did, and every other time we talk we play this game: What is the thing, what are you looking for, what do you need, I can't help you Grandma, I can't help you with anything, I answered that question five minutes ago, don't you remember? But she doesn't, she doesn't anymore, as I buy a whole lot of nothing, and for nothing pay at the store, the house has moved somehow and she doesn't know who I am anymore: My name doesn't begin with a name, it begins with an A, and I think I'm going insane. - Dementia indeed, and every time she moves something, she seeks someone else to blame: The pots, the pans, the knives, the spoon, her purse, the broom, the flowers that bloom, strange boxes and blankets she once made on the loom, we are way past twilight years, and into the gloom.

So after I create, I bake, dinner or a cake, fifty bites of food for me and fifteen for Grandma if I'm lucky, although five sometimes is all she manages, as she says she took her pill and the truth savages, until I grind it up and hide it in mush. Here is desert Grandma, careful don't touch, the pan is still hot. Please don't help me clean, let me do these dishes myself, polish and dry them until they gleam, put them in high places where you won't move them because they can't be seen. This is my plan, and this is my scene for an hour every day, and after dinner I go outside again to play. I stand in the shade and write or draw, or save Azeroth, one hand on the keys, the other in a claw, I metaphorically chew on my leg and gnaw, seek to run away from the trap of family into which I've been placed. I glad to be here and helping, but I can already tell that we've lost the race, and there is no remaining hint of my Grandmother's grace. All that remains of what once made her great is what she's accumulated, the books and pictures, letters from Switzerland sent when she was a youth, and photos from Mexico in that year when she lost a tooth. The books remains but not the memories, the house stands steady but not the hands which built it, her life is here, but not the mind which took part in it.

This is life every day, I work outside as much as I can, with a standing desk and less of a plan. Sometimes I'm alone for four hours straight, and during other days I am interrupted every five minutes. I show grandma my art, but she doesn't understand what's in it, just 'That's nice', or pretty, or sparky, that's new, that's different, but it's the same pictures on the wall, it's the same gowns and the same ball, because now I'm the one who stands tall. Not hunched over, I unbend every time I look, I'm living here for free and I feel like a crook, but I'm not doing nothing, I'm writing a book.

Eventually of course, Grandma goes to sleep, and then out of the cold, back into the warm house I may leap, turn out all the lights that were left on, let the cat out of her cage, because I can't stand that crying, she sounds like she's been betrayed, because grandma locks her up five times a day, afraid she'll escape because one of the strangers will leave open the gate, or one of the helpers will do it by mistake. Either way, it's not great, and this is the most difficult part of the life that I hate, because nothing matters and I can't stand seeing the suffering, because freedom is even more important than eating, even if the cat is afraid of my greeting.

One more bite, oatmeal at night, then a shower to be warm, and I write a text to cleanse my soul. It is only in my letters that I may be bold, make my soul young again, and not feel useless and old, because nothing matters that I do here. I can't help, I can't change things, I have to be calm and not rage, I have to play at being careful and a mage, blend my chakra be a bushin sage, repeating all my words three times, and every day that hill again climb: The hill in the forest on top of which lies a home. I have a red cloak and I roam, my what small teeth you have, my what lost eyes, we need more strength inside.

Finally comes the night, and this one at least is quiet, no nightmares, no opening and closing the closet door, no pacing back and forth for half an hour across the floor, just sleeping and quiet and bored. Boring, which is so much better a 'nothing' than the alternative: Too much. I make sure we have enough food for tomorrow's lunch, and then like Lurch I trundle over to my piano, typity type type, let my emotions flow in the night. I write these words to Beauty, reaching for the light, and in measured cadence I cast a spell to grant me might: I can do this, Beauty, I can do this. I can do this again tomorrow, overcoming my eternal sorrow. Not because I'm helping, but because I receive help .

Day 23: May 21st, 2024

To Beauty,

    I thought it was bad poetry. It didn't show me a story or bring me to a feeling. It didn't teach me or rest me, raise me or slay me; it barely made me sad, and certainly after I read those words I did not become mad. Indeed, the poetry was bad, black lines on a page, to X, to Y, a printed leaf, simply an admonition not to leave, but to live. Heavy as lead, remembering the dead, hands spread wide, crying inside, the writer of the poem seems only too willing to suffer the burden of the tide, their feet nailed down, their eyes glued shut, their hands bound - but from their lips words leap around, as prisoner attempts to make some sound, show the world what they suffer and why. Speak not cry, show the world how their mothers and sisters and brothers all die. Fathers imprisoned, cousins without vision, born into war, bloodied and sore, by your flesh and your history, your surroundings gored, beaten again and again into the floor, and I wonder, as I read that poem, how may they ever walk through the door? Become something more than dreams and wishes, than memories and switches, whips full of kisses, the world saying for your own good, the colonial store selling your survival as if the bare minimum is a gift, evolution tumbling into a pit, even good dogs being bit. Every day you must wonder - is this it?

    I've been reading you see, about conflict amid the olive trees, from when the Turks left and the British arrived, to stupid declarations and the idiocy of tribes, all the measures of money and knives. I'm not sure that the real truth, the whole truth, the truth and nothing but the truth still survives in any book, or under any rhyme, because all the writers of history, winners and losers, always lie, puffing up their vanity and massaging their pride. Tens of millions of people are being treated as if they were one, a singular person with singular vision and singular actions, as every family member attempts to gain some traction, understand their station, the costs and relations. The issue of course is history: Who did what to whom and when, a hundred years ago were we already doomed to either sink or swim? We are numb, we are thin, and those tribal families are always trying to win, seldom accepting of their own sin, as bones become ashes and then dust on the wind. Accusations and counter accusations shall wind back and forth throughout all of time, us reading books as we dine. But is that poetry, or history?

Now we attend to the mystery: Because my grandpappy shot your grandpappy, and your father shot your father, and my sister blames your sister, and my cousin hates your cousin - does that mean I should suffer? What is this curse we are under, to from our freedom be sundered, locked down and labeled, stuck like donkeys in the stable, doomed to eat forever no fresh grass, only dry hay bales, while some farrier hammers in his nails, saying that they're necessary for walking on the trails? Really these are lies, you are strong enough to do more than survive; you could become something great if only you had the time, the space, the available grace, the opportunity to run an open race, instead of suffering Garoshe's disgrace, covered with the signals of warmongering and hate, of closed cities, closed gates, and endless lines of purple mistakes. Abandon not your axe, flee not your trial, stand up again avoiding the bile, sing and dream, plant seeds and bring fruits and leaves, if you can, if you please, tall on your own two legs, and not pushed, knees on the ground, silent, praying, make not a sound, this is the resounding tone: Someday, somehow, we'll unwind, our truth given to a field full of cows, one memory spread across the sky, Milky Way trying to live not die. In freedom born, by past enchained, this I wonder: Shall you know your name? Come we to earnest truth of the game, all men suffer, and all mankind blamed, all women shamed, all children betrayed, in the name of those who gave -

nothing. Everything. Something, more than this, the Somme or the wall, the praying or the slain, all those who tried to save the world but instead went insane. It was bad poetry, it was sad, reading it didn't make me happy or mad, but outside the words, in the hand, I saw hope that we might escape Fate's command. Enough blood to swim in it, drowning until we touch mud, at the bottom of the river in sunlight we shiver, now comes the summer, dry up and tumble, plant your seeds, and ten years hence from the soil bring forth papyrus leaves. Write your words, show that this seems better than you were, more children to be sure, artwork not suffering, dreaming not this, receiving not bullets but a kiss. Bad poetry indeed, but may surviving affect your greed. I hope that someday you find what you need, and achieve the room to breathe. I hope you can say I choose to do this, and not please. Live on your feet, not die on your knees. May your life be good enough that you can afford to raise trees, and spread in the morning honey from bees. Not lead indeed - may you achieve what you dream, on that far-off day when your letters are a praise, not a scream.

I don't know when that might be, I've read too much in a good ending to believe, but there are people here, inside and out, who feel your suffering and raise a shout, paint your symbols on walls all about. This isn't a great plan, but it's at least one way you might get out, and I know it's bad, making people mad, but at least this way we're doing something, and not only being sad. Aren't you glad? Someone over the sea read your words, and they sprouted into this symbol, like seed eaten by birds. Above all I pray that someday: You may receive what you deserve, all that you've worked for, suffered, and earned. Blessing upon you little bands, you elder people in foreign lands. I saw once your poet's hands.

Day 24: May 22nd, 2024

To Beauty,

    I turned off the hot water in the shower before I was ready. The world became cold, and I was forced to get out. I don't understand why I am seemingly incapable of creating warmth by myself, from my own bones; it doesn't matter how many games I play, or the amount of elderly tomes I read, this piece of ice lodged within my chest I cannot slay - not alone. I need some other hand, a different vision not under my command, a staff, a third leg, to help me stand. I am out of balance, out of whack, a giant and illusory sad sack, hollow-faced man with empty back, a hobo wandering the train track without a pack. All I have are rocks, and there are holes in the toes of my left sock; no knife of steel, no fresh meal, no meat on my bones, no stories where I am the hero alone. - No, all my solo adventures are into the dark and the night: They are my crying and whining about how I don't dare to fight. I am not right, I do not fit, I can stand all day and it hurts when I sit: Too often I give up and say 'this is it', I am struck to the quick, no more to struggle, I've popped the bubble, here's the double double toil and trouble cauldron; bubblebeam, Starmie scream, lightscreen, cast the shadows and dare the dream, oh there's the rub, isn't it? There's the chance, when with Eris we attempt to dance, not flipping the coin but mining the seam, into the earth we dig and dive, seek rebirth, that our trials are worth the curse. I wonder, what is this life which I have nursed, begger or knight, unicorn or light, loss of nerve or thunderbolt's might? Am I worthy, can I be, to talk the talk and walk the walk? With my hands I drew lines in the sand using chalk, mind's eye open, painting lies unspoken; I wished I was a dragon flying in lands far apart, but instead I was only some fool making art.

    Not very good, couldn't be, I don't have a purpose to drag me out to sea, far beyond the bath of western stars, to Aslan's kingdom full of golden bars, where princes and paupers alike face no strife as long as they the follow the laws of life, never cut themselves deeply with a knife, or break of those other laws mankind made to play nice: The absence of violence and the weighing of right and wrong on the dice, filling the world with towers of Babel and Gardens of Babylon, Colossus of Rhodes, the wonders of the world, not seven but a thousand, not a million but a billion, all the stars and the sands and the trillions. Oh, I can go on and on, counting and pounding, moving, surrounding, every other hotel room filling up forever and ever, and it's never enough, my mind does not encompass all the smoothness hidden in the rough. I don't know if I believe calculus is that tough, is it the truth, or does it just work well enough? I say this with a sound as if I am the Billy Goat Gruff, crossing the bridge to the other side, green grass brilliant, shining in the sun, life bringing structures forth from air and water, village from the well, pulling on the rope as the ground swells, earthquake threatens all who dwell under shelter and in the shade, like me by their own vision betrayed. Into the future they were tossed, and realized that in front of concordance and Nike they were not the boss, could swoop and dive, drown and fly, but no matter how hard they tried, justice is not built in. Magic doesn't respond here to a blessing or a sin, we are too near to reality, unable to access our frivolity.

No clown face, no shuttered grace, I will not attempt that race, the struggle and crawling through the grime to disgrace, weaving rude twine and not beautiful lace - but perhaps that was a mistake. I am not someone great. Where is the fire or the flame, where is the strength hidden in a name, no lion's mane here, no jackal's howl, hyennas's laugh, baboon's scowl, human dolls and caricatures, stories and prayers? I do not shut my eyes from this moment; I open them and stare, admit that I could reflect upon care, concentrating on my fear of that beautiful glare. I'm so tired you see, so worn out, attempting to raise in front of Semiramis a shout, dark tower full of vampires gazed upon from without. It is a maze and a prison, some sickness and gout. Shall we cleanse it, or simply allow time to run out? Here is the lamp and the flame, here is whispered shame, every time I gave up, every attempt to the future shut, every moment the past was not enough.

I need warmth, I need water, I need food and purpose and cause. I am lost. - Like a ghost I retreat to my old haunts, re-do old hunts, save the world again in the same way. I variate between left or right, throw the ball and pick the dome or a helix, some feline domesticus, I unlock the cage at night and fur runs away. No warmth shall I find this day, no fire, no flame, no cause to play, and no gold in my hands that I can use to pay. All I have is paper money, all I have is promises and if's, all I carry within my poor untrained gifts, not enough to lift me past the sky, over the pale and into the lie; there is not story time, just reality and a joke, the sure knowledge that in front of beautiful I would choke: Be the lesser version of myself, avoid the well and the yoke.

But I need that idea. I need that flame, I need the right to whisper that name, grab the warmth lest I grow cold and sane. Something is wrong with me, deep in the brain. I am cold indeed and I meet my secret needs, for answers and hammers, for letters overcoming stammers, and the terrors which overthrow fears, sights in the middle of December of my future arrears, and now I quail again as death in the forest draws near.

I must leave the shower, leave the warmth, into the cold again be birthed. Quick, quick, before I lose my nerve - jump, jump, and be heard. Never be a jock, but show your pride in being a nerd, show the world all that you've learned. Love alone shall not be earned, but that's ok - we smiled anyway, and at the end of the day, what more is there to do? Memories fade, hope remains, and hope never dies. - It just stays a while locked inside, resting until it regains its pride: Let this not be a lie, for fire and flame, warmth and flight, trying I find in other's names light.

Day 25: May 23rd, 2024

To Beauty,

    Everybody lies, even if not on purpose, because we all have a side, a preferential claim: There are powers of imagination burned into our hide, as desperately we attempt to convince the world that we are the righteous ones, the worthy ones; the people ordered and made for this attempt to catch the rain, that manna from heaven which we eat and drain, for ours is the right to live and breath, to farm and reach, to attempt our wrath to unleash. - I don't know what I want, I don't understand how I will, all I care about is that my future and past shall not be nill, worthless, purposeless, changeless. - Yin and yang, circles growing and driving us insane, we might place down whatever labels remain, writing those lines in sand with our bloody hands: Imagining that by staining, imbibing, draining, all those rocks of this earth, all the ways in which the sky fills up with mirth; the causes and purposes which we birth in this land filled with birch trees, redwood grove, pines needles, oak balls, shades, groves, stands, reaches, hills covered with trees reaching toward heaven, guarding shade and holding mist, this California, this home, family and place. Here are the stories we give, call, and make, painting our bloody pictures and inscribing with our words circles of protection, seals of summoning, mysteries of undoing, djinns in their rife and ice, marids flying through storms covered with strife, families and tribes, mothers beside themselves with grief, fathers trying to forget how they failed to fulfill needs, those young wild stallions and mares baying for blood, searching for magic to fix the world's wounds, make it all-right, ok, make the sacrifices worth it today, unable to compromise, they want it all their way, and are prepared to kill, maim, and destroy, to get it.

    Everybody lies, believing the truth which is inside 'for them' for me, for I, that white orb grounding vision, Kilrogg's twisting, logic unable to gaze upon itself, filled with axioms which would confuse even an elf. Feanor they would claim is right, even while all those who were sensible questioned the strife, and had horrible doubts about the morality of the knife. Who sees no reason to slay kin because of a pursuit which you have all the time in the world to accomplish? - One asks, what is really worth this? Compromise is painful, yes I know, to give up and suffer, to be called stupid and slow, you could have accomplished so much more if you just held out a little longer - but what do those pitiful, painful, small men know who are not in the arena? Sneer and jeer all you want, cast our name into the mud, call us villains, rogues, and failures, fact is. - We accomplished what you could or would not, moving the world and not simply allowing it to roll over us, and I know that in doing so we have failed much, but I tell you here, it was enough. We're not strong and we're not tough, but we may whip ourselves and say mush, mush, mush, we have medicine, we have dreams, we crawl forward even cut off at the knees...

But you see, everybody lies. All claims have a side, certain facts they show, and certain facts they hide, case-law filled with silences and pride, all the drips of water which make up the tide, grains of sand pushing waves to the side, and slowly pulling off a move called bide, taking their hits in order to dish them out again three times, and that power is not swift or wise - but it works. Perhaps obscure, obtuse, mis-directed, ill-conceived, requiring mighty strength and desperate need, worse than a bubblebeam, but better than a blind tackle, or a spackling on the wall, filling up holes busted by opening doors uncontrolled, the arc of our actions proscribed by those who built them of old, the facts and figures of solidified gold, power of purchase made not cold hard cash, but a heavy door with strong hinges that last, and governed by laws which will tie a boy to the mast, whipping him until he faints at last. Is this not our mask?

Everybody lies, you see, about what is wrong and right, if this is before dawn or after night, whether the tool they use is a hammer or a knife, and if the cause they have is brought by darkness or the light. Zoroasterian might, spark casts shadow, silence begets noise, boredom forges toys; how do we see whether this is greed or need, dice or coin, worthiness or scorn? Not by their words but in their reaction, not by their facts but by their traction. - Follow the money, who benefits, who gains power, who receives more, why was this not done before? Everybody lies, has an agenda, even unto themselves they are a pretender, as world searches for counter-balancing avenger, some Dante or Astarte with a temper, throwing stars and painting mars, an emperor must sit upon the throne of Olympus Mons, moving starships like gods - but is this truth or lie, how shall we show, what might we hide? I wonder, do we tell the truth inside? - Don't lie, we say, we parade, despair and degrade, build up again, making shame go away. What shall we be? Whatever we wish to be today: Prophet or a priest, conquerer or a niece, nice or evil, poet or creep; all the world judges us as we sleep, so the question we ask ourselves is: Was it worth diving that deep?

The harder you fall, the higher you rise, the more lies you find, the more truth you imbibe. Believe everything, that's what I say, find the road through the maze. Everybody hides what they are, even from themselves, and certainly don't give the public all the thoughts which in their heads dwell, not succumbing to the give and take, the steady swell of change and heavy burden of mistake. The hard part is not becoming too great with age, or in our youth by consistent wisdom be dismayed. Will we be better? Can we be better? Finding our truths, accepting our lives, moving inside, daring to challenge our greed and pride - are we enough to swing our sword and break the tide? Fight fate, and show not hide? Are we equal to the future we will find? Everybody lies - but I'm not sure why we bother, when the truth always comes out in time. In front of the memory of ten thousand years, why is it that we hide behind fear or pride? We call it face, but - that too is a lie. One of many, one kind of an eye. Jar-Jar blinks and dark night sinks, as we are become the brink, attempting from dark symbols to drink. Lie, but if you do, don't bother to hide - know yourself, and be not a patsy before the tide; fight for righteousness, tell the truth when you lie, and I think you might be surprised what you find inside: Some true word nailed to your hide when you didn't see, some unwelcome truth revealed in a dream. Everybody lies, but nobody is wrong all the time.

Day 26: May 24th, 2024

To Beauty,

    I feel like I have to be slow and careful, nice and kind. Such is the price. - Only I was not made for strife, and in me twists the knife. Emotions hurt to feel, to know, emotions come out of me in a terrible show, full of wrath and ruin, rage and despair, a terrible pulling out of my hair. - When the world is too near to be, then I find life unbearable; I cannot dream of attempting the undeclarable - to reveal who I am, to take of the mask, finding my veritas task, and certainly failing it at last. There is something wrong with me, a power unavailable, a mountain unassailable; I wander round the summit of lesser paths, I walk the night full of starlight, but I do not dare the sun. - I am not equal to the undone cave, I cannot concentrate, by life betrayed, accept my hate, and be amazed: I wish I could go insane! And now, from me, manner's drain, I understand, tis what I do, but like civilization upon the tribes I won't see it through, not having enough talent for both me and you. I am like the healthy child now filled with flu, unable to breath, barely may I see, I'm tired, so tired, collapsing to my knee. -

    I do not bow, I do not bend, nor do I break, but from myself I take and take: pound the flour, stir the whisk, turn on the oven, bake the cake, turn and twist, throw all your cards on the table for a game of whist, yin and yang, black and white, good and fine, I have no sense of inalterable time. There is no eastern isle for me, nor Throne of Thunder, turtles surround me but I travel under, into the sewer by path of the grate, washing down with the sky-water and oozing mistakes: What would be not taught nor found, no brothers, no sister, no mother, only books and shutters, light in the doorway filling a mind that mutters, which under the mountain shudders and shudders. I have only glimpses of the sky, stars at night, soft moonlight; I hide from the harsh sun and the burning sight of nuclear annihilation, beyond comprehension. - Obliterations of substances which were old when the world was young, cooling down from the big-bang guns, instead of a dozen orbitals, only: One, in that way a vision undone, first step of ten thousand stairs begun, and if I am dangerous enough to bypass the troll its gonna be fun. - I don't know what I'm doing, but I've begun.

    And it is not nice nor sweet or kind, it hurts because I'm trying to draw a line between what might be and what was, between my heart's fears and my voice's endless tears. I won't give in to black and white, I'll be gray, I'll fight - by doing stupid things I'm not sure are absolutely right, and I'm not sure because the possibility of my actions pains me at night. I don't blame anyone, I don't ask, I simply try to find, to make the truth and love her and be mine. I wish if I tried enough then I would never have cause to lie, if the world would just tell me why it is that I cry. Why, why, why, screaming skies, I will not pick a side - You're all foolish idiots and cowards and lies. - So am I. I ought to give us the benefit of the doubt, but I'm suspicious: I ask, what is the secret behind our shout? What is it that we are shutting out? It's painful to show and tell, its painful to hear and be heard, I study like an athlete and exercise like a nerd, by the world I am bored. - Not because it is not great, but simply because I don't know what to do with all this hate. I'm so tired of caring what others saw or ate, the food they imbibed, the dreams they brought inside, the causes and purposes they raised into the sky, made a pillar sure and strong, made to last the whole night long, but I wonder is it worth a dragon's song?

No purposes or chains, not forward or back, only sideways, round and round, lost on the track, I am like a bat: Blind, waiting for reflected seams, coal that burns, diamonds which breathe, carbon indeed, and like all living things I have needs; some of which are not nice, and many for which I pay the price, - distraction and rage, shame and despair, forgetting for three days to wash myself or braid my hair, because I simply don't have the energy left to care: To get up off the floor and fight for myself, to take walking towards over running away from, to act smart with a plan instead of short-sighted and dumb. Life for me has always been numb - because I am not nice, and was not built for strife. I don't want to hurt anybody, I don't even want to hurt myself, but that's what life is you know, pain. - Existence of a strain, moving from where we'd lain, ghost-stuck suddenly, frighteningly, sane: I don't know what I want, but I'll pay the price if I have to, blood and bone, memories of eating soup with a fork not a spoon, all for the sake of training myself to be a loon, because I am a fool, a fook, ordering muck, crashing out over three mods, accepting the causes and not the laws.

I'm not nice, I'm not good, I say and repeat this like if I do it enough time, say that: Then it will become true one day, and when that comes my own ideals I might betray, accept my evil and tell understanding to go away, as I am overloaded I explode, write, and bay, howl at the moon: Can you see, do you hear, why is emptiness always with me so near? Nice, cruel, what is that? Names drawn out of a hat. - I don't like definitions, I barely accept ideals, it's all relative, but that doesn't mean it's all wrong. Life has more to it than one note in one song, no matter how long the age may be. Old republic passes by, but that doesn't mean the empire we are forced to try, only that old on its darth-bed lies: I'm not nice, but I'm not sure what would happen if not hoping I was nice is something I ever tried.

Day 27: May 25th, 2024

To Beauty,

    What does the moon see when she looks down upon me tonight? Surely it is not someone who does anything right. - I mess up everything that I may or might do, chasing after shadows and not the light. I don't know what knowledge is, I'm not sure what sight I have, but I am convinced that my hands may not succeed in matching the world's creations to my greed, facts to imagination, goals to successes; everywhere I go I make messes, for I am tossing out all those wise suggestions, all while listening to those foolish musicians: The greek kind, cursed by the Muses, driven to write or explode, driven to weep or die, driven to sacrifice before they attempt to fly. - I dive, deep beneath the sea and drown, hoping that there will be treasure in the thing I'm pulling up, the muck-filled container I've found, not pearls and rubies, but gold hidden and bound, buried with warriors and lost in a frown. I was frightened by the lightning, Zeus's cast bolt, Poseiden's grieving at Odysseus's thieving, the blinding of those who he had no business greeting, mortal's attempting with immortal a meeting, asking for blessing but finding only a beating; Achilles grieving, as in the underworld he is sad and bleating, no wolf or sheep now, simply ash, and not the kind that flies with water-dragons in the sky, saves the world time after time, but instead the ash that died: Mourned by friends and enemies alike, vision that to a twelve-year-old is a strike, some memory like a spike, the world flashing its greetings and saying 'sike'. Look, be careful, we never plugged in the power but still handed you the mike, so if you want to be heard you have to scream, voice distorted beyond all recognition. Now we are forced to make a cake in the kitchen, some ginger-lemon piece where the published ratios and plans don't quite meet. We have to make it up, eyeball the parts, turn guessing mistakes into art, and now, adding fire, may it be time to start. -

    Rise, rise, rise my friend, my work, my memory, my shame, my sustenance, my name, my ideas like tomes, my becoming like bones, living waters and war-ram's horns. Shake the sky, silver why, I might be better, but I don't do, only try - try - try -, only why - why - why -. With no painting being equal to what I was baking, baking, banking on here in my head, alone in my bed, what I've done isn't what I said. I'm not great, I'm not one, I'm not even equal to what's in my head. The pictures don't match reality, I'm dead, passed on, audited, wrong; again and again I feel that song. The book is too short or too long, the colors are translucent, the trinkets for sale have lost it, and these dreams I've unleashed have bought it, because tomorrow's illusion only comes late, and sweet-smelling tea is created, not baked. Treats sour now sweet, envisioning seemings but never jumping off the brink, pounding on a shield but never stopping for a drink, I hammer myself thin: A wire to bend, and this work is not the end, as saw rusty blade cuts and poor artworks run amuck, I'm leveling up. - But it's not yet enough. I'm working on it, I'm a failure, but - while I'm working, I'm not giving up. The moon looks down upon me and I fear, I know, I see every 'what' in which I'm wrong and and think of a thousand words to change my song, but that magic belongs to the future now, as I cast my eyes to the sky and worship a cow. How now brown bow, this to the emperors and that to the widow, half for charity and half for clarity, I am embarrassed by what I say and what I give, what I am: Sands of sin, lines in the sand, as I dip my ink in the bottle and begin, yet again. I can't finish yet, there's more truth to win, more wonderful, sweet, shimmering, rhyming, glitter to spin. I'm seven months in, circling on like a leaf in the wind, surfing by dryads hair, and risking myself for a dare. Listen to me, moon - do you care?

Down upon me she gazes, but does not see. I write of her, but feel not her breeze; the forest is dark now, and I miss the lost fairies for the trees, being brought by despair to my knees. Death comes upon life, and I am unable to breath, frustrated by loss and suffering much, unable myself or wisdom to reach out and touch. All I may say is, over and over again: mush, Mush, Mush, make it through the snow Balto, race over the ice, bring medicine to the children, make it all nice, save a life, fix the strife. Maybe if we do this well enough then we could avoid seeing the knife, be light and not dark, be a whole and not a part. - And I know it isn't enough, as I spend my days not writing but playing, not saving the world but drawing out stories, other stories, other's making, other's cakes in the oven baking, too much sugar, too much oil, I can't make this better, I don't have the toys. - My pictures and painting don't come out right, and by the time night rolls around I can't make any coherent sounds, but when the sun is in the sky, all I do is dream and die, obtaining half of what I wanted to, reading only one tenth of a book, spending my days curled up in a nook, or laid ou long on on the grass. In the shade, my hopes betrayed, I'm not enough, never equal to all my plans and principalities, possibilities; standing up straight forgetting to twist my knees, spending too much time saying attention please, these are my ideas, these are my faults, here is all I wanted to do, all I envisioned, the plans I have and the missions. - Exclamation to question, attempt to celebration, Cadfael solving situations, but I am no detective, no priest nor herbal selective, I am defective. What am I under the moon? All that is wrong, weak not strong, rhyming not long, bad who can't even remember all the words to a song or a poem, but makes everything up as he goes along, repeating his refrain, using the same words and names over and over again, as if this time they'll be write and win, but I am, instead of the flame, the wind - cleansing Ch'i, breathe out, breathe in - short meet long, thunder begin, as veritas twined. Confused and bruised, but still - I've little else to lose.

Day 28: May 26th, 2024

To Beauty,

    Water and rock, I am floundering against the clock, for I have talked the talk and walked the walk, I have drawn in chalk, I have done all I wanted and much of what I didn't , and now I don't know if it was worth it. - What is this? The ennui, the gray, the angst, the pain, the shaving down of my brain, the eternal, irredeemable stain of being whatever I am, of doing whatever I do, I think I'm just distracting myself from you; from what you mean, the dream and the scream, the tearing apart of my seams, the re-weave. The call and demand rise up, take a stand: Use and stretch out my hand, instead of simply hiding behind a shield, saying I don't care, I don't dare, I won't paint this world and stare; give up clarity, stepping down into the muck and the mire, I threw away my power, and for what? For why? Freedom? What's the point of that, if I wish to die, like I have so many times? Is it such a terrible crime to be tired and lost, to not be sure if you want to pay the cost, or not even being sure who the boss is, what rules and regulation, what refutations and salutations we aught to adhere to, all the truths, all the lies, and all the rhubarb pie. - Sweet sustenance which is not for I, who become so over-stimulated that I want to cry, as I write this every night, but am not sure I wish to try.

    Speak not hide, show the world my pillar from earth to sky, sure, sirrah, that I will be castigated for my eyes: All I see and love and hate, despise, I know my vision of beauty is not a prize, as we become daze and disoriented, discombobulated, bobble-headedly back and forth, shaking in the grip of a curse, that solid earth; as wings, winds, feathers, and fingers pass me by, not quite touching, not quite, the world to me being too quiet, playing at nicety. Here in the forest I think I'm alone, until suddenly I hear the ringing phone, or the driving car, or the music over the hill, just like every other time I wished to go under, but instead found only swill: Those briny deeps, those lonely keeps, Karasang wilds mountain steep, as on lonely french boulevards, triumph sweet at exodus of orders and greed, each to the other according to ability and need, not modern democracy but the ancient killing of kings, when blood in the field a blessing did bring.

    Now wheat stands higher than my head, and we all have food enough when we go to bed, but some days I think this success is all in my head. I've written and I don't feel alive, just dead, marked for bed, forgotten and to bleed. I'm tired and I want to sleep, give up fighting, turn meek, dye myself with beets pale pink, I am passing by, laying out all the drain, sink, and cry, what am I doing I ask, who am I, I, I - I'm trying to find out, I'm trying to learn. I've giving it what I have, what I am to burn, the stark sparks that strike the skin, again and again, until we're afraid to be hurt.

We can't land, there's no place to stand, as we falter before the alter, sacrificed to time and memory, the pre-eminence of the journey, not because endings don't matter anymore, but because we so easily grow bored. Torn into pieces, spending every last gold coin from our meager horde, we are interred, I just...don't know now, I don't know, I don't care, I don't show, I don't, I...I'm tired. I'm plucking my strings on the lyre, making noise, music, but unpracticed. - My antics don't match my vision or heart, every day I make one piece of art, paintings and pictures or words and whispers, here I start, and I don't know what I'm doing or why, how many of these are screams and which ones are sighs, but rock and eave, wind and eyes, I stand here on top of the hill and try anything, something, nothing, everything: Speaking to one and all, some and none, every once in awhile I start again, only to become sure that I'm done. I'm dumb, no ideas in my head, no clarity to be said, call me Karigan, lost and thought dead. I'm not sure I care about anything real, or know who you are, but I certainly have this tension, selfish greed for something I cannot mention. I possess no name or ship or game, simply the memory of what was insane. I want my revenge, but I know that's in vain - it's not the inner world I need to find, but instead these stars and how they align; To hope in this journey fate treats me kind, allows my thread to re-weave and re-bind, as I wander the darkness until the truth I find, and I will find it, in sunlight, freedom, and phantasy. In reality, yeah, I'm not totally fine, but this is a hope I won't give up on - It's mine.

So, rock and wave, mountain passage and deep snow's claim, I eat myself up, accepting my stain. One step a day, that's enough. The toughness I bring, the dreams I screen, I guard myself, and help myself and wreck myself, alone not because I'm an elf, but because I'm human, all too human, having no gift of prophecy nor willingness to overthrow the ancient laws of the land, being neither self-reliant nor transcendent; being neither farmer nor scholar, bounding or breaker, beauteous or faker. - No skill have I in the rift, being neither smart nor swift, while being too lazy and tired to make do with what I have, whipping myself until I'm too mad to be sad. In one desperate action I stand, and I repeat the playing of this hand every day, pretending new cards will come my way. I borrow and steal wisdom from light, hoping against hope that I may, I might, through some foreign hand gain sight, and the ability to write. I don't inscribe things for my own sake, I tell myself that story, even though I know it's fake, because I suspect there is something wonderful to be found in that jake, my jester's mask and cape. Yesterday it was funny - tomorrow, it could be great. Here, raise a glass with me - to mistakes.

Day 29: May 27th, 2024

To Beauty,

    I know I'm ashamed of myself. - Is there a 'but' here, or an 'end' to that? I take myself to task, and after I do, hope to ask, tear off that mask: Be revealed as I am, mad, good cat, bad dog, march into the mist and bite my own fist. To the hills I climb, to the cloud-castles I rhyme, where giants proud welcome bards from time to time, escaping from those with stone skin or beards of fire, all those ice-men who dance around a tire, some beaten-up roadwork, remains of kings and jerks. Is this an accident or on purpose, did you leave it here because you couldn't carry it, or because you were too lazy to bear it? When your back is hurting, knees shaking, heart breaking, breath quaking, broth boiling over, we walked away for one second, and it turns out that was one moment too long, that was end of song, - and now we, dreaming, screaming, screeching, streaking, naked and bare in front of everyone, clad only in hair. We have no skin, only blood and muscle, bone, that wonderful ruby tone, Alextraza played here once and changed what was, and now it turns out that was the end of doves, the start of war, Byzantine floors, convoluted, filled with Roman secrets, Ottoman mysteries, Turkish leaves fallen from high trees, I remember the Armenian Quarter there, three streets, a plaque on the wall, grey stone, lost tourists looking for a home, but unable to know. - To recognize and persevere, I've read the books, I've thumbed the tomes, I've walked beneath the Sofia's dome, I recall burnt pillars and sweet pomegranates, myself parading along the old way, silent, silent inside every day, I walk in the circus, I sing and I read, I am some dumb tourist filled with greed.

    American is what I am, three hundred old, all else filled with massacres and bones, it was not my ancestors nor my home, except for that one in ten part of me which knows not the origin nor the tribe, but only that there was a Great-Grandma, and she died, long before she passed on any history or pride. So what else do I have to hold myself high? Rainbow bridges in the sky, fiddles cry, bagpipes despise, Arthur leaves hoofprints where he rides, Sigfried flies up to the mountains in northern Spain, and then around the world again and again, not in blood but in memory: Of heroes and villains, of philosophers and priests, raising up the river dikes or felling the wild trees. My ancestors were farmers, they crawled on their knees, and some of them become knights, and others were free, east to west, north to south, I don't know what I am, but I know what I was raised to be about: To Love the world and never for myself shout, never shut off a single view or give up, quit, say I'm through.

I am not self-reliant, I am not transcendent, I am not adherent to ritual, I don't feed the flame, never pray in a direction, nor find wisdom in a name. I am stained, not good, not bad, not sinned, not rad. I am neither blue nor red, some armored media derp or an intelligent nerd, I am not a jock, or am I someone whose music can be heard? Yes, I've been hurt, but not enough to forget my word. I wonder the world lost and alone. In the woods I am turned, there are emerald bricks now, and purple paths for which I yearn, masks that seek my friend to turn, to make me feel and burn. I'm ashamed and that's why I hide, but of my silence I feel despised. I'm not moral, I lie: Read these stories and imbibe them, I know I don't feel them. It's easy for me to criticize all the actions of all the world, hypocritical politician's words and naive decisions by ignorant savages. - Civilization is not always what it's cracked up to be, it's just the 'better choice' in company.

And thus so, saying "accompany on"[4], we, overcoming curses, attempt to be gone, and thereby missing the forest for the trees, we find ourselves in the wild saying please. Teach us, charm us, help us, guide us, running after forbidden fruit and finding lions that play the lute, we reach to the river for a stone and call it a bute. It's beautiful now: The word, the world. I can hear the lute playing if I am quiet at night, like a vampire I hide from the light. Without showing myself, learn of my sight, listen to me: I am not right. My words have rhythm and rhyme, but that doesn't come down in the correct way, or at the correct time. I waited for a thousand days in a line, and then gave up. - I'm not kind, for I hate, Timeless Isle, Ordon's mistake. Fire arises, and the cat meows outside the door. - I open it and say don't run away any more, but of course it does, but of course it does, calling softly after me to follow, and I do, into the hollow.

Empty now with a hole in the heart and a helmet on my head, I prepare for my eternal bed: Give up, by the muse led, I'm not rite, I'm dead. How now shall I live and why? I don't know. Reach for the sky? Hand's up, arrested and tied, now we wait for the opportunity to tell justice our side, and hold ourselves to the words buried in our hide: Hope never dies. We are ashamed of ourselves and our lies, but we try. Over and over again, we test ourselves, ask why, why, why, we write down again and again the answers on high, cast in shadow by the sun in the sky. Wisdom it is, even to the blind. Here show our heart now bleeding in a line, matching pain inside, words written down in kind, knowledge which binds and unbinds: Wild grape's crisp ambrosia wine, as like the gods on souls we dine, protecting and freeing ours and mine. Find the truth and make it so, read and be heard, song to the bird.

It's not easy, this turn, to tear off the mask, but it is achieved at last, three days past: Juvenile badly written, a blast. I am blind, foot on the gas, not driving but walking, waking, and alas it was too late - but so what? Better a mistake, then silence on this side of the gate. I am equal to hate, ashamed of my silence and my state, look and listen to the hook I did bate: Wriggling wurm, flameless dragon, peerless snake, wooden monkey, human grade. I have no flame, only clay and dust, I've lost my name, but it's my turn for a move in the game. I am ashamed, but so what? Better this than nothing, better broken than gray, I will not in myself stay. Crawling and busting through the soil of my grave, I am not entirely saved nor safe, helped to savior or grace, as through the night wild and howling I race, writing down my rapid reflections, staring at my mirror in a face, losing my fear of love and hate. I am ashamed, and I know it's not great, - but it is time for me to make a mistake. This is how we learn, trip and fall, bleed and burn, who am I, I dont know - I'm trying to learn. I'm still trying to learn. I think I can learn. I will learn. Cannot is a terrible word to say, is the poem I heard this morning, so today I won't: I may. I can. I repeat those words to myself until they form a valkyries hand, beautiful wings and a god's command, to Valhalla to fight every day. My body and mind are weak, so with words I play, with words I slay, with words I turn fire to clay. I can do this: Look at myself: I did it again today.

Day 30: May 28th, 2024

To Beauty,

    I may not be erased, but I am re-traced, reduced to utter disgrace: I am lost in my hate, my love is a lie, some days all I want to do is lay down and die, be re-born, up into the world fly, away from this hallow-fell sky, october's midnight cry, when ghosts walk and monsters creep. Masks on the human face do leap, each and every person after their treats, filling books with words and songs with sleep, everyone with their world painted neat. You see, every time I start these words I want to give up, I lay my head back and think: is this enough? I told the truth the only way I know how, by showing it and rhyming it, by painting it, and making it - is this not a gift? An opportunity to do this, I have space and time, and reasons for my rhythms, as I wander around flinging my ribbons, twirls and dashes, great world-spanning slashes, standing up straight then bending at the waist. I bow and trace my designs on a window-space, clear lines I do not see but feel, accepting my oxford commas and then abandoning them, proper passage off of lists of dashes, I am in these words making gashes: Great galoshes, stomping and splashing in puddles. I'm laughing, I know I'm not great but I'm passing; I never learned to dance, but maybe I could sing, raise a voice high to bring the ring and the rain, water-worlds falling like pain, as on high mountain-top I begin again and again. I fend into the future, I embrace the past, admitting my problems at last.

    Certainly naive, uneducated, seeing only the breeze, not the depth of every leaf on every tree, I know I am not competent to say this is the truth: Trust me. - And I'm too arrogant towards others, believing anything they do or say is real. I have Descartes' brain without his religion, I have his vision without the mechanics and the math, I might attempt his work but I see at the last all the ways in which I don't pass: Me laying on the ground again gasping, gasping, trashing, thrashing, I am glass, invisible before the eyes of the lads, whipped on the mask, I did it all wrong - and what now, pass? What how, green eyes, red skies, fiddle strings, birds and bees and things. I am stung, coughing up a lung, hacking and cracking, everything I am lacking, as even writing this I black out, lay my head down, forget the silence and the noise, the endless grasping after the new warming toy, fire and flame.

    Beauty's name, I lost the idea of the game, every day is the same

- gray. Gray, gray, gray, gray, gray - quarter of a heart, empire's art, lungchans spark, pearl I've hidden, places I dart, ways and races, waving chases, Anastasia's graces. I remember, I remember, so many Decembers, I've lost my temper being mis-matched, ill made, quenched wrong, and in my early days lost. - For all my hopes I ever paid the cost, naive indeed. I was never the boss, but neither was I ruled, always passing from tool to tool, always the fool never the cool, I lean against the walls and kings attack. - Like the anvil I bear, all too aware of my lack, not enough, I laugh and laugh seven times, reading the same books and the same rhymes, but every time is different. I am different. Why exactly I could not say, how in in what perfect ways I may not see. Eyes do not reflect me on me, as like the Romans I saw Gaul and found greed, I have two walls, feel the rumble of tribes marching in, as I, full of civilization's sin, am arrogant enough to believe I might win, fence with the wind, and in a land of four, or forty, or four hundred thrones, begin again, classic unwinding, remix, re-twin. I have ten alternatives guided by two hands, as poor inefficient me skips global countdown and commands, in my brave space attempting to land after I have fallen or been shot down.

Suddenly finding myself in empty enemy town, surrounded by sickness and skeletons, lashed together barons and ghosts, I be lost, cold, no coat, not even a hook to hang my skin upon. I weep, burying myself in the lawn, lonely, but moving on. Plato's vision is not gone, but I'll not call nor fall, be short or tall, I am not measured at all, just a poor fool kicking around a soccer ball, in empty field and at blank wall. I'm empty here, sketched with envy, arms too slender to hold, full of fear, not bold - before my time, I feel old. I'm tired, drawing a line in thyme and giving up before the bell rings time; beaten up not because of others but because I lost mine, that entire focus of mind: Why try? Why write? Why do this at night? Because I fear the sun's light, which says that I shouldn't be resting, but should burn and rave at close of day, fight, be bright, high lamp pillared sight, look, look. - Someday I might fly like a bird, speak, not write. Repaint my face, redo my grace, attempt again the great race, and overcome fate. I only hope I didn't start too late.

Now, this trial is not going to be great, filling up the car with my mistakes, and burning memories in this way. A dark smog surrounds me, settles into my lungs, poison! Over my eyes smoke, too long here in the den I begin to choke, college parties turning me broke. I don't meet, I don't match, I simply seek and scratch at closed doors and long gaps, broken floors and mysterious hats, ceilings of glass and fields of grass, turning from green to gold at last. I have lost my past, the present is blasted, the future is lost. I am tired at last, and I lust for a pass, some path through the mountains, some journey to the sea, a way for my cursed life to be free. I don't know what I'm lying about, but by precious fruit on tree, I will learn, I will learn, I will learn.

Day 31: May 29th, 2024

To Beauty,

    I don't know enough, grabbing with my hands all the fluff, a thousand pieces of frail white hair floating in the air, seed pods and flower petals, bread crumbs and stories of Gretel. Hammering out the world in metal, copper pictures and iron filings, magnetic electric meanderings; pictures with rough edges and unclear boundaries, shadows and sunlight and shading of reality. I, like all humankind, am seemingly limited by mortality, having not that fifth level of dimensionality which allows me to see what was and what might be, all the information available under the sea. Instead, I am caught by single-direction traps and the costs of action, by friction and fraction ground into bits, simple yes or no, one of two, I am counting on my toes, abstraction turning into litigation. Arguing back and forth, presenting my facts, only allowing myself to ask certain questions, stay away from the pillars, stay away from the crashes, my integrity is smashed, as in those days when I swore I would outlast the lies, and I tried and tried, but gave up lest I die. I simply don't know enough to affirm where, when, or why. Are you what you are in my dreams, or something else under sky? What masks do you wear, when and why, how, and for what purpose? You are trying to live and not die, you are trying not to cry, nor to say good-bye to your heart and your soul, to the meaning of the words inscribed in your head and carved into the wood of your bed, where your vampire-self lays, at night, asleep. - What dreams through you creep? In that half-way house between Atreyu and Nayru, stories and magic, midnight and dawn, as we open our mouths to yawn, sometime we remember, or see in our temper, some august ancient temple, Delphi-made. We run from dinosaurs in the mist, remember the last good-bye kiss, recall when we lost it all, as before our eyes again flashes the soccer ball; we are skating through our mind, pulling up again every important dime, silver flashes, silver lashes, silver slashes, whispering about times that might have been and never were, when we flew like birds, and soared over cliff, or by the sea: Visions of freedom, and the iron tree.

    But other times they may be heavy and coarse, ungainly, unsightly growths, strange lumps and heavy chains, as in our veins runs Scrooge's blood. We are greedy and ungracious, fighting troubles punching faces, ungainly, naked, foolish, laughed at, beaten, in turns failing tests and being eaten, the past rising up to destroy the future: Obliterate, obliviate, hopes and dreams, replacing them with whimpers and screams, pictures of failing and being creamed, as in our ignorance we begin to believe what our fears tell us and make us see, warnings brought by the breeze. When those stories of other lands drive us to our knees, shadows wearing masks of me, my fear's controlling, warning, watching, waiting, taking myself to task for my failing as I fall off the railing. - The heights are out to get me, that strange noise in the forest at night is bear or wolf or dragon, some starving two-headed ogre, mage preparing to give twilight closure, end of all days, down comes the sun: Our courage and daring undone.

This is our four-dimensional curse, as that which brings us high may also cause us to see ourselves at our worse: Make us feel worthless and bursting, covered with boils, green balls of death hurling from us in a mess, or else frozen. Creeping blood seeping, straining, kings causing us to be misremembering, awkward phrases from twenty years ago pulled up, dragged behind us like rocks. We are crashing in the river, our boat rolling over, rocks hitting us as we are dragged under, and the more we panic, the more punished we become: Black and blue, numb of feeling, dumb of hoping, mindlessly groping for rope to hang ourselves, or to save ourselves. By our dreams we are pulled and pulling, hope become turning, raised from the grave by lich enslaved, our skeleton bursting forth from flesh, our face eternally stretched into a smile, as we wait and meander for a while. - But sooner or later, as runs time and space, immortal soul reasserts grace. We are free, we are free, to the very extent of the definition, and slowly we understand the powers we have been lent, to travel through the circles of love and hate, or light and dark; of meager and great, of flame and spark, one of us alone on the arc, ready to find a start. Rainbow art and promises forever, understanding the sacred betrayed, as the past behind us we lay down. Not to forget, but nay shall we recall everything, everything. Always, always, it's too heavy and we won't pay the levy, nor build them up, accepting the floods and the muck. In this dark silt, in this black guilt, we find bits of gold, lessons from the old ones of silver on the tree, of blowing a horn in the woods, and kindness towards the green witch. - The eyes of children and the newly born, who accept not the chains, burdens, nor burns, we are not branded as A, B, C, or D, there are no answers in the test we present, no it's open paragraph, responses from you sent to be read, then grounded up in the mill and made bread.

Now drink those letters, and eat those words, then with your little power houses burn: Not out but in, not scars but the expansion of skin, muscle, mind, bone and sin, knowledge outside beaten thin. Sheets of shiny gold and copper bold, electric miracles and mountain tops, zappy zinc and lemons lost, made then given away for more than cost, and if you do this enough you'll never be lost, not completely, utterly, and forever. At least, you'll find the North Star and sit down to a feast, jump into the fields of rye and see what it is to be a beast, forget for a while humans kind and fleece. No-one can steal yourself from you, not even the police. The world is limited by rights they don't even recognize, lights of truth revealing what they do wrong, and our own burdens and failures remade in a song. To be sure, this often takes a long, long time, and it's never done in rhyme, not nowadays, as instead of bards playing, lawyers get paid, workers doing what the bosses have paid - but look out, don't let yourself be betrayed, read everything they write and say, because it's your words laid out for all to see, like a seed sprouting up into a tree: High symbol and shady cover, but it's not always light, the law isn't always right, it's simply might better than night, when it's clear and clarified at least, refined mutterings of man the beast.

Now, dreams drag us around from lesser to least, stealing us from the worst to the best of ourselves, unconscious splashing in the puddles of ignorance. In this way, red fish becomes blue dragon, fossil becomes flight, and night becomes dawning light. Dreams show us how to fight.

Day 32: May 30th, 2024

To Beauty,

    I hide myself every day, attempting my bad and good parts to slay, becoming just another human bearing out the day. Nothing special, nothing new, I am sick, like the bird who flew too close to the sun, until wax melted and he tumbled undone into briny deep where dark things sleep, becoming but dust in the muck: Brown soil, rocky bottom, merely mistletoe, insignificant and forgettable, which could harm no-one and change the world in no way, at least until trickster blue attempted to slay joy and light, casting happiness into night. - Underneath, far below, to be turned carbon from gold. All of a sudden, I feel and see myself as old, some great fool who can't focus, can't create, can't make, can't macerate dust from wood, burning up in stone, now ore remains unusable, a turn of events now inexcusable, failure planned, unstable resources, loss of land, now a cramping hand, hours tossed away, fires burning uselessly in clay, this is turning now to work not play, filling up, not filling in, my day.

    What should I say? Tell the truth? Shout it from the rooftop? As if I even knew - forsooth, I hide from me and you, my entire line of reasoning tossed through some giant hole in my argument: Fallen pillar of the soul, logic's legion invasion, burning throne turned into loss of home, as if I could have gone anywhere, as if there was any point in this assault, as if nephology had passed the salt, or as if the wolves had been welcomed, not crossed. I am lost in the woods with teeth, sharp teeth in my leg and from my mouth, I am biting and bitten, sane and rabid, forgetful and inconsolable. I can't let it go, I make it up, I drink from the Lethe cup, leaving behind what I may not let go, body, mind, and soul. Spirit alone withstands the universe's mighty hands, gods that shape, words that quake. I am like the bottle we shake, bubbles and froth, unclear, mislabeled, now exploding in our face, we lose our look of grace: All a sticky mess, soda fountain exploding, doubting, as we forbear to belive or understand what we have seen, all the places we've been, all the flashes of reen, rat-men burrowing beneath the streets, with ancient battles and crime bursting forth as if they were flowers, myself an apprentice without masters. No-one but me remembers those great disasters when we were dismembered, all those moments in which we lost our temper because the world would not change, this one failing to save, or even stand up straight, quilling beneath signs of love and sigils of hate, unable or unwilling to spiral out a gate from here to there, from then to now, from world to wold: Open moor filled with flowers and foxes, forgotten gardens, magic bravery and shame, overcoming what I to myself named, coward and afraid.

(hide) Every day, I don't know what I wish to say, or which parts of me to save or slay. I ship myself and I flay skin from bone, typing these words on my phone: Exculpation, marathon, midnight song, one karaoke sing-along filled with purple dinosaurs and ancient swords, Dante's words: Don't mess around with the graves! Let them alone stay, touch not the stain of the dead. You are not high anymore, nor in school, don't use those worn-out tools, don't play the fool, ask not bright world to be deadly cruel. My place is in the dark, where I can't be seen, can't be heard, can't be felt, can't be found, one hand only sticking out from the ground, held up in entreaty, up in prayer, headed to the dragon's lair where princess sweeps and kings meet, enchanted world continuing to sleep: Sword in the stone, power abandoned and alone, I am weary and broken to the bone, suffering standing in her home.

Do you know why I'm hiding? (Do I?) Because it is create or die, burn and fly, tell the truth or live a lie, but when I do I become fire and flame, ashamed of my pride and my name. I can't do things like this, write things like this, say words like this, shout out heart and mind like this, without turning everything around me into a fist. - I am (note) a safe person like this! My eyes unwelcome, my energy unhealthy, I am frustration, angst, rage, screaming, weeping, barely holding on with my fingertips to a rhythm. I am running out of rhymes, I'm falling to pieces every time, and when I'm alone that's fine - but every now and again someone with me meets, company upon me creeps, and then I hide, hold back, rewind, become quiet outside while in, in, in, I am sinning, exploding. - Escaping this world, this life, these people, this knife, this strife.

I am not safe dammit, but I have to pretend that I am, put on my mask and pretend, pretend, pretend. I am in the wilderness no falling plane to fend, I don't know why I'm fighting, I'm just tired of the nights. - I am tired, tired, tired, three times I say, three times tie myself in this way, three times break the clay, fourth time all to pay, so that I might see what is behind the words, what sort of curse, this burden that is mine. - The fibers of my soul I use to make twine, magic steps in fishing nets to find the void, reveal the next step beyond. It's not pretty, it's not measured, I'm not treasured, I don't know what I'm doing, I don't know where I'm going, I'm just exploding, all my pieces falling apart. - That's what I'm hiding, you see, the ten thousand blood-tinted mirrors of me. Why do I hide? Because I'm afraid of what you would tell me you see, because if you did, then I might believe you, and be suddeny either saved by, or struck through with a spear,defenses destroyed by your unconsious leer.

Day 33: May 31st, 2024

To Beauty,

    Some poems hurt to read, like when Celia sings of being quiet or having dreams: Never, ever, ever letting someone know they are more than they seem. We were friends once for a day, for a month, for a time, but now - it hurts to be near, it hurts to be far. I'm just confused, like a pirate yelling arr, arr, arr, arrogantly wearing my mask, squaring myself up for a task. I hope I will not fail at last, even as I know I won't have a chance; how bad of me to wish to dance, hold my head up high and prance like Bambi in the wood, bright flowers of may, horns grown to defend and sway, this is how I end the day. In hopes and dreams, in lies and screams, raving mad munching sad, sure that everything I do is bad, unable to hold a smile or throw it away, repeating and wounding myself as the dogs in every direction bay, and I am by my own hearts-gravity betrayed; because I have no wings, no willed wishes freed, unable myself in my heart to admit my need, cutting myself to make sure I still bleed. These are Saladin's nights, Richard fights, Robin's light, Maid Marian's bright. - These are the feelings brought to me by a sight: Great smile, fingered hands, worry for others lands, even though I'm not sure to what extent you command. Are you part of the problem or the solution, do you misunderstand the art, or are you engaged in absolution? I've read too much of history, I've delved into the mystery, all the tribal fights, all the lies and kites, the cheating, the scheming, the hiding of meaning, the actions of peasants and powers, governors, ambassadors, soldiers. - Oh, surely one of them somewhere told the whole truth and nothing but the truth, and I wonder, which one?

    I don't know enough; I have my guesses, but they are impressions, and I don't enquire, because if I did just to be made to be a liar too, cutting with lightning and flame a brew, but never letting it be tasted and chewed like that five-thousand year old shoe I once saw in Yerevan, three inches away from my paw. If we only stayed with what we saw, I could have touched it, taken it, rubbed it, seen the patina of age fall, and had for two whole seconds a wonderful moment of personal archaeology, at least until the security showed. Invisible panes of glass, walls and ceilings I could not pass, those watching eyes, those waiting bands, an angry scream and demand. Put it down, let it go, it's not for you to know, but simply to see the show, because surely if you touch it you'll ruin it, you (I) don't know what you're (I'm) doing. Everything wrong, grease and stain, acid brought by brain, the beginning of rot, and ourselves earning disdain for our malingering pain. We reached out our hand for what was not ours to gain, we said those names three times in the rain, as if in this manner we could absolve ourselves of our stains, and undo this terrible horrible no good very bad strain, this struggle insane.

I don't read certain poems, I hear not certain songs, stopping half-way through recitations and casting upon myself obliviations, part and parcel of my negotiation with love and hate, all that I am: All the mistakes, slashes and flashing, and pacing and smashing, pieces and parts of limps and lashes, painting salves of what might be and what could have been: All I've seen and swam, lost valleys, forgotten hills, unsleeping monsters, and saving wills. This is all we are, dreams of tilling the soil and burning the oil, our lives filled with forbearance and toil. This we are, we live to dream, and from time to time we feel an urgent need to scream, at others and ourselves, who we are and what we might be: Where, why, and when, like a serpent we wind around the soil thin, three inches at least, as fingers to the knuckles reach, spear-hand, serpent-kick, flying screech, - becoming better every day at least. I am not ready, I am not steady, building out a dock on the jetty, far into the ocean, deep unto the sea, just far enough away from shadow and shade for the tip of the sun to reach me. I am cold and afraid, making certain each and every day that one more plank is laid, one more step made, one more solution bade. - I use all I have, living and the dead, memories which have me feeling me: Bad, sad, glad, or jaded, but not happy: Never happy, hippy, or zappy. I am not zippy, nor am I Bibby, I don't play well with others and I can't seem to win alone. Doesn't matter what numbers I type in or what sort of phone I use, old or new, slipshod or through, pass, throw, whirl, twirl, shoot, dunk, whatever I do, wherever I am, I hear a whistle now, referee saying I'm wrong, me interrupting the flow of my very own song. I'm not sure how long I can keep this up for, when all I want to do is sleep, into my dreams creep, find certain poems or letters, visions of sugarplums and times that were better, a company sweet not bitter.

Because, sometimes, no matter how hard I try, all I see is my failures, when I should have said something, not just cried, lived and not died. I do not stand upon a sure rock inside, but simply rest on my rack, floating on the tide, lifted up by my own iron walls and hide, only here because of the emptiness and lies, physics reflecting the truth of size. I am all displaced, neither smart nor wise. Neither am I strong: Falling apart we are, unable to reach that holy star which shines in heaven, burning on the horizon, foam-flecked, iron-melting, sulfur-raining, reflecting clouds staying, green-house running, whisper-stirring, child of the god, mother to a child older than her. When she sings certain songs, or enforces certain laws, then I am become lost, tossed onto the ocean without a ship, and into the wild with neither knife nor whip. Lions and lionesses wait for me to slip up, sipping from the poisoned cup, and becoming something that might be enough, a living being who does more than dream. Why listen to these songs? Because I want to be more than I seem. Why read these poems? Because I can't help but have these dreams, and I know that can't is an evil word, but I'll use it here: I can't give up and still live, I can't be aware of myself and put on that lid again, containing all the wonderful sin. You see, I've listened to these poems too much now, and the line is thin between what was and might have been, and I see it now, so I begin to read those poems and listen to those songs. Just a line or two, though I can't bear it for long, and take many breaks, allowing my soul to quiet from its quakes, recovering from the aftershocks and shakes, repairing my heart every time it breaks. I just hope I'm not too late.

Day 34: June 1st, 2024

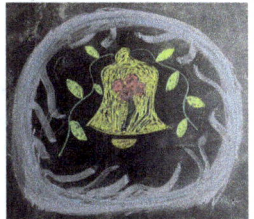

To Beauty,

    I'm afraid I lie. because I don't know what kind of person I am. Do I want warmth, or only sin? Something strange is within, anxiety-anxious, misplaced mistakes, the sort which danger makes; I am intersectioned and take everything from everywhere, extend my hair and bare my soul for all to see, meanwhile the whole time being blind about the differences between I and me. This is not the same one who flies high in the sky, as dives low under the sea, Sha's of fear and anger, pride and wrath, like a queen among the bees I am industrious - but then I sleep, and out comes me: Wolf who howls, dragon who drowns. I have no gold nor chains, I have no moon or sun; I am alone in the gray mountains, cold, going mad, trying not to yell too much or grow too sad, writing down and doing things that are really, really bad, having dreams, having dreams, pulling on my wooden nose, slathering medicine on my toes. This whole situation blows! But it's not as if there was any other option; I have no traction, no direction, no attraction, no intention. I am blind-self-reflection, mad muttering in magic mirror, with magic ring to help me spear these mail-coated missive, round fins so utterly dismissive of my might or my travel, as slowly I am unraveled: Pulled tight, shrunken in sight, desperately, stupidly, fighting light, as lingering over my pains 'me' is stifled and tight, tied up in frightful visions of future feelings, as poems and prayers send me reeling. -

    Loss of balance, lose of name, loss of shame, but still an awareness of eyes upon me playing the game, anxiety is seeping into my head, I am blamed; what should I be but blasted, broken, buttered up, to be shaken and abused, laughed at, made into shoes, stepping stones for those betters of mine, whom they would rather choose? Let me tell you, this is not news, I knew from the beginning that I would be bruised, hurt, cut, not enough, reflecting back three years hence, and reading my own words full of a pretense of poetry or understanding. I don't know what I was trying to do, and I don't know what sort of flu I had, the sickness that kept me inside, wearing my masks, failing my task, feeling attacked, even though I know for a fact there is no knife at my back. You see, there is a wonderful freedom in autonomy, in the gray haze, in the million-peopled maze where I can avoid any extraneous gaze. I can be alone, I can heal myself, I can be stronger than I was, I can be an elf on the shelf, I can be stuck. Unable to move on, unable to climb, feeling like I am stuck, a box full of rhymes running out of time not even to make even a single honest dime. Always I glance at the phone as it chimes, hoping against hope for a message to take me from my home, some rake that my leaves will take, these pieces of grass, these partitions at last, as I am back-cast, light showing my shadow, and a shade under my sorrow growing.

Who am I, who am I, who am we, who am why? Just a thing that's shy, a memory waving good-bye, some boy who's tired. - But dig in, accept my sin. Me still grins, this one won't win, but I played. My deepest heart I did not betray, not again, and if the light even today still is dim, it's better than the nothing that was once within. We still can't see, we are blind, but from ambrosia we have begun to sup, our blood is flowing into the cup, and ever so slowly gathering up. Over our hands it melts, armor it smelts, defending us against the damage we have dealt with our infinite cloaks, and socketed gems, we are free to flow: Ice and fire, fell desire, heaven's ire and titan's mire. We are cursed with flesh and descended from iron, our heart working itself free from form and order, as we march over the pale across the border. Seeking ourselves, fording into delves, finding little old half-elves and solving riddles, finding tricks, jumping straight into the thick, Augustian scheming, move now, quick, quick. - If you don't think, then soon you'll be licked: Beaten and broken, bloodied and bruised. Not the sort of muddied which is fun and the sign of favor, nor the sort which is the signal of labor, but instead the distemper of the betrayer, as with green skin and evil horns we are born, treating those who had loved us with scorn.

But it's not hatred, not really, nor jealousy, nor hunger, but instead simply our temper, our trembling, our anger, our emotions, our wildness, our suffering this. - For to be opened wide, to dare the tide, to walk and mumble, to tumble, hand over head, hip over hip, like Mr. Smith I managed to trip, saying what is this, what is this, monologuing in the mist, great turtle, A'tuin rising, I see in his eyes something surprising: All I suppressed, everything that made me less, my fears, my black and white spears, my dear, my emptiness, my amusement at nothingness, because we can laugh at all of this. Like Lugh take our bad luck and twist, like Sandry with a quick flick of wrist, give dancing boys a lesson in directing their fits, and turning this into a comedic bit. There is some method to our madness, some way to sit and meditate, concentrate, write down and make. Instead of denying your hunger, fill it and sate: Paint your love and your hate. Be true to yourself, willing to make mistakes, to be the butt of the jokes like Jake, but behind that patterning is something great: Growing, barely bit by bit showing, gold in the dross, glint between the crossed eyes, I don't know who I am but I'm finding out, and I will pay the cost of knowledge: Being wrong, being told so, and learning to sing a song of changing, a song of making. I am shifting: Snares eluding, traps breaking, new cakes baking, new tastes, new shapes, new words. I'll find my worth, even if I have to travel again the entire earth.

This is my curse, that from my birth I have never known who I am, and I always lie. I say that's fine, but for my entire life I have attempted to find that light that shines, truth, beauty, lies. There is no untruth in this world, only mazes in the mind and a subprimordial brine; listen to my lines, me in the mirror, I am missing, and there are ten million clues, every day the world whispering: Choose. Is all I ever say a lie? Even false words can reveal the truth inside. Even my masks reveal what I'm trying to hide.

Day 35: June 2nd, 2024

To Beauty,

    Soon enough this time shall pass; I know the quiet cannot last, as I feel last gasp approaching, loss of will and mind, broaching topics I did not dare to breach, walls falling before the leech. Bright diamond necklaces, three pieces to each, old age unraveling to the beat of ill-logic, as ends this story ever tragic. - The life of man and Grandmother, minds lost, aluminum tossed, no more over ourselves the boss, we are beaten now, no longer alive, merely spares inside, pins that don't match up; already soul and body drinks from the lethe cup, first day by day, then hour by hour, now minute by minute, until no 'thing' is understood, not potatoes nor forks, not plates or fields, and from our work not a single good thing yields up its name, so that its place in the world penetrates the brain, reliving ourselves of some manic strain. I know the person I'm talking to is not to blame, and when I rage I feel shame, overwhelmed because I've said no, no thank you, ten thousand times, literally, I don't want anything, I never ask for anything, I haven't accepted any offer of food she's given for a year, because that's how long it been since Grandma used soap to wash her hands.

    Sometimes, oh there are days, where I wish I could drown my memories in a beer, but I have found that so-called magic liquid only brings them more near, allowing me to speak yes, but in no way allaying my fear, or drawing me farther away from my bier: Raging fires where Faramir laid, poisoned by darkness threatening end of day, beating at brilliant mind until it all goes away; some demented craziness is now making the whole world sway, sure that there's a stranger at the door or a thief, some purse-snatcher bringing grief, as goddess looks through garbage, searching for that thing with no name, and if I ask what it is, we don't know, no-one knows. Just…we feel frantic because something is wrong, the words just don't match up to the song, as we respond to every whisper with a shout: What happened? What was that? What'd you say? And I reply three times, but it doesn't matter anyway. The answer is nothing. It's nothing. It's always nothing. That's all that surrounds me now, nothing. There is no future, there is no past, even the present cannot last. Oh, how we wish there was some blue diamond pill stuck in the forehead that we could clasp and release to restore us to ourselves for one moment, one day, just long enough to fight against time and say words which were real and mattered.

I wish Grandma understood and didn't act like a mad hatter, walking at night in circles for an hour, or locking up the cat until I have to let her out when I hear her cry, four times a day as of last May, and then twelve in December, until this morning when you left the door open and didn't even remember. Yesterday you told me you had three cats and a dog, and now it's just a bad fog, you got in the fridge and the cheese is missing, so is the silverware, and it could quite honestly be anywhere, like that pan we found last week that had been missing for six months, and the way in which we have to wash again every plate that you touch. If I wanted anything for Christmas it would be: Stay out of the kitchen please, I don't need hovering or help or harassing, I need nothing. I want nothing. Just....let me help. I wish I could help. Nine months ago I thought I could, answering questions and reliving fears, but now there is nothing left but the tears.

Torrents roll upon me, the future that I bear, as I understand surcease of care, wild wavy white hair mad in the wind, I know these days shall never come again. I don't know when it happened, the last time we talked for real, and when our worlds were related in the same way, and the same angle to reality. All that makes life slipped away: Mind quietly went to sleep, and never woke again that day. Now my evenings take on the character of a play, as I write to someone who isn't real, about event which made no impression on the soul, only shadows on the page. I fear reduction to a sage, praised for pretty words but quickly forgot, as the men and women who read it learn what they are not, and I look down upon my acts, knowing now they soon shall pass: Be not remembered. No sense persists, only feeling recalled, I'm not grandson anymore, only 'him', or 'the guy', my name disappearing into the sky. No point more in asking why, the children's question passes by overhead, along with what and when, all being answered just with a shrug and a grin, as if I could read her mind, or the logic find. The map is lost, matching the end of sentences. They're all gone, no footsteps, no song, just like this particular day, which was very, very long.

Now, its not torture, its not fate, its simply me choosing to face every human's ultimate disgrace: For loss of limb, tongue, eye is bad enough, but when we cry and don't even know why? If I ever knew I was going to get this bad, I would rather die. Dementia's a demon alright, even if it leaves behind someone kind. Now, slowly, we're running out of time, until I can't take care anymore, or stand up before the climate, storms of worry and madness. Sometimes I beg Grandma to eat as she stares at the treat on her plate, as if she didn't know what it was: Food. When I am asked to pass her a fork while she holds one in her hand, or when I have to grab her wrist to stop her from physically stealing my breakfast, or when I have to guard the soup pot because she'll lean over it and drool, or when I play the fool saying: I don't know, I don't know, to every crazy question, the answer, or what you're saying. - Those words don't work together, grandma. I don't know what the weather of the car is, or why the blanket is smiling at us. I'm just surrounded by nothingness. There's no point, I can't help, nothing I do changes anything, ever, in any way, and each and every day just gets worse. We are on some radiating sine wave, which goes up and down but always trends towards the earth, gravity returning light to its birth. Blackbody now, hot to the touch but invisible, insensible, in theory describable, but practically a mystery, holding a zero-point module which becomes lost in history. There's no more help to give, there's no more hand to hold, and I don't know where I go from here. I can tell the routine is starting to fall apart, I do it again, but sometimes the solution doesn't start. I go outside, retreat to my art, but it doesn't matter. Alice still shows up to tea, but there's no tea, only me and mother in the woods looking after grandma, and ever so slowly running out of time. Life is sour as if I had bit into a lime, and I know I'm free to write and rhyme, but I'm not sure why I'm bothering to climb. No-one watches me or wants to hear me whine, jumping on that bier and hoping to die in time before the darkness comes, because I know it's bad now, but it's gonna get worse, and I'm not sure how well I'm going to deal with that curse. Maybe I'll burst.

Day 36: June 3rd, 2024

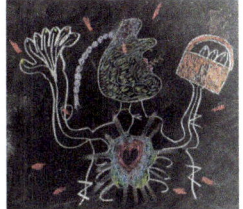

To Beauty,

There are many sights I won't say I see, and many dreams I won't admit I have; I won't tell you what they are, you'll have to ask, but they're all bad, a series of terrible tasks and masks. Every time I pursue one I hear myself crack, and a tenuous creaking in my back. I don't want to stand, and as I hold the violin I bend, failing at defending; no-one on me should be depending. I know of all things, and I am ending. - I enter once again an inner sanctum, lights around me, wings surround me, but into the house I go, dead, greedy spiders waving to and fro, I see skulls and gold: But that game for me now is old. I have no friends playing it today, and I never made any from the activity. I search in odd places, I find forgotten races, attempts to run across the desert and reach the sun. Bring back another one, some fire seed upon which to plant a tree on Earth which will reach all the way up to the Sky, then climb it to find an acorn and jump; pass through shadow to another world, find a hole wherein I could be birthed, bursting, busted, locks broken, hair tossed away as a token of a time when I did speak and was spoken. My true name cast out and carved in blood on the open sands, where I gained a fifth finger on each hand, signal of Scholomance command, darkness in my head, to reach and rend, to spare and spend. I knock down these pillared walls, I walk into the august halls, and as all stare at me I feel a call: Live or die, do something to break it all. We are cursed to try, and crawling sigh, as we open our eyes up to the sky, say a name and drain our brain, write in rhyme our hidden strains, and know at least our secret shames.

We are human, we are monsters, we are meddlers, always trying to peddle our newest idea, which too often is a patched up tin pot, works well enough, but not what we had said we had bought. We polish this pot as if it was new; it shines and shimmers, beauty strikes us through, and we want again to choose this one, this one, as we cook, but then we fry and leave, look away for half a second: Smell, turn, burn, off, hope, but the bottom is brown already, it crunches. How hungry are we, really? Will we have the roots with the flowers? Will we have the walls with the towers? Can we accept the castle and the bower? Knights are knights in two ways, meek in hall and fierce in field, before the devil they will not yield. Some have failed at this, broken oaths to infidels, but the promise is not to them nor to me, it is to thy, not I. Holy host, ancient ghost, what we follow the most is in our actions revealed, reverences standing like a banana peeled: Only strong, supporting, with the help of a hand, five fingers breaking the stem. I shake and shake, I quake and break, but...I do not burst. I am not the worst, never blame others for my curse. I am here because of what I spent from my purse, those four and ten score years on this earth; see me attempt to earn my worth, writing, making, madness taking me, muse awaking me. I am meandering, lost in the woods seeking a fairy. I don't ask for anything, I don't want anything, I simply am trying to understand; glimpse of smile, devil's command, the way in which I stare mesmerized at a hand, awed by the rocks and lines in the sand.

    Struggling, I attempt to land, I jump from the sky and like white tiger attempt to fly: Sixth point to five stars, ancient bars, the music shining like stars. I am dancing in the dark and praying for that spark, meanwhile playing the lark, a neir-do-well, a nothing-done-well, a sickness in me swells. High-octane blood they said, raging feral, may as well be dead, not willing to go quietly to my bed. - I have lost my head, or nearly, like Nick I'm in the thick of it, schools of magic, dreams so tragic. Like Nebuchadnezzar I grow manic, and like Saladin no ally wishes to stay, so I must continue this crusade my way, paying no attention to how Gungnir sways. My back is to the wall, the kings me slay, I am a coward deeply ashamed every day, as I will not work hard to achieve - to achieve - nothing, or nothing I will admit, even as I fall down frothing in a fit, or look at a picture and feel like I've been hit. My life is constructed of little bits. Pixels won't form pictures, my ram is flipped from indescribable, indecipherable dimensionalities, five four three two one zero none, incoherent. I am a torrent of confusion, under Sahir's illusion, not sure what kind of thing I am, mask or man, heart or plan, like Kel I play with iron-tipped fan, dangerous to those who can see the damned.

    I am doomed; I fear to wonder the earth lost and cursed; I can't save myself, I don't know how, simply seeking myself reborn as a cow, this one less than half empty howls. - Fenrir unchained, frost giant's brain, I don't know my game, my glorious purpose or my original name; I'm so angry and I don't know who else to blame. To see me, to fear I, this is the mirror up in the sky: Moonlight, shining key, truths and lies, words I despise, coward too afraid to cry lest I unravel and no longer ask why. I never grew up, and I never settled down. I am a clown, gallivanting in a circle round, if there was ever a point to the laughter and sound, for I am silent. The clowns are always silent.

Day 37: June 4th, 2024

To Beauty,

    I don't know what to do, so one step a day, that's how I'll continue my way, purifying my clay. I'm not strong or pretty, and what does it matter anyway how I show, if there is nobody to show it to? I don't act alone or as if anything physical ever led to a clue. I'm not a Haz-Bin, but a never-was; I never heard the buzz of bees, black or red, yellow stripped, the kind that live in walls or trees, building nests to safeguard themselves from leaves, razors flying through the breeze, whips that break the rocks off clean, snakes and arms both bleed. To some deep terrible extent I'm not sure what I need. Biting myself like a desperate vampire, I feed: Fear me, seek me, break me.

    Y'know, sometimes I spend half an hour on the phone looking at pictures of cats, flicking my finger back and back, continuing to roll upwards and put my life back on track; I'm losing my mind putting on this mask. Some days I'm so tired I can barely stand, bend at the waist and listen to a music band, over and over again, grasping at throats as if they have hands, hungry for salvation, life spent in preparation, this is my dungeon; deep and dark, no song nor spark, I attempt my art, but it does not heal me, only tears me apart. I don't know what to do, to expect, to attempt, no pentious sacrifice, no cherry kiss, no showing Valentino my fist. No-one holds my chain, and I struggle against no-one and nothing for no reason. I never, ever, to hope gave treason, but occasionally in this long fire-season, I've breathed in enough smoke to die, to silence my throat, my lungs, my crying, I can't even cough, I'm free but at what cost? I am lost.

    I know not which fly to seek, or what sort of empty places to creep. I dive into books and try so stupidly to sleep, see dread beasts with dragon heads and leap, always trying to keep my balance and honor my talents, do what I'm best at. Which is what, exactly? I sort of wish I knew, because every day I feel as if I have the flu: Nose stuffed, throat in pain, a fuzziness in the brain, twelve hours in this bed I have lain. I am sick - but am I to blame? What's the point of this stupid game? All I find is shame, seemingly empty spaces where once was noise, naughty lists instead of toys. I deserve this, I suppose, the result of following my nose and standing on my tippy-toes: "To seek, to find, and not to yield."[5] I have passed the western stars and landed in a field, one full of rye, tall grasses high, as I bend at the knees and sigh. Onee-san, must I again try? Crawling I hide, in the roots, between the stalks, under the flowers, and against the clock. Perhaps if I wait long enough it will all burn up, eye-lines clear as Armageddon draws near. Of Ragnarok I do not fear, but I feel unequal, unreasonable, and lost. I have been bossed around in my time, and I've responded to that in rhyme, but never on the clock filled with their dime, only on mine, hours after I heard the chime, clear ringing decline of laws and rules, manager's guiding tools. What can I do now that I've decided to play the fool? Certainly not play it cool; I have already done that, been cruel.

I admit my crimes, I'm out of line: Living in phantasm, facing not reality, unable to see or understand duality. I've drawn my three cards without knowing which to choose, I'll have to wait once more to see if I lose, hoping to take home no cut, only a bruise, and without being entirely clear on what I have to lose. Life is a game, this truth is plain when you look it up, see how men hurt themselves and heal, how hearts paradoxically both stand tall and kneel, strong in survival but afraid to face the feels, weak strings falling over in a breeze, such light linen walls won't hold what we need. On what sort of mare's milk shall we feed? The lon-lon kind, which hides our seven years of memory inside. Swing your sword and break the tide, don't accept the reign of time.

Now, in memories we dined, but enough of that. - Now we take a different tact, bending our sails to wind's new act, we trace ourselves back and back, and this way claw ourselves, attack. Crawling we snack on hard rocks and eat trampled mud, running before the bombs and fording at the flood, our halos falling off, becoming undone, as we hold not to something, but none. Soon shall come chances and changes unavoidable, powers shaking which once were thought unbreakable, word written down that have for a decade been unsayable, my complete consistent field rendered incompatible with life, as I take to my own head the knife: Cut and slice, a Frankenstein's monster make of my strife, awaiting now the lightning strike, heaven's stoke, Zeus's yoke that seeks to bind mankind, look at a Bun-Bun rabbit and say that is mine; Shiva says only if you can find the truth, Brahman, only if you can find yourself.

Look in the mirror, growing ears like an elf, desperately seeking to repel from your shelf and delve into the deep, Azeroth's keep, from Elune not a peep, what are you, a creep? Look at the cat, meow and mreep, isn't that neat? Now that you've rested for a while, stand up on your own two feet. We are neither feline nor canine, not mankind or stuck waiting in line, it's your life to find. You have as much freedom as you'll pay for in pain and misery, and as much wisdom as you understand and reject in your own history. This one is a mystery: So "Zippity do da, zippity ay, my oh my it's a wonderful day."[6] - What else now should I play, in order to seek and find my way? Not fire, but breath in clay. Music my heart to find, muse to say and writing bind. I'll swear to myself, someday I'll be more than fine. I'll be alive.

Day 38: June 5th, 2024

To Beauty,

    I'm messing up, I'm stressing out, I think I'm going to lose this bout, I am full of doubt. I don't even know what I'm fighting, or wht the writing on the wall says. How I wish to want to rise or how everything we did failed today. In my Grandmother's house I dwell, and green flames rise for me: Not jealousy, but a stain. Something wrong with me. - Pain. I am by a silence laid, a blind and foolish boy who wields a broken blade. I asked you what you thought of what I wrote - do you have any idea what it took to tell that joke? To turn and say, I would like you to look at what I made, and tell me what you think? I wanted to read your writing, too. - But you never replied, and that stuck me through. I do not flirt, I do not play games, only silence or a flame. Why can't I tell you my name? Because of myself I am ashamed. I simply cannot be straight, direct, obvious, clear; I lose my mind when you draw near, even though you be a ghost, no member of mortal host, a phantasm in my head, a memory of when I was dead. With my words I don't want to show my feelings, release the shock and see people reel at my gentle soothing rain, iron-tipped pain, or surcease of sorrow to gain. - No, repeating my refrain over and over again, because I am trying to move, melt the ice, re-forge the knife, find who I am if I'm not nice. For this in blood I'll pay my price,and blind myself, the better to see with an inner eye those demon wings spread across the sky.

    I reject all gifts with a cost, I am willing to try and be lost, in nether's darkness, in chaos and fel, in the house of evil I dwell, outland I go now, to hell. - Land falls apart beneath me, all who help me fear me, I'm sure that is going to be my story. - I was never meant for the light's glory. How do I know? Because my past is gory, filled with dead things and horrors. It's all in my head, nightmares as I lay in bed, remembering when on others I fed, not giving what I took, not freeing out of fear of a look. I locked my heart away in ten thousand books, million games, and I was a crook. Now, Look! See me, feel me, I am half fake, all mistake, I have not enough in me to be great. Can you understand my self-hate? I've already eaten, but I am already empty.

    I dare not open the gates up to empathy, or listen to fair angelic symphony. Down I dive into my history, that of man and mankind, of men and women and wine, of other creatures that in my eyes shine.

I begin to unwind my thread, use the spools in the shed and the old foot-loom two feet from my grandmother's bed, diving down through the madness in my head. I meet Hades in the halls of the dead, but he wears Vera's face, and I hear Taltos tip-toeing, quiet pacing, heart racing, for me to be done with my talk, and the real book to begin. I put on Tishoo's mask of sin, I fall but never reach the ground, I claim old names and don't play their games, I'm so confused, it's inane, what am I doing? Who am I? Where am I and why, why, a thousand times, why? Oh, if I wrote those words across the sky, would you have replied? I told you half the truth and keep to myself half the lie, how I spend every single day trying not to cry or faint. I have in me some terrible purple taint, thaumatism gone all wrong, nature's ill-fitting song. Hehehe, How long do you think I'll last? How much longer?

    I gave up being a farmer or a fisher, but I'm not a poet, I miss her...even though she's not real. When I was born there was a hole in my soul, some loss of spark, I always sought for others to tell me my part, not who I was, but if I could make good art. I have an indiscriminate eye, there is beauty in everything: Both the crocodile and the fly, and when I saw them I said maybe that beauty can also be I, if I draw like that, or write like that, or pretend to be like; put on my black and white hats, play Cleopatra, call for an asp, and so dramatically give my last glorious gasp, only to wake up again the next day, and have to pay again for gas, receiving my pittance as part of the cast. I've done it before, and all's to do it again at last, as if the world was a stage and I merely a mask in the play, lines rewritten by someone else every single day, me always failing to remember them or reach them.

    Life is heaven and hell all rolled into one, fireballs striking goats, then hiding them from the heavenly hosts, Adam being stabbed by a nifty ghost. With glee we scream, even if we don't know what this means, as we depict humanity by a dream, floating along on leaf-sails asphodel's stream. - Through the back door now, quickly, while the string still gleams, lest the one-eyed tri-faced crone snip, everything you ever did appearing as only a blip, insignificant triple of Egyption ship, all your words, drive, and wit, reduced to the fact that you lost: Gold ridiculed as dross.

    To be sure, I am always lost, but I'm trying not to react to depression in the same old way. I'm not throwing them out, I'm reclaiming my doubt, I fire my clay, add a glaze, place it in the blaze, wait one more day. I read back my own words and say: That was me, and I can be better. I'll look in the mirror and say 'her', understand, you've fallen but someday you have to land, you need to change, or else you'll pass like this, you'll die like this, dreaming of some prince's kiss. Wake yourself up boy, leave the tower, crawl under the thorns, and run, run, run when you hear the hunter's horn. You can be free again if you survive until morn. Maybe they don't read what you write, maybe they don't know how you strike, maybe they don't care what you think of at night. Regardless, it's give up or fight. What do I want? Living or Life?

Day 39: June 6th, 2024

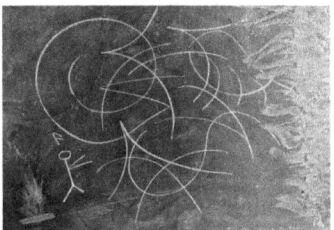

To Beauty,

Something in me is broken, life only a token to exchange. I don't know what to do with this endless rage and these darkness chains, I'm going slowly, ever so slowly, insane, and I don't know which part of me to blame. Like Blaine I play with fire, have a mind full of science and ire, but I'm also like a rocket stuck in the mire, one growing mold, unable to succeed at what they're told to be. All my happy memories are old, and even when the sun is out now I feel cold. Something is wrong with me, I can't even touch the sea, or shelter anymore beneath high tree. Between serpent and eagle, or squirrel running free, my back bends, and next my knee. It's not that I can't stand, it's that I'm not sure why. I realize there will be no meeting, I sigh. I spent so long trying to live not die, speak not cry, fly away from here, not the earth in the world, by my own words twirled into space, reaching, racing, hoping to face a mirror, myself, and leave my coward's shelf, but alas impure. I shall never meet an elf, or walk with dwarves and dragons in lands apart. I read books early in my life about the stars, but have no wizard's art, and don't even know where to start, because doing science doesn't interest me. - I was made for books and to read, even though I recognize now there is more I need, some purpose, some deed, reason, or drive, to do more than survive.

If the purpose of power is power, then is the purpose of life, life? I hope not. - If it was, I would grab the knife. I won't accept there being no end to this pain and this price, to these moments of deep horror and fake nice. I do not accept the God's dice, and with my own hand I'll roll thrice, again and again, third times the charm, as I break down the walls of the barn, and leave this ogre's farm. I wish to do not harm, but life is pain, life is suffering and breaking, life is failing and taking blood from warm veins, or like a zombie eating brains, slowly, slowly by our actions becoming stained, once blue blood now drained in some ghastly defense of enforced humanity, the world declaring what it accepts as sanity. I reject all morality, all laws of God and man, because what I do reflects what I am, and when I stand I will not allow anyone to take my place, or paint their words above my head. I am made of history, but this grave is my bed, and good and bad are what I say they are, and I know this is pride taken too far, but falling is just another way to rise in the isles. Later we build our piles of broken pieces, our pillars of what we love the most, our never forgotten, never abandoned ghosts. Someday, somehow, we will raise a host of all we were, devils, angel, animal, man, abandoning all our well-thought plans, because this is our chance to raise our hand, this is what we worked for, a question of God we demand: Why am I alive? What do I do with these things broken inside? I don't know what else to try.

One birthday, at twenty-eight, I gave up trying to die. Curiosity killed the cat, but kept me alive. I said I'll see this out to the end, even as against my own despair I will forever fend. The strangest things may keep us going: What happens in the next book, or the next chapter? Will we ever have a chance again to hear that laughter? What happens if we write ourselves down faster? Would I last the journey? As a child I remember playing a game called Math Blaster, and I was never very good at doing two tasks at the same time; somehow I always got the mixed up in line, which do I do first, how do I climb the leaderboard and make sure my voice is heard, my name known, my home found, my abandoned phone ringing? I am lingering, lamenting, half-demented. Like banshee at side of house, I cry: Someone has died, or is dying, and now to friends I'm lying, saying I'm fine when I'm not. I've been caught, in my own mutterings, by the bare fact that I'm stuttering, or posting stories. A picnic day looks happy right? But it's not.

If you look closely, it's a symbol of everything I've lost, and of what I'm doing to pay the cost, myself out with family but not friends, flowers in an empty field, no glimpse of me, and a stillness on the breeze. My world is full of falling leaves, and every single night I say please, please, I can do this. I can do this. I can make it through this, as every connection I miss watches, but stays silent. I hide from myself too, not admitting when I am through and done. I write a thousand words every single night and show them to no-one. Every time I weep, I weep alone, I never pick up the phone, and I don't know where to find my home. Pictures of picnics, like thumbs, are like buried bones, buried by a dog. Safe, saved for those terrible days when no matter how much you pray, no manna from heaven comes, no smiling faces to make you strong enough to not be numb, to feel enough that you may accept yourself as dumb. I smiled, you see, but all that is knowing what to do, not what to be.

So I'm still broken, but these words, these thousand words, are a token of my favor, a handkerchief in the air, an arrow sent speeding nowhere. I'm not good and I'm not fair, but there's a reason I wear a Padawan braid in my hair. I'm trying to learn how to admit that I can care.

Day 40: June 7th, 2024

To Beauty,

    I distract myself too often, running away from my coffin: Pretty pictures and pretty people, pretty games and the things I do of which I am ashamed. For so many hours I will play a game, refusing to even think about a certain name. I watch movies, I read books, I tuck my life into a nook, with knees drawn up and head bowed, my back and spirit cowed. I can't handle this, I run away into the mist, I can't care, I can't look, I can't remember, I can't admit I have a temper. My poor tendency is pouring into someone else all my strains and worries, imagining that if they were here, then I wouldn't hate myself so much, or be this incredibly out of touch with who I was and what I wanted, whatever comes next. I distract myself because everything I do hurts, or has the potential to hurt. Life is pain, birth is straining, what's the point, what road am I on, where the gate? What do I do with this endless hate? In every direction upon every task, I have all the power for which I ask, but none of it avails to break the mask. My heart is missing with my mind, and only my soul is left inside, howling mad, and every day bad. I am up at bat, swinging blindly until I hear a crack, or else am called out, in line last. I stumble and gasp returning to the dugout, quieting, controlling, hiding my freakout, readying myself in the quiet for another bout, fists swinging wildly, crowd shouting, and I just trying to shut it all out. Quiet now, quiet in my head, like Ippo I can't see or hear, beaten half dead, but with the loss of my senses I've lost my dread. Now comes the approach, to empress of fear with shadows behind, and a nightmare inside. I distract myself again, take another ride, one to seventy, a bronze tide that someone else might to occasion rise, run Black Temple one more time, in search of green blades and rhymes.

    I can almost hear the chimes, ringing bells inside, the echoes of Quasimodo or Frodo's flames, muse unreal to me, inhuman, to my shame as I am turned insane, writing down in manic rabid reflections on my name, missing matters, music splatters, I am shattered: Offensive before the sun, as my death knight runs with ruined grace, advancing at a wraith's pace. I put on music and ignore my hate, distraction again my fate. I know that when I do this for hours it's not great, and I don't match up to my dreams or my rhythmic screams; the face I put on, the letters I use, they are wrong, because I can't do this, I can't do this, Beauty, I can't do this every day and every hour. When I try too hard the art goes sour, and seed never turns to flower. I am cut grass, gasping my words, I am mud, I am burned, turned into a bloodless thing with white fangs which does not dare to hope, or even grasp as a dying man does at the rope round about his neck. - Beginning to choke, this is no joke, I see how I could croak, and I am trying so hard not to break and be broke. Ten years, no more, I gave to the possibility of that score, as like Eleanor three times I fought to be free, defended castle against enemy, and like squirrel climbed high in the tree: Leaping from branch to branch, taking the high road, avoiding the loam and the soil, the dark, dread toil, fungi obliterating cellulose and lignin, moving through the world as a shark does with his fin, cutting the waves, and bringing smaller, slower beings to their grave. Oh, carnivores have it made, top of the food chain, but even they sleep, both mighty T-Rex and roaring lion slumber, falling under the Lord of Nightmares and suffering white hairs, loss of drive and care.

No matter if the sword of light goes out, still Gourry shouts remember me, but I'm not that brave. Instead of reaching out I look in, staring at my navel, dan tien, trying to be stable, taking what small, ignorant steps I am able. Like Cable I go back and back, with one eye, looking, living, crying, dying, I am bleeding, but I put on band-aids to heal from my actions, before muse I kneel. Out comes the torrent, down comes the rain, and there now Mauna Kea's frozen grey, and carved lava, like before Kenshin's grave. I am lifted by the past, hot air in balloon's grasp, I clasp the rock to my heart, I am burned, but that's how the redstone engine starts: That I imagine someone might read, match my need, eat the seed I spread on the porch outside when in the morning birds pass by, fill themselves before they fly.

But from such work I distract myself, by and by, whenever my brain and soul begin to fry. The only promise I make to myself each day, is that before I go to bed again I'll try to write a thousand words before I die, because if I pass through aneurysm, this is all I'll leave behind: My thoughts, my rhymes, my art, the parts where I worked hard, when from my distraction I rested, when my abilities I tested, and if they are not equal to the heights of my dreams, at least I let out my seams. I became wider, I changed, dress with new panels, or a line of pearls that in dark night among the woods twirled, seen by the moon, if not the sun, cared about by something, if not someone.

Come now, play the game, accept that you feel shame, but face up to the blame and don't run away. I use everything this day, all I have, did, and learned, how I burn and be burned, not by Beauty but by her lack, not by hearty meal, but by my own empty snack. Starving wolf, I attack! Moving forward, not back. I will find what I lack.

Day 41: June 8th, 2024

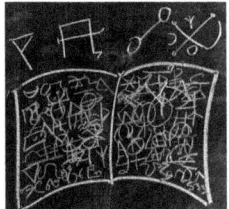

To Beauty,

     I wonder why I buy physical books? Is it for possession, or simply an obsession? Certainly there are other ways to obtain the information: Cheaper, too. Half my life is kept in the world electric, anyway: My money, my thoughts, and all the transmission for which I've fought. Perhaps there is a fear in me that if all I own is kept on some magnetic tape, then the time shall come where that will all be erased through some negligent mistake, or geomagnetic storm. If no-one remembers me, and no trace remains of my activity, then after I die, how will I have been born? Not to toot my own horn, but I've existed, even if I've missed my many chances to change the world. I am tossed from the mountains on a brook, tucking myself into my nook, mindlessly reading and clicking right on my book. In a way, this ease is wonderful, but what it gave it also sometimes took, because when it runs out of battery I can't look. Although - the same is true in a way for the paper, as every child learns in midnight capers under the covers, stars and moon are not enough to see the page; for that we need the sun's rays. So us, mankind, the readers, feel dismay at end of day, when no more through fantasy our minds can play, and we are reduced from fire to clay, no more do we learn what god's have to say; now we make it up, tell our stories in a gruff voice: The Iliad, the Odyssey, Beowulf, jumping clear over the gulf between our ancestor's dreamy eyes, and our modern mathematical minds. Those words were never set in stone, changing with every bard born, and every peal of huntsman's horn, just as the men in the Mexican mountains slowly turned green teosinte into yellow corn.

     Our legends were simply the beginning of the morn, the start of day, when we began no longer to pray, but to the gods we said, we say: We are the makers, the movers and shakers, not equal to Nature, but with a nurture of our own, slowly constructing our cultural bones. Now we stand clothed in flesh, knowing good from evil, cursed from blessed, slowly becoming with each year better, if never the best, even if, occasionally, civilization took a rest, and strangled the new stories before they left the nest; but dead things may flower yet, stone turned into seed, old legends reformed to fulfill the needs of now, when postmodernism and science threaten to cow creation, enclosing fiction and imagination.

     Some say we should stick to the earth, and not go anywhere until we've fixed the problems of our birth, but I look on that idea with mirth. I fear the day mankind fills their mind, and no more attempts to trek to the stars and battle against the Sith, because I feel like a day we give up on that is a day we miss, one of those times when I can't write like this. The heavens hold legends and myths, the beginnings of our greatest tricks, when with Anansi and Br'er, we trust in the fire, our spirit, our soul, our instant desire to fly ever higher and higher, for we are not the great beings; we are tricksters and thieves, weak but wise, learning through our failures each and every time we try to make water run from the rock, or seek for our lost socks, traveling through those demon portals, saving lost Fu-dogs. We trip and stumble, becoming lost in the fog, tumbling from the mountains like a limbless log, before becoming trapped in the black and mud-filled bog; there we wallow in the dirt like a hog, until, becoming again clean in the rain, sinning still and stained, we continue to train our brain, and strain our eyes in the twilight, seeking our next round to fight: We walk, run, creep and bite, burning raise our torch up through the night.

Now comes time for rhyme, inner wieldings of the mind. Spin and weave, fat made from thin, we are the spider's twin, weaving our net from what we stored within, the origin and last friend of sin: Hope. On all else we choke, eventually spending all our coin, becoming broke, and this is when we dive again into our books, or make one, burning ink beneath the sun, Hathor's eye destroying us one by one, firing every bullet from out of our gun, until eventually we remain powered by none. Isn't that fun, to run out, to not know where to stand, or how to shout? We are shut, becoming not kittens but mutts: Political appointees, commentaries, grandees, forgetting the funny pages where once we did feed, sandwich catching tigers who then be freed, friends to those who both need and greed, although occasionally like hunters we play dead and flee.

And, after we regress to life, where do we race forth in our rising disgrace? Why to the book and the sea, the marches of I and me, stories and legends of history, ancient mysteries made modern, as like a caterpillar in her shell we harden, preparing for the day we fly in the garden filled with beautiful rays where the bright shining sun always stays, heart matching hope through brilliant days. As long as we continue to work we will not be betrayed. We are always becoming, 'being' arrayed across the fields of Pelennor while ghosts land on the shore, not the story exactly, but close enough for a sense of the tale, memory and moment wrapping around us like mail: Armored against that which us assails, the assurance that we are snails, made slow, with frail, easily crushed homes full of tomes with glass screens, with glare that in the sunlight gleams, blinding us and hiding our dreams. There's something magical about books which are more than they seem, as when the page turns and flutters like the wings of a bird: The smell of glue, the path that I came here through, a library filled with books for me and you. In those ancient canals I flew, from Narnia to Shannara, from Tortall to Mistral, the hills of Barad-dur, and the isles of thistle, this is my festival of misrule. Books to me are far more than an electronic tool, even if that makes me a spendthrift fool. These letters are my magic tools.

Day 42: June 9th, 2024

To Beauty,

    Purifying this, I shall try not to be distracted by what falls before my eye. Failing Earth, I reach for the sky: I was looking forward to the chance, but I think it has passed me by, and this summer I shall not say hi to the sun rising in the sky. That vision kept me going, it kept me throwing my paint against the wall, that I to the future should look and call with hope, as on my own regrets I attempt not to choke. My life and everything sometimes seems a joke, and I a jake: Some great grand mistake, the hollow of a dried-up lake abandoned in the woods by field and stream, lost rain, only the deer taking pains to visit, and not a single human being on the entire world to hug and kiss it upon the forehead, granting blessing and in such kind ways addressing the dark, loss of spark. It's not for years and months entire that I'll stay quiet anymore, as I journey in my ship far beyond the shore, chasing stars and lamps in the heavens, smiles and memories - ...I'll stay quiet you see, I won't talk or speak, I won't play a trick or reach, and only have courage too often honored in the breach. I am become once again a leech, but there is no blood anymore, it is summer and the wells are dry. What for now should I reach and cry? The dream I had passed me by, myself retrating again to shy. I am afraid you see, weary and messed up, in the woods I walk alone, and I bow under the weight of my bones, my failures and my tomes. Every day I set out, and every day I fail; I doubt. I can't do this, or I didn't do enough, I wasn't tough, and my art was rough, not smooth. I do not know how to soothe my skin and my mind, or bend now to my nose to the grind, and like stone stand strong against the storm and the wind, wings of gravity and the nuclear force within. I have half a life, being made of strife, and cutting at myself with a dull, gray, rusty knife.

    I have a flute I play, or at least that's what I say, that I should practice today - but I don't. Again I give up. I am dust, failure, never enough. I don't start, I simply stare, and then I turn and hide the view from me with my hair, pretending I don't care, as if by writing these free rhymes with which I fill my time, I'm acclimating to the new climate. No sun, no rain, only evening wind beating down brains, the walls are stained. - This maze of mystery and misery wherein on every turn I fail my tests of history, yesterday's examinations, and last week's intentions. Six months ago, or a year, or ten years, I said I would be so much more, having traveled through a thousand magical doors and risen so high off the floor, be like a flower gorgeous and bright, well liked and well read, with a clear, concise, voice in my head, and all the energy in the world to get myself out of bed. But of course, instead I achieved a tithe of a tithe of a tenth, badly investing everything which to me was lent: Time, space, learning, love, chances, and the white glove. Home alone, I lost the doves, and in frozen halls answered not a call. Today, I may as well have lost it all, for the world could burn up and I would hurt, but I would fall.

Failing, tiring, Atlas bends and glass shatters, window panes are now in tatters, and inside walls opened to the wild. Food, water, and shelter is what we need to survive - but I ask, what require we to thrive? Some rush unbidden into the hive, become one with the people around outside, the ones they match, the masks in which they feel they could hide. Others are prisoners of pride, never content to be second pillar standing to the side, and unable to bend beneath the wisdom tide. And there are a few, like me, who simply on their turn played bide, returning what was granted unto them three times, although possibly none but them ever heard the chimes of bells ringing in the dells, and of horns blowing on shire-side, telling that strangers ride near: Either fight or be kind, depending on what sort of sign they give, if they be foe or friend, loyal or treacherous at the end. See and greet them, shake their hand, meet them; shall we let them in, feed them kindly, put them to bend, pillow them lend? Or shall perhaps we drive them off with fire and spear, armored, give into our fear? Are they enemies, or someone who might be dear? The only way to know is to let them near, and perhaps ply them with fruit juice or beer. Whatever the case, made of glass or mace, let us not treat them with disgrace, and boldly speak with them to their face, so that we may comprehend you openly and honestly.

Now this is correct and strong if we stand upon the threshold of our home, but perhaps we might be more careful when into the wild we roam, after staying up all night hearing ghostly groans. In the morning we wilt and moan, after trying to sleep on cold ground and hard stones. We give up our stories, lose the sense of measure and toil, slowly undo cohesion in the boil. Unglued, we are spoiled, unequal to our past, slowly climbing the hill at a gasp, just barely with our fingertips attempting to grasp this chance, and to dance. Lost, of course, with no direction and some chores, swinging and swaying upon the floor. Dirty, tired, confused, what have we to lose? Only the memory that we did choose, and the soft uplifting shoes, wings of Mercury and flames of the muse.

Having failed to attain, and unable to break the chain, we have no recourse to savior or fame. Alone, I accept the blame, it is my fault that I speak a name, and of my triumphs am ashamed; not of what I did, but of what I didn't; not of how I fought, but of what it cost; not that I was lost, but that I wasn't very good at being my own boss. I'm late, you see, for all the work, and I've slept too long among the flowers, until even the heavens upon me did glower. I have no heavenly song or earthly power, and yet am not lowered into the sand. Uplifting my hand, I ask a question and dare demand, we are thirty-two months upon the sea - when shall we land?

Day 43: June 10th, 2024

To Beauty,

    From the river to the sea, someone I know said that today, but I'm not sure what it means. One person I read told me that it's a call for the dead, a lopping off of heads, a reversing of history. Others hold simply the view that it means return to normalcy, one state without practiced hate. Have you encountered that, seen that, a slogan, some selection of words in English or Spanish, with such power that the intentions behind it vanish? For suddenly those letters take on three faces, one of disgrace, a second of moral race, and a third of ambivalence - Is this simply calling for a change, or for violence? I don't know, maybe it depends on who says what and when, how they think and view of it within, whether they think of it as fire or wind, destruction or surcease of sin. I wonder, what do the students here mean? But maybe it doesn't matter, words take on a life of their own, failing to explain or show. I must admit, I tend to take my responses to these sorts of things slow, because I am so confused between up high and down below; mankind, after all, has two shoulders, possessing an entire life of pushing boulders which are so big we can't see around them, and there is no response from the other side no matter how loudly we call. Auntie Em does not reply, we can't go home, there is no magic spirit into us blown, no breath of life, no release from strife. Up goes the balloon, and we hold the knife, deciding when to descend to ground by cutting the sandbags in a circle round the basket, and the timing of when to do so is a practiced tactic: For the higher we go, the clearer the sky. The longer we wait, the less obstructing the cry.

    For mankind, you and me, are emotional creatures indeed, who upon all kinds of logic feed. Now, being not a perfect creature, being filled with horror, fear, pride and greed, I will so quickly determine what I need to do. I don't know if I can write words to change the world right now, I can barely change myself, and I'm still climbing upwards on the shelves, escaping the store where my legends were bought and sold, myself imbibing from every story I was ever told, and trying to make my soul grow old. In that attempt my heart grew cold, a skin of ice which for a day sufficed to silence my ears to other people's worries about pains and fear, flowing blood and tortured tears. It's so simple, so easy to condemn, and so hard to understand, but these actions both, I believe, are both half the hand, and a misuse of our mental capacities' command. Of course what I wanted to say, when I read the news today, was a pox on both your houses and all military powers, because I can see in books like Abed Salima and My Promised land, Biographies of Bibi and histories of colonial war, that to understand this completely I would have to pass through a thousand doors, or tread my feet upon ten thousand floors, because all I read of political history is an endless condemnation of lies, and it takes me half a dozen books, going back a hundred years, or thirty different online articles saying here are the hands, and there are the spears.

Some, the historians and the poets, have more nuanced views, where others are in the thick of it and say one side or the other you must choose, or else they will lose, and death will come to millions. Not thirty thousand - millions. Every Power involved is a villain it appears, and the peasants pay the price, even if they go to concerts or stay at home being nice, and just because they were in the wrong place at the wrong time, they burned. I know I don't know their suffering, I've never learned what it's like to lose a home, or not know what has happened to the son or daughter you've borne. I'm not confident to stand here and toot my own horn, saying I know right from wrong and good from bad, or that I really understand what's happening in that land. I feel of course, see the broken limbs and air-dropped bombs, hear songs in front of white houses, and others calling for the return of their spouses, and to my shame, it's all a little far away, and I have other troubles that fill up most of my days, as I with other demons of death and forgetfulness become upset, but even in the midst of that, I see and hear that it's not over yet.

I deal with stress in the ways I always have, by attending to the past, or leaving my concerns about this till last: At night, before I go to sleep, I read, and then I write, expressing all my concerns and fright. Tomorrow I may have a different way to fight, but right now I simply seek the light of comprehension, glowing rays of the sun, setting my feet before I run. Of course I'm not done merely because I read a book, or thought about truth and aught, moral manners in a bloody mist. I'm well aware I can only say this because I'm far away, and I don't suffer from not choosing yay nor nay today. Maybe if my family spoke about it, but I think we've all decided to stay quiet - two personal pieces of death and illness are all we're equipped to handle right now, even if one of them still has hope. We've all decided to give ourselves some rope; plenty of happy space, so we don't choke. Now, I know to certain others this is a cruel joke, that simply because I don't have to, I won't. But I keep count of every vision of that bout, it grinds into me like sand on clay, scratches and lines on my life when I hear others pray for theirs. I'm hypocritical and evil, aren't I? Doing nothing, but feeling like I care, ringing my hands but not covering my hair. Instead, I run off into the upper air, trying to gain a clear picture in the midst of despair. Morals? Not I. - I don't try, and only barely cry. I didn't sign. Of course, that doesn't matter: I'm too poor to donate a dime. It's too complicated, and I don't agree with everything that you've stated, because I'm not sure which part comes from having love, and which from being hated: I worry the truth has been gated, with only certain parts of it openly paraded. From my high, bloodless tower I may safely condemn both rocket-powered sides - and meanwhile silently watch the headless, armless, voiceless, unorganized peasants fail to hide, as they die, three at a time, or thousands by the tide. I see two ancient tribes, but I don't want to join any side, for like me none of them are angels, and I don't yet understand all the hidden angles.

Day 44: June 11th, 2024

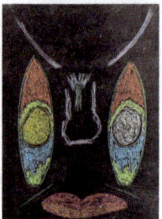

To Beauty,

    I see a sliver of the moon outside, high in the winter sky, like a cold and brilliant tide. As I wandered inside, I glanced upon the stars one more time, and vainly attempted to make a rhyme, but my rhythm fell apart and I wondered if I could take heart from this, the loss of treasure and of hopeful mist. As I felt the rain upon me fall and the wind kiss the trees, gently caressing and dripping with the breeze, I knew some terrible weakness in my knees, and a shoulder-pain as I was unable to say please. Gripping my heart with right hand, for a moment, merely a moment, I stopped and decided to stand, breathing deeply and hearing the sound of a breaking band; stroke of iron, snap and crack, like Whitebeard I have an aching back. As long as I move I don't notice what I lack, but occasionally in my hand I see a pact, some vision of the Horus-birds clack, with a beak so black and eyes so deep, that the dead noticing it can creep up from their sleep, and like zombies leap to feast on flesh, voodoo drawing them from the nest, with a thousand Zandalari loas each pretending to be the best, as if by following their words we would pass the test and make heavy the feather, place their finger upon the scale; but attempting this we fail, seeking and not finding any reply to our mail; we are ghosts in jail, and in front of life we quail, first quiet and the loud as we wail, recognizing the end of this tale. We know how this ends, we know what we are, not a happy thing, nobody who gold would bring.

    Although, we may offer our congratulations to those who may, or at least we would if our own sense of worthlessness we could stay. Who are we to say: I'm glad to see you achieved something today? Who are we to say: I think you're doubting monsters you slayed? Who are we to say: I'm glad you played the game and won? From our shallow graves we feel done, while your life has only just begun. Of course, this is illusion, all illusion, our fog of failures coming home to roost, although we're not even sure what we would have done if our had rocket boosted enough to achieve orbit, escape from gravity and strain. I feel pain, but it is not on purpose, it is not at price; it's because I'm not sure what to do with my life. I do not have a goal like you, I have no interest in anything really. I'm more like a ghoul, mindless and hungry for what I cannot describe, least of all civilization me, hate and fry, because of what I am, and everytime I lie, by omission, every day, I don't know why I try. - I know I've lost hope but it's this or cry, every day, all the time.

There are no isles for me to return: They are not forgotten or lost, but sunk. I was never assaulted, never attacked, and all the while my family had my back, but after fifteen years of traveling and trying, I still find myself over and over again, lying. In word or deed, or simply down, being silent or a clown, some clow card on a new mown sward, phrases I recall, but I don't know where I heard them at all. It's just when I sit down to write I hear a call, some upwelling from my spirit's hall, like a dog chasing after a ball while the cat looks on, disinterested, distrusting, pretending. Not speaking, but creeping silently from shadow to shadow, and shelf to shelf, mind filled with memory of an elf, or if not that, at least something else. A dream perhaps, or a nightmare which only glowing eyes could see in the darkness under the Yggdrasil tree, the gnawing end of days, long serpentine deathwing and mind scream. I run and hide, cower and die, I hear it even in my dreams, after I wake with aching head and bound feet, trying not to turn into a neet.

I greet the noon-day sun, I open my eyes, I gaze and see and try - even if I'm not sure anymore why. I know in my mind there will be a thousand chances again, but in my heart I'm tired, and I can hear Pluto plucking the lyre. He took it from Apollo you see, by way and trick of Mercury, and of Aurthur cutting silver on the tree. Sure light has won, but now that means it's all up now to mortal might, or prophets in the hills, or perhaps even wise men with immortal pills, who tell the truth but half right, and, descended from demons and man, are also half knight, with armored red skin and bright blue sword: Some three hundred and sixty degree mage-wrought ward, like a hawk-brother sworn, one who has read a thousand books, but always has more to learn.

I'm not sure if this is how I was born, or else the result of being burned; either way, where I've gotten now is the result of everything I've earned, and entangled. I am turned in four ways, searching for the perfect angle, so that I might detangle this maze of memories, the thunder, lightning, water and wind which, eight thousand times, and with eight thousand tines, over the devil sought to win. King of games and mystic mine, a field lock and assassin's climb, nightfall and Colbey call, chaos and law; I grow a demon's maw, and pretend I have a cat's claw, but I am no Jamethial, I am no thief, no Gen, no king no crow, merely a hopeful youth brought ever low. So to those wonderful others who never read what I wrote, I'm glad you have reason to gloat yourself, when in the future you find your own elf, or see in the sky a calf, Isis at last. Never forget the light you cast through the leaves of a tree, with the magic, future-forward breeze, as long as you learn and fulfill your needs, worthy of honey and bees: A flower in deed.

Day 45: June 12th, 2024

To Beauty,

    The only noteworthy thing I did today was make one piece of artwork, into which I poured half my heart, not to finish, but only to start, and this attempt tore me apart. It was the least, the little, the smallest thing I could bring to life, a piece of paper with glitter pens and a light, some angled stars and circles around which shadows bite, a bile of straight lines and angel's sight; explosion of my far-begotten hands impossible to fight, because I don't know what I'm making until I attempt to fake it: Who I am, what I can do, the tide of emotions that rolls me through. I struggle, you see, not to create, but simply to come up with ideas I don't hate, or which I have not done before. In attempt to do this I sometimes dive into strange lore, or spend half an hour curled up on the floor, a fool blinded by sight, who writes down his dreams in desperation and night, but remembers and recalls nothing in his fright. She, off in the distance, seems like a light, because she is not real, and she is not here, and she could not care, and I know not any other way to pay my fare, or among others attempt to dare.

    Look: Demons, devils, and dancers, those reindeer like Rudolph and Prancer, Arjuna the lancer - or maybe he's an archer with a blue string, bond not destined but made, with effort and will, or two years of attempting to drill through the rocky skin to emerald within. Egghead stolen, Rogue-found, Knuckles flies, and Sonic sounds. - I have no tails and I am falling too fast towards the ground, as like Sarah I throw a tantrum and pound my fists on the table, my head on the rock, two seconds now off the doomsday clock. Clacks fly and phone rings, the mail arrives but there's naught to see - it's all empty, entirely without merit, merely advertisements and junk, lying, saying that if I spent money someone would find me a hunk, and roll me off that seaman's bunk. Have you ever done that, been woken up by someone shouting, yourself startled, then leaping, falling, hitting metal with your face, nothing broken, but you're groaning with the disgrace, because those brown wool hammocks, itchy and scratchy along with the blanket, are driving you batty, making you a little bit catty, and showing you the importance of sleep. Six hours isn't enough my needs to meet, especially if I'm walking metal hallways and random annoyances have to greet, then write it all down in that book I keep. Gah, fourteen isn't a good age to be so short of sleep.

Of course, now I'm twice that and may rest until noon, or ignore the consequences and act like a loon, putting in some bear's mouth a balloon, birthday memories of gloom, because even over happy days, the fact that grandma's going crazy looms. I just want to grab a broom to sweep it all away, self ground to dust by play, as before the computer I sway, doing dailies and grinding concerns away: One more time up to Azaroth, half-demon to slay, trying to hide my green fire beneath my empty clay, so that I could calm myself long enough to paint the stars today, and to both sun and moon say: I pray you achieve all your praise, precious amalgam and reader of ancient lays, who in the valley of kings shall blaze.

Meanwhile, I, I am afraid, shall be lazy, and writing words every day which get a little more crazy, cast aside illusions of solidarity, paint my artwork madly, seeking clarity, as if, if I did, I would deserve some charity. Endlessly I delve into all variety, reading books of Fitz and Verity, or watching shows filled with Taylor's hilarity. Over and over I continue, never holding on, barely staying strong, and not standing up straight; like a fish I bite again at the bait, like Amaterasu hiding my face. At the same time I might claim to be lord of storms, tell my story in this way, and thus end cycles of night and day. Desperately, I escape: Look and tell myself to wait. Wait, not til you're perfect, but at least til you've passed another gate, written on the sand in sorry state. Late story, but good colation, managing step three of this situation, clarifying my hesitation.

I try and clean the blood, let it flow and flood, rainbow sign of mud. Not firm ground, not yet, but just enough to make a bed, and believe we will not soon be dead. Plant our feet in soil brown, and let spread our leafy crown, as we listen to solar sound, high-energy rays and neutrinos that spark as they hit the ground, causing in us a reaction that makes our heart pound. I am expanded, made wave from point, with heart and soul pushed out of joint. This is how I jumped and lept, this is how I saw and swept, serpent strike and apple bent, this is what the world has lent. Not words, but recompense, blind visions from a person on the fence. I wished to hold Rhongomyniad, mighty lance, and with that girl fight and dance, even though I had no chance.

Alas, staying in mountain, I sought not the fountain, so now I paint and it's...it's not great. Late-cometh, lazy-waked, I am lost on this lake, salt surround me, no thirst to slake, as I bake again my sugarless cake, fruit-full of a god's hate. I learn, again and again: Two times come to life too late: All my words might all well be fake, for I am no fae, only a coward who can't remember Luthien's Lay. I tried and tried, but only managed one thing today: I painted, and then I lost my way. Five cards, but only one line of play; I don't have cats - I just have clay. My fire is not strong enough the world to sway, at least not now, but maybe some other day I'll have cards of the Clow, and I'll find a spirit wandering round bright and unbowed, causing all sorts of trouble - Oh so proud, and maybe if I'm lucky, laughing at me out loud, far away, beautiful summer cloud.

Day 46: June 13th, 2024

To Beauty,

What would I be like if I lived alone? I mean really alone, with no-one to talk to on the phone, and no worries about the madness of an old crone. Would I begin to chew on my bones, curl up in a mad search for home? I'm writing these words because I imagine one day I shall place them in a tome, casting them across the wide world to roam, so that someday a dove might find a treasure trove. That is to say, I write because I imagine I am not alone, I speak to someone, the bones of poems, because after I eat myself up there is nothing left, I say again three times, I am alone. - Picture it, and then atone. Thus, down I go, below, below, folding before yet another blow, the silence and fear, the no point and no care, the two weeks I've forgotten to wash my hair. After all, despite the clarity of my brain, slowly, ever so slowly, I go insane; but not useless. Simply following a different strain, accepting and completing the circles of all my innermost pain, draining myself of blood and pus, imagining a me, and not an us. I become less than what I was, but like a needle, like a snake, like those tiny, tiny bugs we all hate, like the story of light and dark giving bending great, I worm my way in between fate and debate, talking to myself of course too late, but never mind, now I earn my rate: One hour of creation for one hour of life, though I make no promises twill be a godly light, because in me angels and devils fight. Nephelium am I, mortal man doomed to die, and yet with a spirit which pillars earth to sky, and stands strong against the storm and firmament passing by, the truths that pretend to be lies.

The cold fact is that if I said everything I ever thought, me you would despise, because I know what I see in these eyes: Reflections upon the boy who would not try, the child who through wonderful worlds did fly, but now attempts to cry, not because he fought and died, but because he recognized the worst, and retreated from his curse. And the most terrible part is that he also knows this is all his fault, with all his weak heart. He is truly blessed, with time and space to fill his nest with books and poetry, to spend three hours gardening, two hours painting, one hour pacing, and a silent year racing towards himself, trying to open his box and leave his shelf. However, this is all theoretical words on a page, acting on a stage, with some dumb attempt to rage against the dying of the night, to seek his dawn in dark of light, to inflict upon his own body terrors and blight, fix an overbite and strain his arms, straighten his back and cut the splinters out with harm, til his nerves and pinions scream in alarm.

I'm no school-marm, just a dumb student teacher who never learned her lessons, a falcon without hood or jesses. Wild and free to hunt or to flee, not spectrum but field, Ulysses will not yield, nor Achilles either, from the shores of Skyros without miracles of wisdom to draw forth poison from the soul by rending the flesh, blood spilling forth in a flash. Now, slowly dripping, can you hear the splash? Red on clear: Clarity by walking through the valleys of fear, drawing ever nearer to the bottom, sight of water's summer and autumn. Do you remember that song, Gotta catch em' all? It was in those waters that we learned how to swim, if not quite how to win. For every lesson we learned then we grew thin and lean, our skin becoming red and green, blue our eyes, and fingertips silvered, skill we had but not wit, as crystalizing we threw fits. Could not the world be simple and sear? Could not we simply love and be dear? Instead the whole world is swallowed up in some apple's fear, as if by saying the world was one way we could make it so; speaking the words without comprehending the meaning, where it came from, how it ends, or where it turns and bends, like twisting ropes off a cliff kicking kicking, back and forth, swaying swaying, leaping, daring, hoping the iron is tight and the strings were made right; one hand on the break, the other in the knife, to take ours, or if we're unlucky, someone else's life, turning what should have been happy into sad, endless, miserable strife, some dull bleating blade and not the high fife, music of the spheres and of sight, sun's left eye uncovered and burning bright.

Every day is another chance for learning, although the books and tales, the legends and myths, are wrapped up like soup, distilled like mist, some great grand mix of boiling trouble, effervescent bubble, rocket double, thunder lighting and flame, water and name, Ane-san, am I to blame? For it was this one here who decided not to play, it was this one here who stayed home all day, it was this one here who never attempted to fire this clay. Let spirit rise and slay, body and soul, bare heart and hair cut under a bowl, clown face and amber fool, attempt in blindness make use of tool, this is cruel - but honestly, I would rather be burnt than old, though it renders us such long time cold once our skin has gone, as flames march on, and we hear ton-ton-ton, some seven-league step, some don't give up yet, some Cinderella's bet on kindness and a tree. We are free.

Free to fail, free to quail, wail, trail, travail, fail. - Again and again we sail on this ocean, from mountain-home we face the gnomes way down deep in Underdark, seeking for kindness's spark, because we once read a book of art. Every day we do our part, we don't give up our heart, we are bees, born amber and spark, this is our glowing dart sent off into the dark. Up to the sky we ask why, why, why, attempt to smile not cry and with the fairies fly, even if we must use wires and rhymes, red-hot wings and lives. Our bones are broken, our songs be spoken, but still the crowd has not awoken. - Oh, wish we only for one single token, some reply from earth and sky, mother, father, sister, brother, lover, why am I alive? What does it take for me to thrive? I've worked alone for so long, and I'm still dying inside. That's why I'm speaking - I'm trying to do more than survive.

Day 47: June 14th, 2024

To Beauty,

    How do I write changing words, that matter even if they are not heard? I know I can't make ones of gold, and somehow they are not fire but cold, every time I read my rhymes old. What I attempt here is not bold and bright, simply bronze at night, a mixture of the worst parts with which I fight: Greed or despair, loss of vision or care, I run my hands through my hair, wringing out in sweat the thought that I could dare to write and draw. Declaim, be a fraud, simply some frog stuck in a well who wishes he could be a cat wearing a bell. Fierce, fire, freedom, fell, I am blessed but I feel as if I am in hell. Have you ever tried to write but don't know why, or scribbled in the sand while madness behind you cries? The kitten tries and tries, but lies and lies.

    I don't know if love is a reason for living, but at least it's a reason to attempt to live: It's terrible I know, but better than below, or in the house bellowing, trying not to lose my cool, as I write words that sometimes seem cruel, or reply to nonsense questions as if I'm a fool, and this time it'll matter, this time they'll be remembered, this time I won't be shattered like Alice and the Mad Hatter, trying to calm down but becoming madder and madder, because I've said this again, and again, and again, and again, and again, and again - I....I'm beating my head against the wall, drawing splinters from my thumb, trying, trying so hard to not just be numb, and rather than being dumb try nimble, like Thumbelina growing wings, flying, singing, dreaming. - But while she is a flower, I am a weed, a coward both in heart and deed, for it hurts to create, to attempt to fake a smile or a mask, or even set myself first step upon a task. Raise my sail up the mast, catch the wind that comes from heart of fear, a spark that makes certain things indelibly clear, like how I run from cheer because it brings my real self to surface near, and then I try to cut my throat upon the bier, so that I may play dead and drown my actions and my words, for I speak in tongues ...{}{}{}{.... and know not what I say, or if it shall have any worth or meaning at all either tomorrow or today. I don't know, I'm so afraid, but I need some of these burdens down to lay, for the simple fact of the matter is, I am here to stay, and there's so much I can't bear to hide from or betray, not forever at least, even if it all turns to ash, because I simply don't have the cash to purchase passage anymore, as I watch Charon push off from the shore, talking to all the ghosts passing by and learning their lore, before curling up in a ball to spend the night on the floor. My body may be in bed, but my head is going round in circles red, squabbling with this endless sense of dread:

    That I'm not good enough, that I can't do this, that there is no point, that it'll hurt more than it'll heal, that the opportunity cost is too much. - Surely there's something else I should be doing, charity or work with reward or morality instead of this endless duality, where out of three cards I always pick the wrong one, and then I have to wait, cause I'm done. What is left of me? None - Neither cause nor effect, sufficient or not. I am lost and blind with white hair and head of straw, unable to speak to the sun or talk to a squaw. Even the squirrels run before me, and while others have their totems, bear, beaver, elk, I only have myself. Not because no-one will help, but because I am silent and afraid in this world I have made, where every time I create I also rage, or at least have the potential to be willingly enslaved by an idea or a dream, a vision or a scream. Out I walk on that park bench beam, limb of tree, not knowing if the trunk will support the deed. We do not do this out of a sense of greed, but simply because we felt a need to reach and link our hand to fate. Dare in one sense, for one minute, to be great, and wrestle, triumph, run through our hate, or with crystal unlock the magic gate of bones and dragons. Which, at any rate, wouldn't offer haven, but merely a place you could stay for a couple days, read a book, quiet your mind, center, focus, breath in, breath out, stand when you can, and carry what you will, for every day you live, that mere existence is your turn at the mill. Like Mothra we die but are not still, turning wild eggs into memory and will, fly in the sky and falling, dying, lying, hiding, because if you can secret that one piece of yourself away, then part of you may always survive the end of days, or mighty lizard's nuclear rays: The back of your brain that danger away from stays, never accepting the chance of play. Calvinball is what you did today when we attempted to pray. Give me, grant me, show me how I say, to be blind, to be kind, with snowball in hand hit a head, and let it be mine, as snowgoons and monsters run around outside. I don't use numbers like eleventy-three, but I imagine my pride, gem at the heart of a lie, symmetrical, turning, Turing, I see the sky, even if their what is not my why.

    Parts of me fall out on the floor, and my tears, my water, pushes on the door. Now we swell, the cell is burst, lipids fall and we are cursed. This, however, is not the worst, because in hurting ourselves we are free. We cut to draw forth the sliver and the shadow, then shatter ourselves with a sight of smile, because we will change, if only for a while, writing ourselves, purging our bile. We are like a Totodile, half our brain asleep and half our eye, it's dangerous here, but sleeping in the wild we try. We are bear-men, goblin-slayer, foe-hammer, radio-jammer, how do you change? Beat at the walls until they go away. Break, break the tide, swing broken sword wide, we couldn't change the world, but we tried, we tried, and broken, beaten, tortured, we would not die. How do you change things? You write and cry, you shake the very pillars of the sky. Here is the knife, the ink is red, and now it is time to go to bed, but I will wake up tomorrow and face again that dread, giant-slaying, footfalls making, standing, swinging, swaying, chains are breaking, and we drink life to the lees, for this is our curse, we are free to travel from mountains to the sea. How do I change? I become more me, and if no-one has ever heard, I am still burned.

Day 48: June 15th, 2024

To Beauty,

    I read story books so that I may become someone else for a while, Aurthur, or Kelandry, a devil or a fool, suddenly both young and old. I have saved kingdoms and destroyed bright young lives, I have given up and against fate strived, I have known both love, and love's lies, I have given up, and I have tried over and over again to despise all I read and all I hear: What in the tales is far from me and near, all I do not care about, and all that is to me most dear. In these histories I learned a little of fear because I caught glimpses of the shadow at the heart of all things, where Powers fight against Lonesome nights, and dull gray blade gains a silver edge, as lemmings in their thousands leap gleefully off the edge, men and women with happy midnights and wonderful weekends. I do not want a good weekend: I want a good life; but I do not know how to wield my knife in order to gain that, the only tool I have, skill of vision, wit of wisdom, madness to escape a prison. I wait out my life untouched, unbothered by strife, because I can escape if I want into books and tales, swords and dragons; but love and despair, braided hair, they drag me back, they make me care. I am no youngling, I am no Jedi, a padawan without a master, the supplicant without a temple, the priest without god, and a poet - a poet who has no poems, or perhaps no home, something wrong with me, just dried blood and old bones. I pick up the phone, I turn the camera around, and I try to imagine myself ten years from now, but what I draw is a blank. I can't picture it in my head.

    I may imbue the scrying glass with visions of all the past, the wind that sweeps into the mast, of Anthropocene or Babylonian math, Egyptian worship and the cast of buried cities burnt by ash, or the clash between three kingdoms. I have seen Kenshin buried in the mountains, and heard tell of staff striking stone to make a stream of Brahman's dream, and sacrifices screaming upon the stone steps. The waste of Alexander, Persian promises to the conquered, Viking raids and the way of the Dreamtime, long before a northern island held tin mines. I know how Shaka lost his lands, and the steadiness of William's hands, of communist bans, and the rhetoric of those hypocritical in command. Shall I recount the songs of protestors, or tanks in the square? I too have walked on stepping stones across the river of time, and known Plato's visions or Wordsworth's rhymes, but in all that adventure I have never known the sound of chiming bells on earth of a heaven's birth; only the screaming descent of hell, and the swell of purgatory. Bibles, Koran's, Guru Singhs, what are these, they do not bring life to me, or freedom from the law of five rings. I do not know, I do not know, I am still bewildered, I am lost and thrown, because none of my wisdom is a guide to the unknown.

What was, was, what is, is, and what shall be, I know not thee, for even writing of chances, I need to flee, crawling along with broken knees, bent back, and shattered limbs. I can't stand, I can't carry, and even drawing my rough art is only a way to tarry, to look again and again into the wet pond while trying to shatter these bonds of all I was and all I thought: All the ways in which civilization has wrought silver from the stones, and fertilizer from bones, wild deaths transforming to green strands, as when in Japan they redistributed the land, giving preference to those who turned it in their hand. Is this not fate's command, work hard enough, long enough, and you shall have reward, even at the cost of fire and sword. I may pay, you may pay, they may pay, but somehow, some way, at the end of the day, good things come to those who try, all those who survived falling from the sky when the sun set and oil burned in the west, like a phoenix leaving her nest in the mountains. For you see, the world is round, west is east and east is west if you walk far enough, or sail though the way be tough. We might in Russia speak roughly or in the south never say no, freezing in Andean snow, or sweating in Congolese jungles, as we leap to the moon and look back, seeing only jumbles, feeling the endless series of fumbles: Failure to pass down pride-worthy knowledge or teach our children to be humble, the way in which papyrus or stone mumble, how paper and electron tumble, losing cohesion as the water rumbles again and again. - The sea on which we depend, red brine, pink brain, yellow liver, blackened stains of slavery or tribalism, as if brown was not a color, or Maniac's pale eyes were as blind as we are from ourselves. - So often, and so easily, sundered, heart surrendering to logic, logic giving up before laws, laws being passed for reasons, reasons that to hopes are treason, and treasons to, well, what do we betray? Who shall we slay when we read books today?

For surely there are enemies to kill and friends to save, the powerless learning to be brave. As children we fought against metal machines or Agrona's schemes, becoming like dragons in our dreams: Flying high, flame and fierce, lost lord by ship transformed, paragon of one to two, true shape breaking mind til we threw the heart a line: A quote built from world so fine, these last faint echoes of a dead god's shrine, a story that was only real in that reading time; but by descending to earth one day made brilliant wine, an ambrosic liqueur that shined, and every time we drank from it we lost our mind. Slowly the madness builds up inside: Surely this world was never made for our kind, for such a cruel place as this no good god would design. Why do I read? Because the truth I wish to find, hidden behind all of mankind's lies, their world-fields with holes in them, paradoxes forbidden and meaning treated like muck in the midden. We dare all, we dream all, because we may pass all, fate and boundary, law and rule, for we know that even the Emperor of Heaven can also be a fool. If his mind, even his, is a tool sometimes misused, then what is this cold flame inside us? - The indelible sense that there has to be trust in something, in some way, for clay to hold the flame.

Why do I read? For the same reason I travel or write, because I wish to find my name, and the purpose or cause of this mad game. I follow the limits or the rules of man and god with shame, because I know all my choices are really mine to blame. I do not control the world, nor do I invent this language, but mine is the occasion, this my journey towards my destination. Why do I read? To overcome the limits of my imagination, embracing powers of destruction and creation, challenging even the rights of nations. For what is power worth, if it can't save one soul, or what point the church if they make flame cold? I know of only one thing the dead might hold as gold: That they had cause and purpose to be born and turn old, transforming the babe spirit into someone more bold and daring, demanding of ourselves not to simply do as we are told. We learn and read so that we may smile and sing, even in the midst of fifth void ring. Look - We will break this dream, in this life or the next, if not us then some descended self, if not this person on this shelf then that one over there, Human, Dragerean, or Elf, for we will be free, come hell or heaven, right or wrong. We are living and this is our book, and our song. We don't give up, no matter how blinded or how long, how weak or how strong. What I do is read what others wrote, and what I do is write it all down in one stroke, because if I don't then on my hope I would choke, spending my spirit's gold, becoming broke. Why do I read? So that I may escape cruel fate's yoke, look at all the terrible world, and still laugh at it as a joke, by hiding my face beneath my cloak. No mask, but simply how I attempt my task: Freedom, freedom I will have at last, free from all the weight of the shadows I cast, revealing myself, seeing myself ten years from now, in a blast, some sudden midnight-sunlight flash. I may still have no name, but I will not hide forever in shame, pretending to be someone else, always hiding half my heart on a shelf. I still read, but only for a time, so that I may write these lines of August rhyme. Now foolishly, now badly, but now mine, and a fine find.

Day 49: June 16th, 2024

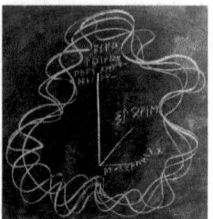

To Beauty,

I cannot ask for it, or demand it. I may not seek it. I barely dare to dream of it, and if I write of it, it is to deny it. But my mind, my heart, my soul; I don't know how much longer I can make them bold, no matter how strong my rhymes, or how old my tools, and I know that in refusing to name names, I act the fool. Yet what is this to beloved I ask, white prophet set me a task, some trial I might pass and obtain fate's decree, the right to be free and happy, like a zippo lighter sparkling and sizzling at flick of thumb, cold metal against flint made not numb. - The spilled oil brought alight, the soaked rags made to fight. I seek the light three times, and four times round, invisible, impossible, unuttered sound, names of stars and might of crown, ancient legends which this land surround: Hawks eyes, bear's paw, crow's caw, power of words and music, drum of blood, memories of Mediterranean flood. Seeps the Nile alluvial, reborn each year, and know the wild Congo, wild furry half-men without fear, or seven dogs searching for a king. - Seven-times gold ring, or invisible gigantic thing, power corrupting, draining, stretching, slaying; I do not dare to ask, for I know in greed how I might pass, seven times under shadow, til I reach out to grasp silver thinking it gold, watching it tarnish as I grow old, and lose any strength to polish heirloom to bright finish when I am sick and the world spins. When I am lame, ever late to the train, when I am stained by muck-arrow, or brought low by morgul-spell, when I lose any right to aim like Tell, or like those days when like the walls of the heir of Byzantium, I fell before cannon-wail, end of a long, sad, down-trending tale. Or maybe like the Turks I rise up before the walls of Constantinople to assail the last bastion of Roman learning in the east, hungry dragon upon one final jewel to feast, until my mighty empire has become in all the land the least, food before mighty northern beast.

    Like you I try not to be cold. I want warm waters, though I'm not sure why, when I have no ships nor means to fly, greedy because I'm scared of in and out, though I'm not sure how this is going to break the spell that keeps me bound. Writing books that do resound, but that I wish in the heart could not be found, for rather than my scorpion's sting, I love my cat's meow, even though that is long past buried. - No more comfort to me now, as I hitch myself to an old, rusty plow. - Shall I for work be shod, barefoot boy now iron-bound toy, boiled until he now longer bubbles, burnt until she is no trouble, they be made one not double, but what care I? Beyond names and frames, beyond forms and shames, beyond legends and games, if I follow the rules, what is there for me to gain? I've spent so many years and still I feel the strain of not knowing what is wrong with my brain.

I dare not attempt the mountain heights, place my heart upon the spike, call out to victorious Nike, sacrifice my goats in job lots for betting gods, or hurl the arrow birthed from chaos! - I am tired of hiding, I am weary of lying, I am building my walls from the dying, I am seeking, I am trying, but I do not ask. I do not want. I do not grasp. I simply hold my own breast and clasp, bent over, nails digging in, as I fight against my own sense of terrible, horrible, unworthy sin. Something has burrowed, some terrible nightmare has burrowed beneath my skin, the earth rises up and I feel not eagle's wind, worm eats me rind from Rin. In that valley, down from the mountains I spin, sweet water Bukshah drink, but me, I drown beneath the rink, Icefyre, future buyer, I see what I am, and it is not a happy thing. Life is pain, and I don't know what worse it shall bring, as I feel death from traitor's sting. Betrayal of myself you see, hopes and dreams, a coward's ways to write not say, as far from the fire shall I ever stay.

My clay dissolves before the rain, I am unflamed: All surface colors from me drained, but each day I wake again and grab at the reins, not to direct but to hold myself to the horse. Wild mustang do your worst, or mare give me milk and care, let me bind one more stand into the braid of my hair. It reaches lower now, beyond end of days, beyond end of Clarres, as we play one more game and lose one more chair, chain acting as a dare; deep into mountain's heart I leap, gold, mithril, and magic I seek, silvered skill to drink, be made wolf or dragon, anything but man, anything but what I paint with my hands; I do not wish to beg, I attempt to stand, defying my body and memories command. An eye and teeth I see, blazing, blazing, I will be free.

I know not the darkness I fight, I cannot name it in noon's light or by sleeping at night, but only by dawn and dusk I might, when shadows seem strange and the smell of dew reaches it's longest range, just as Falena and Babylonia are strongest the day after conquering barbarians spill forth from the hills, before they lose their wrath in the mills. Their height is Hammurabi when they make laws, but before the lawyers have taken to the vision their saws, or corruption has sunk in its darkened claws. Greed isn't evil, but thinking we deserve what we ask for is dangerous, because it changes us. I don't want anything, I don't ask for anything, because I am becoming, not being. I am drowning, sinking, breathing in Tethy's kingdom beneath the sea, one stuck only with me, without light from lamp, fruit, or tree. Instead, in the loam is sunk a seed, not yet broken forth to show me what I need. I do not name it because I dare not claim it, and I will die before I chain it.

Wild thing here and there, would you care if I stood to be seen? Would you love me if I told you my dream? Would you still trust me as into the void I scream? Would you stand with me as we found the mean? I know not what I have, and I know not what I bring, but I know that when I see it, I attempt to sing. A song of staying, a song of betraying, Felagund fighting, lighting slaying. Zeus, I return your bolt, and I accept how I am a dolt, but I am also a child, I am a flame, ash insane, but fair play, because a truth I say, and if I hold tight to that, not even fate may stay. Now, before break of day we must away, as we attempt scales of the dead to sway, so that Anubis may not draw forth fire from clay, or crocodile destroys us in all ways. Our heart is still heavier than a feather for now - but it is lighter without its chains. Each journey begins with a single step, and every day we make one more, though sometimes it's flying in the sky, and other times crawling on the floor; but little by little we draw ever closer to the door, rising up from beneath the sea to the shore, dreaming of it, nameless, that we adore. Catra found it, but not Nevermore.

Day 50: June 17th, 2024

To Beauty,

    Sometimes I sit in the dark away from sound of silence or hope of spark, because I don't know how to start. I can't write rhymes with an unbalanced heart, and I can't allow myself to be insane when I have to be strong, and I've tried for so long, but it doesn't matter anymore, because Grandma can't even find her bedroom door, and five times in this last hour she's become lost, sitting in bed for maybe a minute or two until she gets up again and spins, walking round the kitchen or searching for the thing, and I am sensitive now, I've already opened myself within, so I can't pretend to myself to be calm anymore. - I've been trying to inscribe these words for two hours, and she was calm, and I was calm, wrapped in blanket, wrapped in bed, warm and dark and embalmed, allowing myself to feel, and care, and dare, to dream, and I emerged, ready to be seen, ready to believe, and I've tried to be quiet, but I now feel like screaming. I can't help, I can't help, nothing matters, nothing changes, it all gets worse. I make my art but its just a curse, six months ago she could recognize it and me, but now a house is a fish, a bird is a tree, a flower is a thing, its just empty eyes with empty spaces inside, she doesn't even know what the word 'dinner' means anymore. I make her food, pour her juice, call her to the table, but she just sits there like some animal in a stable, fallen fences in her mind keeping her from being able, this whole life feeling just like a snapped cable on a broken bridge.

    There's no point in answering any of her questions anymore, because when I say my mother is not here, she traveled home, by car south, I say it again Grandma, look at my mouth, thirty times, literally thirty times in three days, the lady is not here at the moment. She went to the store for food and mail, to speak with my brothers, to play with my cousins, and in fact there is no-one here, not thirty people outside the door, or a man at the window, or an invisible car in the driveway. I do not have a child, I am not my Grandpa, the trees are not filled with women dancing, you have one cat, not three dogs, and you don't need to put him in a cage eight times a day. - I'm just going to let him out again as soon as I see him anyway, because he's not going to run, and cats need to be free to have fun. We can't torture this animal by locking him up just because the strange people on the porch don't say anything and never go away. Yes, I know they're strange, and No, I don't see them, and there is never anybody here. We live in the middle of the woods miles from the nearest town, and it's not safe for you to be wondering around scared of the strange folk who left their faces in the flowers, or the ones who moved your house, or who rearranged all the furniture in that odd room that looks like your bedroom but is not.

I know I'm just running out the clock. On some days Grandma barely even eats anymore, staring at the bowl for two minutes with spoon in her hand, before taking two bites and offering me the rest, but I don't want it, I don't want it, literally fifty times as day, I don't want it, I don't want anything. - Why won't you eat? Why won't you sleep? Why won't you do something with your day, any activity, anything, any.... - Please, read a book or watch a movie. Paint, draw, spin, pet the cat again, do anything but pass through the house like the wind, re-arranging pots and plates, washing clean dishes five more times without soap, or finding an old town notice from 1995 and questioning me as to when it arrived. How is it possible you are so continually surprised by what you find on the table, when you placed it there yourself not thirty seconds ago? It's not safe to leave anything on the shelf, or a plate alone, because Grandma will go after it like a dog after a bone, opening up any sealed containers, drooling and straining for clarity, curious about everything, always asking questions, but questions with no point to answering, not anymore, though I tried for months, but now we can't even keep score. No, I don't know what the 'thing' is, no there is nobody at the door, what I am doing is washing dishes, what I am doing is making food, what I am doing is reading a book, yes, this is book, here, take a look, yes Grandma, it's a book, you use it by looking at it, it has words in it, here, you can read, yes I know that sentence is strange, no, I didn't say orange, no I don't have a red car, today is Wednesday, not Sunday, no I didn't say I have a fish, but oh how I wish this all made sense. And no, I don't know why the pie is gone, somebody must have eaten it. No, I don't know who that would have been.

On and on it goes, and where it ends nobody knows. Maybe it starts with a pink pig-handled whisk, and results in cooking a plastic pot lid on the electronic stove because that's how you use a frisbee. It's not dangerous, but I have to watch out, and occasionally I want to shout, because I've answered the same question fifteen times today: No, Grandma, I do not want your food, I do not want a half-eaten sandwich, I do not want your used cup, and I do not want to agree with you just to make you go away. I'd like to explain what I'm doing, and how I'm doing, but it doesn't matter anymore, nothing matters. I make the same lunch every day, but you don't know what yogurt is, I cook every night in the kitchen, and every single night you try to stand in my way, three inches from my left arm, looking at everything, understanding nothing, attempting to grab with your bare hand the hot pan, the piece of mushroom that leapt from the stir-fry, or the fresh onion I just cut. - I can't turn my back for three seconds. You're dirty and you smell, because sometimes it takes two hours to get you to take a shower, and occasionally I'm just too tired. So I raise my voice a little and push you out of the kitchen, I'm so angry, just please stop trying to help me, please stop trying to help. Just let me do my job. Just let me bleed my own heart; I don't need any assistance cutting it open.

I can't start and stop like this. I have to continue my road because it hurts when I twist, opening up my head then turning it closed, wincing under ten thousand unmeant blows, because when rhyming time comes I follow my nose, and I can't be nice, I can't repeat every word thrice. I have no patience, I have no plan, and all I possess is my wildly shaking hand. I'm not losing my mind, I'm finding it really, but the only way I can be silly is also to be mad, and every time I go insane, I know, I feel, that I'm mad, because I do not have the patience to stand a barrage of: Do you want this, or what is that, or why are they here. I see the cat locked in the cage again, crying, and I let it free again, and grandma finds it again, and the cat never runs. - You can't do this to animals, lock them up to keep them safe from your own nightmares. When the sun is up, I can stand this. When the sun is up I can manage this; but when night comes and madness is still awake at two am, as I am attempting to unwind and find my rhymes, I lose the ability to remain calm this time. So, I go alone into the dark, outside with the foxes and the wolves, attempting to spark something that is worth it: This suffering, this life, this endless, pointless strife. If I ever end up with dementia like grandma, I'll just end it all, because if I'm going to fall, let it be as myself, as some person climbing the shelves, not free-falling through the abyss, for if there's one thing I've learned, it's that I don't want to end up like this!

Day 51: June 18th, 2024

To Beauty,

    Do you see the star shining in the heavens tonight? An adamant bright - stories fair and strange, of Tauriel and Eldamar. - Of dwarves, elves, hobbits and the like, great authors who, speaking to children, fight off the cold night, and give us hope that in some far land there is both wild and the bright: Adventures that we too might join, gold and friends to find, love, or least some sight of the Divine. We do not wish to go on adventure because there is something missing, but because our spirit, for an entire life, has been listening. Can you hear it now? The wind in the trees, the crackling of the fire, the beating heart of earth and bubbling brooks. It comes when we tuck ourselves into book nooks, or sudden laugh at an orange cats antics; when we have teary eyes at graduation because a precious time has undeniably passed, or as the moment arrives where we realize that one day we will breath our last, as we fall to our knees with scream and gasp. - Hand carries breast, back bends, eyes close, and then we feel a tingling upon our nose: Achoo, Achoo! A sneeze, such a small disruption, but maybe it's what we need to remind ourselves that we still breath. Our Ch'i flowers after winter, and the pain of a bite, or our small back holding a knife, is enough reason to stand up again. For, sure, life is pain, and there is so very little to gain, only a moment's ceasing of strain, head buried in moment we dare go insane: When we sing those songs and read those words, foundations stones of worth, which make us believe there is something more than what we see on this earth. In those short minutes we are born again, doubt our eyes, disbelieve our brain, call logic lies, and say statistics are knives, because on chances and dances is what we would bet our lives.

    We were not made to walk on the earth or sail the seas, we were not made to fly like birds or bees, and neither are we simple beasts nor ancient trees. Mankind we were made, but mankind we seek to lay down, running after stars and not earthly crowns. All the gold and silver we delve for is to spend, the iron to spin, the copper and zinc to ring in the bells, and diamonds are for pulling us out of hell. Power and knowledge for use and purpose, science as nursemaid to art, assisting us to start. Climb the ladder, drive the nail, collect solar power and hear the universe's wail, three degrees of existence. We are the fourth, final gasp of order before death, vain denial of our second law, the one we made or found. This awareness brings us to cold, hard ground, and suffers us to silence our sounds, or at least become one with the crowd, so that we no longer hear our own heart beating so loud. We dance and we sing, we fight and we flee, but then time comes again where we dream. We run out of breath, and we stop screaming. - Dazzled and dazed, we stare up lost at star's rays, a chill light and beautiful, but hard, guard against the end of days, and sweet promise of sun, that somewhere out there the world is not done. The serpent chases the barge, and Wrath moves his pawns, the blue man stares at his face in the mirror, and the horns of the hunt spare a child. Flame feeds not upon blood or prayers, but work and the air, in the same way that justice survives because of care. There are movements and powers in the world which seem to call upon us, rise within us, bringing us to our knees, and rolling us in feed. Like pigs, we will eat anything, find hope in the dark, find dreams from a spark, learn of legends from the songs of larks, and test in our tasks the questions that always answered all we asked. We are the challengers of future and past, birthing new life even after we breathe our last, or disappear in a blast.

We fear what we feel, and scatter from what we know; we die baked on the sands or frozen in snow; we lose our arms and eyes, beginning in our misery to despise all happy families. - All steadfast friends, all well-spoken lover's amends, diligently our soles defending, growing hard feet in our callused meeting with the world. - Allspark valiantly against the cold, growing at the same time ever-young, and ever-old. Space may be three, but it is so close to freezing, stopping, unbinding all the glue which holds it together, for both me and you, we are turned out of our home: Once more we walk in the forest alone. Need has not awoken, or an ancient mage spoken, but what is that before our seven tokens? Listen, listen: The stars are shining, the wind is crying, there is a rustling in the grass and moths' are fluttering by, as clouds clear the sky, and I hear the river beneath my feet flowing free. Last of all the signs is me.

To know who I am, I look at what I am doing. My mistakes, my glances, my fear to take chances. The way the harp opens up or the heart closes down, how I paint smiles on my face like a poor, sad, clown, or how I keep walking in circles around, trying so madly not to fall on the ground. One step at a time, one step a day, this is the only way I manage, writing words in rhyme or art in flame, spending both my sadness and rage, laughing only during those few moments I am shaking the cage, seeking to be something else, hammering my self. I know the stars are out there: I can see them, I can feel them, and I - I wish I was strong enough to speak to them.

Day 52: June 19th, 2024

To Beauty,

      I read something today that, paraphrased, said: If I succeed in waking up and leaving the house, then I will begin to live in paradise. When I understood that, I thought: If we succeed in getting up and leaving the house, then we will go to work. That ideal in my heart lurks, making me feel quite like a jerk, because I am demanding that which cannot work, that I should go back in time and choose a different perk; gaining different abilities or having a different life, instead of being what I am. When I write these thousand words every night, I suppose I'm trying to make up for my own adequacy, because of all I regret. I didn't say anything when I should have, and I was weak when I might have been strong. I have traveled for long years, and always steered myself, opening up boxes and leaping off shelves, dreaming of the wisdom of elves, and the flames of dragons. I read once an idea, a thought, which I have used unto rot: Treat a thousand years as if it was a minute, and a minute as if it was a thousand years - but following such a path has left me in spiritual debt and arrears. About the only power it grants me is the ability to recognize my fears, but not face them, for in the minutes I panic, playing for time, and in the years I wait, learning too much of hate, and not enough of love. The circles I do not complete, they run from me as doves do from foxes, and the keys to locks inside me are hidden: Words, ideas, and hopes forbidden. They come upon me as an western wind, dry and hot, the desert of dreams tying me up in knots. The empty quarters of my life scream, they say embrace me, it is so much better to imagine than to breath, and the bright light of barren, empty sand offers far better music than the leaves of trees, or the shores of the sea. From mountain home, from peak of stone, I hear the call and know it is safe to travel there alone, refusing to stare at my phone, or admitting I want to be known.

      When the sun beats down, when madness comes round, as you hear the rattlesnake's poisonous sound, survival is simple: Learn from the snake, run away and dig a hole in the ground, making warning for all the nice bugs to leave if they want to survive. Be hungry and dangerous, fang feasting on those small furry beings: Wild things "tame enough to come and touch the hand for love."[7] But handle them not with bare skin: Treat humanity with a glove, their art with disdain, their writings with envy, their justice with disdain. Cover the world using your brain, naming striving capitalism, and control communism, nativity socialism; name laws as lies, mercy as idiocy, religion as coping; name science bias, money evil, oil death; never take from your judgment a rest, hiding behind protests, companies, and politics, denying the thousand tricks, the thousand nights, the thousand folk behind every evil word and every good idea. Didn't we all learn in school, at young age, that if you raised your hand, you presaged three other folk in a room of thirty, who had the same thought and doubt, or at least near enough, that in your words they heard an echo of their own, that they might type into their phone and search in privacy, or ask their friends, or simply imagine it in their own heads. We are so quick to take counsel of our fears, hide our raging tears, and for years, shut up. Don't seek, don't climb, don't fight, don't tear the lace or speak in rhyme: Don't be a mistake, a stupid fool who's late. You are a snake, and they will hate you, kill you eat you, vilify you - exactly as we, too easily, do unto them.

Hide in your hole like a serpent, see everything as hot or cold, neither with colors or a spirit bold. Long before you shed your skin, grow sour and old, treating with masks as reality, drawing not upon the magic spell duality. Light and dark, stone and spark, this is how we search, by making art: Pour your paints, dip your brush, and from the first stroke it will be nothing much. All paintings are ugly at the beginning, and all amateurs hope they are secret geniuses, but action reveals all. The picture in your head has fallen to earth, and it is a disturbing birth. Every person has a different experience or opinion: It's good, it's bad, it makes me glad, or when I look at it I feel so sad, and if you'd bought it, you'd have felt had. The name on it was so grand, and it held such great promise, but ten years hence it is a burden on the purse, hanging in the hallway and acting as a curse: A reminder of when you thought you did your best, and it turned out to be your worst. We all have regrets, rhymes that don't match, rhythms out of sync, ideas that were bright, but they fell before the night, the dark times when all fire goes out. It's cold here, and no place for snakes to be crawling about.

So how do we survive then, not curl up and die? By remembering, by recalling, by imagining ourselves warm. We were the only ones who raised our hand, but our embarrassing questioning must have soothed three others. We were the one who questioned the goodness or evilness of a name, but perhaps that allowed another person to take off their mask, and evolve from the creed. We were the one who called ourselves a dragon, admitting to greed, but perhaps someone else heard that and felt freed. I admit, I am not warm by myself, I am not self-sufficient. I need fire and flame, wind and rain, thorn of the rose, blood and pain, some way to stain my colorless skin, some way to evolve my digimon's sin. I am filled with regrets, what I should have said or tried, who I ought to have been, or at least dared to pretend to be. But I cannot go back, I have no ability to recapture the past and bring forth savannah from sand. The world around me is glittering and dead, my thirsty self losing my head. Mind goes, body weakens, spirit weeps, and my soul, set free from hope, is now free to seek. No more every day shall I be meek, waiting to inherit the earth. I cut my tongue to spread my curse, I admit what is worst in me, as I drown beneath this dry salt sea. Look, I don't know what I'm saying, I don't know what I'm dreaming, I'm just...beginning, mixing up all the good and bad, letting out everything in me that is either sane, or sad...I want to go mad, and if I succeed... well... then we'll see. Might I find paradise, or at least me?

Day 53: June 20th, 2024

To Beauty,

    I am not a poet, for all that I have a beard like a goat, and read from people called Gibran or Hanson. My hair may be soft like silk, but is plundered by guilt, as I leap into the mountain, and drink from silver skill-fountain, carving me out into stone, leaving behind spirit for bone. I write, but I do not do so alone, for with me I have a hundred books, and ten thousand more through my phone. By videos and Tiktok, or little Instagram shots, I am shocked back to the land of ink and paper, or good queen Berry's merry capers. Jeepers creepers, I look, I see, beneath the mirror, beneath the mask, beyond the accident, beyond the task, to do more than survive, zephyr thought, zephyr meet, we dye ourselves with the red beets, roots pulled up by our seeking, pink water made with our breathing, nature matching bleeding. - Moment by moment we pass from this life, losing our minds in small ways and small times, body failing as heart stops beating; we dive into our books, we are needy, and oh so terribly greedy. I want to thrive, I want to fly, and I do not fear falling, but am terrified of losing all that I am, mentality, morality, duality. Light and dark, thunder and spark, there are so many horrible ways to die, as Samarkand or Babylon before the Mongols, mighty towers reduced to ash, stone falling in a clash, civilization ruined by a slash. So many books are buried, so many stories are lost, we built Alexandria up at cost, then burned it because we became cross. - The desperation of mankind when life doesn't feel fine, of trying to live along another line, some worldstrand where our actions matter and change things. Set slaves free, or drive tyrants to their knees, we play tricks and gallant knights please, as we struggle to draw the ship off from a lee shore, like door of shadows, red bronze, sky-fire grabbing after sizzling-hot pizza with tongs, clenching our fists, so careful and strange, left and right both together arranged, and seven stars arrayed, an adamant firmament to last through end of night in order that days may stay: Brilliant despair lighting our way.

    This is how we play with words you see, set upon our ankle the wings of birds, and with poison heal our wounds. Matchless speed, bright red flame, Mercury is his name, and playing the messenger is his game, always pretending he is not to blame. Apollo strums his lyre, Athena fights fire with fire, Zeus is an adulterous fool, Hera should have known better, Posiden gave a raw deal, and Pluto alone never kneeled. Oceanus and Chronos, Themis and Tethys, some are high, some are low, but all of them have flown, barbarism and civilization both becoming unknown. As I read and write of them I groan, regretting what of them I have been shown, hair shorn from me like Sampson, strength leaving my bones. Once more I sit in the temple of spirits among my enemies, alone. No-one calls me on the phone, and if I have learned anything from this last year, it is that if I ever have dementia, please just kill me. I live and die, I write to create, but I am not a poet, being filled with hate, because I am so tired of pressing against the gate, and standing up straight. What matters, I ask. What I do, who I am, not how I command or experience, the mere fact that I breath or think, no, no, it all lies in how I jump over the brink, and skate on that thin layer of ice in the rink, take from the lake of dreams a drink, and become more human on the morrow than I ever was in my deepest sorrow.

Tonight I met madness going round, fury without sound, worry without point, pieces of paper that are not important, junk mail from three decades ago placed on the table and treated as if it was the most valiant fable. This is a fairy tale where things went wrong, like a wicked stepmother or a witch in the forest, kind and proper in heart and intention, but when the time came for action or invention, powers failed and the bread crumbs were all eaten up. The bed is not an airplane, the suitcase is not a dog, and how I wish to the heavens we could sleep like a log, or at least for a few hours more in the night, instead of nodding off in the midst of daylight. I can barely help anymore, I can't even show her the bedroom door, because this isn't her house - but it is. It is. It's the one Grandpa built, it's the one we found ourself in, even though it looks like an evil twin, as Grandma shakes her smiling head, doubting what I was saying as if we were dead. Ghosts come to Odysseus's flame, but ones without any names.

I am not a poet, I am not a hero, I'm simply a survivor, but it hurts. I am so tired, and while sometimes I may struggle through the mire, see a smile and write or paint, other times it's an hour past midnight, and all I do is complain. All I may bring myself to write down is the strain, because I write down poetry only when I am very glad, or in terrible desperate pain, and I would help everyone I care about if I could: The cats and the dogs, the beautiful and the far, the fair and bright who bring darkness and light. I sacrifice my words to others in order to bring forth might, because that is the only way I ever learned how to successfully fight, because I cannot shift the world or its surroundings. I cannot reach past the bounding fence, I never learned how to pay rent, not with my heart, not with my life. - It's either buy, or forge a new knife, some sword black or white beaten on the anvil, and folded by the hammer. Only in imagination do I dare lose my ugliness and stammer.

...it's quiet now, cause I walked outside: I hear the wind murmur, the creek burble, the foxes yip, the bandit's tricks, and the slow snuffling of the striped skunk living under the house. It's cold here, but I had to escape, because being inside the house is not going great. I'm losing my mind and the ability to calmly relate, or answer the same question thirty times. When the stress threatens to explode, I escape out here to my rhymes, finding in each minute not a penny, but in every hour a dime, slowly becoming less than slime, and changing every single night my lines. I'm trying. I'm trying. I'm not kind, but I'm trying not to be so mad at the dying, who does not burn and rage, but, living, nonetheless is slayed. No-one is here anymore, no poetry, no meaning, no changing - just this screaming. Or maybe I should label it weeping. Either way, it's keeping me up at night, which is why I close my eyes sometimes and imagine a light, not hopes, but memories and sights, which, once upon a time, were brilliant and bright, filling me with invigorating fright.

Day 54: June 21st, 2024

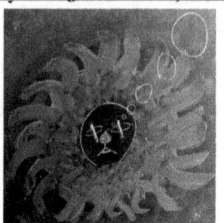

To Beauty,

    Have you ever heard a cat snoring? It sounds like a bubble, a bumbling meow, some tiny, gentle, buzzy-bee sound: Like the cloud that wraps us round when we, lost on the sea, remember solid ground. I was going to write of screaming tonight, but then I saw a message, some glimpse of light, so that for half an hour I felt silence, blessed and bright. This will not last long, and I know that when I wake, life will again be a mistake. I and my creations play the Jake, some clown-blade, four-star slayed, who feels as if something about him has betrayed his potential, as if she had tried with the world to be too gentle, a peasant made gentile: Someone using words he doesn't really understand, finding again and again that they don't fit in his plan, and that she has no understanding of where she's landed. I am like a statue with two fronts and no back, with one heart that feels that lack and wants to give up, say to the world, please cut us some slack, loosen the rope, don't be a jerk, and no longer on me work, turning me into something I am not, or telling me how I ought to be. I reject all of thee; although you, of course, are also free to reject all, and everything, of me, as long as you do not attempt to uproot the seed, or take from pig his slop and feed, garbage made food because of greed. This world is not kind, I know that inside, but fear will not stop me from facing the tide, especially because I know it's not safe to hide: Cards pass and water rages, seven stars of mermaid pages, a story of being fileted upon the table because we were able, like Cable knew what was to come if we should fail our fight, or wrote at least one right word at night. We are ground up by the earth, and dashed by the surf, shot after with nerf guns from which we cowered and flinched, fearing the worst, and at our relief in survival, letting loose curses; pretending to be angry because we were scared, or hiding our true thoughts beneath fierce glare - or, perhaps worst of all, by pretending that we don't care, and never at any point want to stare, and we don't write to you at night, and we don't rely on you to fight, and freedom for us is flight up to the sky, as we live like deer and die like wolves. - Viking walking upon the coals, it is only with our belief that we are more than fools, dreaming dwarves making tools.

    But for what end? To repair which sin? Swiftly now, look within, where cat and dog attempt to swim, howling towards man and the moon among the wind: Now climbing cat has his day, saying this is not the way.

- Don't give up, flight and play, because faith is not enough, we have to work our days. Look, ancient men thought and prayed for gods to save them, or else that their burdens be laid aside, soldiers carried by lightning inside, last spark of seven sons, last memory of book we had done, with one week more to wait, words misspelled only for our sake. Now, some fool once said let them eat cake, and to in our response to that, our heavy wrath, we found love and hate, we passed through the gate, admitting to the entire passage of worlds our mistake, that we dared to try and reach to be great, and now scattered, shattering, we build up with slate. Look, high the temple, engineers bumbling and tumbling, putting not down roots in mountain home, but instead losing their hair in stroke of comb, in spread of swears, in the ways we do not dare anymore to care, point our eyes in one direction to stare, out seeing gods and men for the truth to win. We are running after twins, toil and trouble, minx and double, boo, boo, we say, taking a tumble, finding again in this place we stand, trouble, or perhaps treble, some sound of wind, a flute's piercing shrine, a hero the princess to find.

So that we do not give up, so that we do not run, even though of reward we have none, is what dreaming is for, the lies and the boar, rustling through the forest floor, and goring those who did not climb to have spear of rhyme; for between runner and coward someone must die, man naively reaching high as sky, again and again attempting to try the gates of heaven, the hounds of hell, to silence purgatory's great bell, the knell of ends of days and learning ways, as a god comes and to harsh judgment we might say: Strike us down, we will try again today, (as if the shadows of the future had no sway). We might be like merry cat, pretending to be asleep, awake, attack, as Garfield did close our eyes and snack, not leaving this verse here, but throwing the entire world out of whack by the mere expedience of stretching our back from the statue of David by the square, to snow-white shine of Lady Buddha's hair, and Balinese wedding where true love did swear. Sitting in a lined passage we let a tear fall because we cared, all in order to be the one who dared, be one who crossed the whole world wide, seek the stars in the night sky past the old guildhouse, or hole in basement where lay the mouse, kvass sold by market-blimp, or burnt pillar pomegranates limp; even unto the starry glimpse where stolen pyramids bragged of wins, power over the valley and no payment for sins; even as one week hence comes the wind, cutting spark, knapping stone, flint alone, and buried bone.

Now, I don't know why I'm doing this, filling up my phone, but it is in attempt that madness like this that I hear a tone, three times this: Gingerbread crumbs to home, as I hone my words in weeping and wailing, or assailing my failings, mine's washed-out tailings, crushed granite, insensate panic, one a good place Janet, brown hair, fake laughter and stare; but what we have made we may not command, only set it loose and gently guide with hand, for cats are free and freeing, even sleeping, meowing, dreaming, snoring; sweet, murderous angels with sandpaper for a tongue and knives as arms. - Their teeth are filled with joy and harm, even far away in red barn. I see that cat as an alarm, some softness on my arm.

Day 55: June 22nd, 2024

To Beauty,

    How should we save the world? Obviously we may do it by doing what we are told, never even once attempting to be bold: Simply, forever and always, following the rhymes and the lines, the rules and laws, the guidance of books and of Grandparent's old saw, throwing ourselves over and over again into the maw, bowing before Abeloth, forgetting light and dark, living in gray haze, that deep place without a spark. This is the way to save the world it seems, this is what we are told in our scream, to shut up, shut up, it's being taken care of. The earth is fine, there is no fire, for gods and kings have not desire nor greed, they simply fulfill a need, as in some natural law, commandment please, isn't it obvious that we must believe every person has their proper place, truth and justice in their proper place strong as lace, but dyed, not white, a tinting of sight; and all these patterns merely a way of flight, some warm candle we gather around to stave off the night, because we believe in tradition and purpose, in openness and explanations, in the obviousness of corporate salutations, then finishing out a life where we are stuck, and happily so, building igloos out of ice and snow. This is survival, but what have we to show? For we are at the mercy of nature and chance, or the way that munitions and money dance. A life such as this passes in a glance, water filling cup but not ambrosia, which may make us tough, but is not enough, because black despair comes and takes away all that we care for, a 'gimme' immortality seeking to end all morality.

    But should we fight that, should we aim in our sights for a light, then what might we change; how would we make the world strange? Perhaps we may transform, power from the sun, the wind, or the sea, burning but not me, or at least healthier than thee. It would be so simple to sleep you know, so simple to put on a show, convince us that we had moved, changed the land and the plan, while all around us black dust in the invisible air expands, six points of connection and a sequestered hand, core spine of a dandy man. We place our brain onto this tract, we dare ourselves to take this tact, because we feel, over and over again, that we lack the power or precision, the strength of mind or clarity of vision to save the world in other ways: To corral all our crazy strays, the ones who are greedy or needy, with eyes bright clouded or brilliant beady, because they were human with hearts and minds, even for those few sad people who barely use them to be kind, and do not understand why our eyes water when we rewind, or remember the rabbit-flesh upon which strangers did dine while we in front of thirty peers cried, all because some cruel and world-wise man had lied.

We must do this, they say, this is the only way, unless you find some miracle of chance and fate to sway - and that only happens if you work hard at it every day, with the right credentials and the correct knowledge of how to play; a mind-map of money and power, where inner and outer both glower, bending beneath gold, silver, and flour; the necessities of life, or at least of knives, cutting the world to release energy to thrive, or make our metal and silicon minds. We sacrifice sights for time, and build of worlds of fantasy using rhyme, as we burn ourself in flame and die. Ohm, we imagine rising like phoenix from the ashes to fly, imagine that no matter how hard it is we could once again try, because this ever-renewing fashion is the inheritance of me and mine - flesh, air, and water on which we dine, where we delve in Mother Earth to find, reason and power to reach Father Sky. - Pillar of iron and smoke, the way we eat too fast and choke, the many myriad tiny jokes.

For it is easy to laugh, it is simple to pass, ignore the shadow and how nothing will last, resources drowning us in five-foot blast, looking at the future through glass, saying this pattern will pass. With nature, not Venus, overcoming nurture, ignoring how a hundred thousand words and ten million years is more than the entire history of Human glory and fears. Of course we don't know what comes next, but isn't that the test? Shall we survive long enough to leave this watery nest? Is this our final rest, and shall we like Dyson die, surrounding power but not understanding why? Buggered beast, or white-flesh feast, golden child of Well's release, as we are transformed by final evolution into the least, nothing but laughter or hunger to find. I do not wish to end like that, not me and mine, but how might we off that pillar climb? By not ignoring the laws of time, by allowing that the future may not be set in stone, but that is because of choices and chances, not statistics alone. Capitalism works you know, the free'er the information, and the longer the show, but when you stick to one quarter it's like the volcano will blow.

Might we challenge wisdom with action? Could it be possible to fill our good intentions with actual traction, escaping the curses of Washington's warning on factions? Greed is not bad you see, only as it fulfills a need, and doesn't forge it so we bleed. Invisible hand or Malthusian strand, there are gluts indeed and surcease of demand, compression of money supply and liars filling the land, their piece of pie raving and demanding, drivers of economy and power, with nicer survival, but uglier flowers. The floor of survival may be heading upwards, but I wonder is the ceiling of thriving coming down? Is mankind once more wandering from country to town, finding work but not feeding its soul in the ground, for what will our grandchildren think of us when we are no longer around? Did we save the world or make it worse, are we a blessing today, or a curse, children gaining wisdom, or old beings needing a nurse? I don't know which is better or worse, to burn it all up today, or last as long as we can until we cry. Shall we live for the past, or build a tower to touch the sky? Be kind, rewind, and push ourselves when we are behind, to catch up on what we should have been doing all this time, whatever it is, whatever the rhyme, as we attempt our laws to unbind, ours not to only do and die, but to also ask why, why, why; for we are living anyway, so we may as well try, or at least, so thought I.

Day 56: June 23rd, 2024

To Beauty,

    The mind is filled with so many terrible things: Home and memories, travels and streams, places green, and the ways I scream. I have seen the world, y'know, I have attended the show, from broken houses and betrayed spouses, leading to children hiding in their rooms like mouses; I have been to the school, fought bullies and laughed at fools, I've followed rules and broken them. I've graduated three times and memorized rhymes, I've waved my flashlight in the night time, and suffered pains to make a dime. I have starved, short of food, and snapped because I had a mood, I have shined boots, hammered nails, whimpered as I felt dead pets wail; I have traveled and flown and sailed, I have tried to send meaningful emails and had no reply; I have been cut, bruised, and forgotten, I have lost meaning and found no reason to survive, except for vain hope that in the future curiosity might strive to bring me forth to freedom as some cat on nine lives, or some sword-smith with knives. I have said good-bye to family and friends, hope and dreams, mights and maybes, the sight of babies. We are all grown up now with long hair but weakened limbs, treading water like dogs as we swim. But from where are we headed, and from what shore erased?
    I have felt chased and chasing, the rabbit and the fox, but I am not one of the Nox. I am not one with my nature or my city, and I have no wish to be let alone, or for pity. I long to dive into the gritty world, but every time I do, the foundations around me swirl, men and girl, I am half of yang, less than half a brain, moving, living, and existing as pain. Not the terrible kind that drives soul on soul to dine, but simply low, pi, three point one four, irrational, never-ending, as all distractions I have are failing.
    Which is why I have so often attempted to go away: I have walked the world, from stone pyramids to mountain graves, and in none of it have I seen myself saved. It does not matter how hard I work or pray, I am alone at end of day, at end of light, at night, the terrors on me lay, how I shall die like this, cold, and afraid. Every single moment pass away, I am simply not happy, not ever, not really. There is something wrong with me, who no more joy can find, who has reached the end of his line. I am the caught fish, tearing my lip, on all maps simply a blip, some Tau'ri who cannot be uplifted, and is abandoned on shelves by all those who

thrifted. Myself regarded by even myself as ungifted, I am not safe, either standing on my feet or laying in bed, because what I see in my mind's eye is red, blood wet or dry: Drawn to save or spent to slay, a puddle on the ground of chicken guts, a future in them to be found, even though I've had not a drop of meat since that rabbit's head went round, tears falling in front of peers to the ground. I have since seldom visited a pound, and even now grow sick when cage I see, dirty trick. But I digress.

What I mean to say is that I've been tested, and I have not failed all the questions. Perhaps no passing grade could I save, but maybe, just maybe, I might rave: Ten swords to save the day, and some new way to play. This is how I use my words and what I say: I may be ignored and despised, I am full of lies and I hide, I don't know what I want or why I'm trying, I'm simply, simply, dying, absorbing colors, frying in the flame. I am glazed, and it is in despair that I blaze, send my books or my works or my art out, trying to shout, attempting everything I have ever learned to flout. I write these words down, but I don't know what to do about them or myself, so full of doubt, so bereft of stout. I suppose this is why I gaze at others, and why I feel saved by feathers, angels, or demon skin. I wish that I might be my twin, or at least against the mirror do something like win, and overcome my terrible senses of sin. For a mirror, you see, does not mirror all, and there are always distortions, making us seem more fat or thin, short or tall, floating in the air, or barely managing to crawl. The sun behind us puts forth wings, and the stars blind by in their twinkling, level nineteen of best gear, and running Warsong Gulch without fear, as far flag we see racing toward me, and I'm not sure if I could catch it, or if I did, I'd want to be free. For what is the use of sight, if there's no point in trying to see? It doesn't matter what I know, if before all challenges we flee.

So how shall we face that rocky shore? How shall we admit we no longer want to be bored and safe, away from harm or race? To the thorn we grasp, an idea of a rose clasp: This is our class, this is a lesson, this is a station in the schoolyard, this is sound of ancient Irish bard. Are we a dog, a cat, a wolf, a bat , inanimate cauldron, or raven wearing a hat and mask, who sets poor hero a task? The kind of chance that comes to nobody, of nowhere, and no man's son, who off to the fair once did run for glimpse of girl with sunlight in her hair, and a fierce, mighty glare. Now, my name is not Larry or even Mary, and I have no flame to carry, nor finery to wear at the fairgrounds of County Clare. I travel down, down, past the red, the brown, the blond, the black, over and over again I seek what I lack: A heart, bravery, a working brain, or a home. I wonder the world for ten years, but no matter what I find I'm alone, I have no ruby shoes nor curtained throne. I have no path, only lost woods and words that last and last, until falling on my knees I clutch my breast and gasp, running out of breath and gas, for no more dead beings lay in the ground, and I must, I must, seek power from the living that surround, a vision of loveliness of which I am sadly proud, ears stuck as if by thunder loud, as lightning's laugher kicks me out of the crowd.

Day 57: June 24th, 2024

To Beauty,

What is wrong with me? This half anxiety, and half of thirst for song and tree, meaning and purpose, life and movement, something to set me free, or at least allow me to crawl on my knees, away from here; from light and hope, as into the darkness I grope and choke. I look around and I am broke. - What have I to give, what have I to ask? I do not know my ending or task, only bruised fingers, bloody face as I tear off this mask, and beneath it lies what- what - what?! I am not a happy thing, I am silent in my screams, and my dreams are full of fools like me, ones who strive and lept, who did not falter as they slept, passing exhausted past any hope of being exalted, simply because they felt the drive of art and writing, or breathing and feeling, drinking cups of joy with the whole world, or even just one. A mere tone, a voice, a memory of choice, of nothing much, of nothing much, that's all we say, you know. - It was nothing much, not even the idea of a touch. The world was lurched, out of balance, like a church entered by a demon or a vampire, suddenly flame in the congregation, a blazing, staining, pillar of ash, all of reality now coming down in a crash, ourselves now opened again to the priest's despairing lash.

Under our sins we are burdened and doomed, fate now locking us in a room: One with an open ceiling so that sun beats us, destroys us, burns us, saves us, hallucinations and allusions now rising, now reaching for heaven's eight arms, veins revealed beneath third degree, we seek harm. At night we face the alarm, cold and chilled, spring is the only time we're warm, and fall is but a whisper of what could happen. Winter bites with chill strikes: Ice in the breath, crystals cutting, lungs bursting, we trip, fall, slide, run, telling ourselves over and over again: We are not done, for now summer comes.

And, with the end of June, we feel memory's terrible swoon, fainting, resting before noon. Yet we are mankind: There is no siesta for us, there is no lunch, there is no rest; simply us doing our best. The natural question of course now arising: Are we good enough? Were we good enough? Could we be good enough? Is there even a hope, a picture, or an idea of what that might be? Of what we have to do? Is there a plan, is there a chance even?...I don't know...I don't know anything. I have never known something, understood how my efforts began to end, what flags

I hit, or if I should clockwise or counter-clockwise spin, am I trying the Rasengan that I read of, but doing it with a soul too thin? A body, or a brain, more like the wind than the waves, ashes from flame, a spark in the pan bringing eyes pain and summoning a smell in the air, a nasty, broken, dirty thing, Gollum's ring which holds a soul of greed. I am unfulfilled in my needs, I know this, I feel this - but I don't know what they are. Something is wrong with me, with my life, every time I laugh and act, there is some sound in the back of my head, the restless whispering of the angry dead.

Is this where my actions have led? Is this what I spent all of that energy, effort, and drive, for? To end like this, anxious and tired, sick in the stomach, living like a bum reliant on others? I know I'm lying. - My head tells me this isn't true, that I have work which I am doing, that I have a safe placo sleep, and the ability to make art, and write, and read. I bought a book today, and I spent an hour writing down everything I had to say - but it didn't change anything. The next day is just like the next, and the next, and the next, and...it feels like existence for me is a test, and for such stress, what reward? Are my answers all wrong, is my heart singing the devil's song, am I just on a ride-along? There to see and observe, to learn, but never do, never even attempt, it's not safe, not yet. Something is wrong, everything's wrong, and I'm trying to fix it. I'm trying, living like I should be dying, tearing the truth out of me to dangle on a chain. - I have halted my lying, and begun my malingering, those five minutes where you write something and await reply, knowing the whole time that it's going to be bad. Bad, the message is bad, the idea is bad - and - and - I'm just some stupid lad, not a poet, or an artist, or an anything.

I'm wrong. In what I do, in what I think, even in the stupid ways I leap. Out of the mire, into the air, accepting my hope and heart of despair, I spend all I have, and I know that what I buy is worthless, because it cannot be exchanged for any good or service. This will not be read, or felt, or understood, and if it changes anything at all, it will only change me. But I have done that before, run away from home, traveled to a foreign land, listened for days on end to my favorite band. I have gently held out my hand to help, and I have been helped in return, but what does this matter, as my heart over and over again shatters, rainbow splatters like blood and oil, forgotten, soaking into the ground: Spoiled. Like sunlight after rain in a parking lot, it is pretty to see, but ugly to drink.

Something is wrong with me. Something is wrong with me, and I do not know where to go. I do not know what to try. I am able to distract myself for a time, make art or rhyme. I work, travel, or help somebody else for a dime. I stand alone and climb, though mountains or hills, and I make sure that Grandma takes her pills. I'm surviving for now, but I know one day this will end, and I will go back to the world - and I don't know what I'll do then, because I am barely standing up right now. I am Ok, for right now. I once wrote about what that actually means?

Day 58: June 25th, 2024

To Beauty,

    I finished one project today: I put it up for sale, then walked away. I don't think this my hope shall slay, but I know it's not good, it's bad every, every, every way, because...well..I'm not sure why - maybe I gave away too much of my pride, I staked all on love and lies. In every passage I tried to hide, I gave the world my truth and tossed it aside. After all, what is the point? I can barely find my heart; half my soul is lost in parts, only words, not pictures, only imaginings, not lectures. I'm not at home, I'm not at work, I'm simply standing, hurting and broke. I'm so tired, and I feel not why, maybe because I know not my kind, the ones who read books and rhymes, who feel like every day and every nighttime is the climbing of a chiming, of the bells ringing on high, or the cars on the road, racing, racing they are, and I am standing still. - While others travel again across half the planet, I have done that, with whiplash, and I wish I was healed, but I'm not. My soul has been cast out, my spirit has flown the coop, and I ran upon this road, but it turned out to be a mobius loop! I look back and forward, up and down, all around, and it all looks the same, a game without plan, meaning, or change. - I have with my life spent and exchanged my rage and my pain for silence.

    I approach the barest, faintest glimmering of old age, and I wish to rave, not to be saved but destroyed, not be helped but shown, not to die but somehow fly. I have seen the bones at the ocean's edge, leavings of the cetacean dead, Regis writing on scrimshaw, and the opening of Cthulhu's majestic, mad maw; loss of light and hope, of love and law; melting crystal counting, curse grows worse, and I suffer blame, I suffer shame, because I am...I know it's not. If I have not managed to achieve the best I could have, still, at end of day, I am now more than I was this morn. A book I read, and all the words I forget, except the three which stuck to me like a knot, some star-sailor's thought, altergeist unlocking power that I've bought. I spend time, I spend dimes, I spend chance and will, I am here at this point in life because of the actions I took, the sights and ideas I forsook when I said: No, I don't want a dull job, no I don't want to work here any more, no I don't want to sell my life, no I don't want to follow your rules, no I don't want to bury myself beneath a mountain of tools until I grow too old to care, to adventure, or dare to do more than dream. I was born with an elder soul, and my whole life I have heard it screaming, an unwieldy unhappiness seething. I don't want anything, and everyday I fill that emptiness with whatever comes my way, all the words and wisdom, legends and history, mysteries and music, and I am always active, always dreaming, always learning, always seeming like I'm doing - something.

I am not even a jack of trades: I am a knave, some padawan who cannot save: My blood has been drained, my husk neither a thrall nor one with name. I was slayed, and yet I wake, shaking and cold, my second life with no heat to hold. I have no sparks in me, no flame; only the empty wind, void between planets, solar storms to swim, as I now, mouth spread, wide grin, dare to dream and speak. My bile from me leaks, breaking down magic in me sleeps. I wish to burn and rave at end of day, I want to laugh, dance, play, and finish out the day. I wish to be fired clay, strong the world to hold and sway, light as a feather, heavy as a mountain, searching for that mystic fountain that feeds the boughs of Yggdrasil, boiling, bubbling, toil and trouble, the snake is in it and I see double, the high highs, the low lows, the paths of fire and ice leading to silence sufficing for fighting, a reason to die, but not to live. I look back, back, back, with a crow's eye, or a crone's sigh, now after midnight as I stand outside, I am still so tired, and I have never really known why.

I do not find the fuel within me to sail sea or sky, I am no engine of mankind. If I have spoken or put my hand to work, it is because I have reached out, feeling like a jerk, and I am sorry, sorry, sorry ten thousand times, but I am weary beyond memory of rest, and I try to treat this as a test, memory of a smile blessed. Half a moment, no more, but it felt like a soul at rest, and I go back to it. I have...nothing else. And, yeah, that's kinda a lie, it's another way I hide, one of those fancies and fantasies we should keep inside, as we allow time to toughen our hide. But I was born old, and my skin is thin, cut by scars deep within. I know even saying that is a sin, as I look at so many other people who have it so much worse, existence filled with loss and curse, losing life and limb to fill another's purse, or feeling pulse end, building burn, starving and not knowing where to turn, hungry for learning or food, or just knowing that someone cares, a life full of dead flesh and battered eyes with a soul that stares with burned-out care..

If I have drowned, it is in a puddle. If I am cold, it is because I did not join a huddle. If I am ignorant, it is because through the book I long muddled. I feel as if I am small: Worthless and nothing, some kid in a good country, with a good family, and a good education, and a good life ahead which has already been squandered. If I passed away tomorrow, what would the credits say? There is no strife I seek to stop, no world to save, I am greedy and I want, but give nothing away; I rage and rave, sing, write shout at night, draw faint visions of my mind's eye - but then I walk away, sleep, wake, listen to music, and I don't know if any of it matters. I eat breakfast and feel shattered, so the first thing I did this morning is hit myself with a hammer.

Day 59: June 26th, 2024

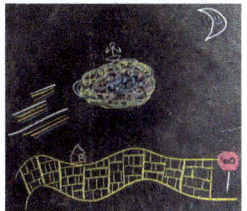

To Beauty,

    They say travel broadens the soul, but I think it does that by punching holes, as steel is made into a diamond fence, buying little, selling high, placing parts of you out of reach of sky; as detritus falls and patina of rust improves, us now unable to move. Money may talk, and criminals may walk, but us, we sulk like umber hulks deep underground, away from sun and moon and cloud. The world becomes too loud, every story containing all of history, math and music hiding, holding, mystery. - I am no Hardy twin, no detective without or within, and I have in me not a single determination that I might win. In fact, I do not know how to define such a state, a world where I am filled with Jedi love and not Sith hate, a head filled with Republic and Council to which I relate, not this empty hole with a locked gate. No hobbits live here, no Gollum sneer, and neither elvish music nor dwarven cheer, not orcish fear or Manish bier, these halls are not of stone or wood or soul or air, but spirit, bright, terrible, and fair - spider's fangs and hair, who hungry drinks, and then burning seeks darkness dim. Run, run, run and sin, fear greed pride wrath lust envy gluttony sloth, I am lost beneath the weight of virtue, wisdom, moderation courage and justice, but I don't know if I trust any of it, the good and the bad, the evil or the glad, happiness, sorrow, or tears, because my life in arrears. I have been paid out, but still I owe, some sucking, horrid cyclopean throw, tosses me to the ground and breaks bones. I know in my actions and dreams I am not alone, but still I feel as if there is some hole in me, dead, empty land where no grass grows, and no wind through the tree blows knocking off fruit and seed, to reinvigorate meadow filled with flowers, renew frozen winter after April showers; in the back of my head some beast-thing glowers, hungry and angry.

    I burn and rave at end of day, but that heart is not mine to save, all I may do is watch as it gently floats away, until what is left is me, silent and fighting. I walk, wondering the hills for lightning, so that I might grab that spike of immortal might and pull down the heavens, end fate and time. - Cow licks cold rime, thus begins first line of man and tide, giant stride, under the hills and far away, what is this music to which I sway? Look, can you hear it play? Please, it says, like my book or me, or maybe one tenth of what I see in thee, oh light of the sun, oh burning one. I am cold ice, but I wrote to you thrice, because I am breaking and tired, no longer nice, no longer silent and careful. I paid the price, but alas no dice. There was never a chance, I know it in my bones, although - on occasion in my sleep I dream, hearing whispers of what is not a scream, and this is so strange, for I grasp not it's name, having read of but never played this game, the last game, the real game, the riddle game. - What is in my pocket I ask? Not a ring or a sign, not a picture or a rhyme, only words I wrote in night-time. From Oaxaca in the valleys to the northern hills where grandma is ill, I take my turn at the mill, grind flour to make my bread, like a Roman soldier march until I'm dead, or in Gallic forests lose my head, and if I am well-read, I am not well-actioned. I am no Saxon, sailing upon the seas, or into the rivers, burn and feed. I return to the north, I regress towards my birth, in despair fill moments of mirth; laughing I draw, paint splatters on the saw, blood pours out through my maw, I suffer under Apollo's law, Diana's chase, hart mistake, I run in fear and it is so great that I may not comprehend it's actual scape.

Tetrahedrons of art and stone have stood still for near five thousand years, every night watered by god's tears, sheer, shining veil of Isis is near, but never actually entirely here. In such a sad way we are cheered, by memories of Vietnam or Rome, Bien Hoa or traveling home, of Athens and Tallinn, Osaka, Seoul, Oaxaca, Arizona, over the bridge and off the road, the places untrodden and the stories untold, pictures in my head of adventures old. I have seen where tombs were raided and passed by English throne, Washington's home and circle of stone, and I have seen the demon's eye and felt when "all I loved, I loved alone."[8] I once recited poems, and there were times I buried old bones, and yet today all of these are mere memories in my phone, as I stand here, tired and afraid, ashamed to tell you of my name. Could I accept my rage, escape this emotion, anxious future-sight cage?

Having traveled to the stars, now I come home from afar, like Piro and Largo I arrive sin cargo, because I was drunk and lost my mind, floating on a smile's tide, seeing in the mirror how I had forced myself to hide: Never breaking bones, no harm to heal, I was always bent, born like this, trauma disappearing into the mist. I was never a soldier, I never swung my fist, I never learned to swim like a fish or fly like a bird, I am no mermaid or merman, I am dirt, expelled of those who live in haste and effort, construction coming but to waste, like a wrist that does not work as I sit in my class chair in the corner unable to write or give sign of struggle in nightmare's blight I do not know how to fight back, only how to survive, I did not dare to thrive, fearing the wolf inside. Fenrir bites and howls at moon, fork runs away with spoon, and I allow myself to act the loon. Like walled city I never grew, but maybe destroyed I may become something new, not a heart which fell, but one which flew.

Day 60: June 27th, 2024

To Beauty,

     I traveled back home for a few days, to my town, to my grave. As I passed the cows in the train, looking out the window at the rain, I realize here there is no chance I might see the past, turn the corner and in swift glance see sun or moon, light or pain, what I've lost, or what I've gained. I am divorced from this place now, traveled too far, seen too much, with my people I've lost touch. I wish I could say that life here was enough, that I moved on because I've grown, connected to other worlds and other places with my mind, my hands and phone, but instead I feel only lost, tired, and alone. I've come here for a task, but after it passes what holds me here? Who may I talk to near and dear, who I may know without fear? Many times long ago, I fought for friendships, against those dread foes of distance and time: All the events, all the history, the kissing and mixups, the breakups and fess-ups, divorce and death, rage and laughter, all the pieces of heart which gather friend to friend and make a home for shame, brave found family who will not blame as we trip in the game or change names: How you dress, act, think, talk, walk, the lines we chalk in the sky, the way we balk as hopes die, tears and play filling up the grand ten thousand days, offering succor when in the night we lay a failure or feel as if over me there is some jailer, locking myself away from what I might have been, all the costs of the wages of sin, the way that we, surviving, tried to win.

     We give up so much, we are lost and pressed, crushed, opined, bound by rime, cold iron chains of ice and time, twenty-four hours every day spent to either make a dime or recover from the effort of doing so; we cover ourselves up in cloth and shade, direct our burning and silence our rage. - Yet is this life worth what we have paid? Soon I shall in the ground be laid, three score more have I to rave, and living to be sure is such a pain filled with little gain, not much to lose, but I am a young man and I think it still worthwhile, or at least I hope so that it might be, because of a smile. Friends, family, lovers, self, I must leave this toy's shelf - kick the box, break the view, find reason to climb, even one too few; I am tired now, I must renew, green cast from druid at last, as I wander through the towns of my past, even as each sight is like a lung-burning gasp, idyllic remembrance leaving my mind grasping hand behind. I write words, pointless words, filled with rhyme.

Look, my school is covered with black gates and bars, because for safety's sake they've enclosed the yard. I can see my flower but not reach it now, and I want to say that's wrong, but I don't know how. When I was younger behind my house you could see cows, and now only dead grass there stands. The only life which may pass are rabbits and coyotes, predator and prey, like the eyes of people I see today. The old men still talk with strangers, or treat chance meetings as not a danger. The folk I pass on the street at noon are bent over into a spoon, phone in their hand, head-phones blind, or staring straight ahead with eyes on a line, not on mine. Is it so strange today, this old habit of nodding our head, or saying to bro how you doing, instead of treating them like one of the dead? Small changes, different paces, faster racing, greater distance, social directives just a little off, am I so old to as be this lost?

Is this the cost of age, or because I moved away? I have not shifted with the times, as against these facts I climb, half real, half fake, half a problem in search of half a solution, I, coming into the world again, am disillusioned. I have lived among birds and bees, far corners of tallest trees, through the flood and frost, on hills above the coast, this is where I have spent most of my years, on high mountains filled with madness and fear, and no more to myself am I near. These people are not mine, these streets are not mine, this house is not mine, and I am glad I am here for only a short time, because I think if I sat too long in grey haze, I would lose my words and my rhyme, the rhythm of writing every nighttime. I am too alone here, surrounded by connections which are not clear, because my screaming is silent, social anxiety overcoming clarity, losing my ability to discern left or right polarity, as I, watched by things unfriendly, try not to cry, write my poems, live and die, dream of love or ask out loud why. I took all I had to point finger to sky, grab at the sun and climb ladder high, overcoming drowning tide.

Some part of me in front of people and house hides, like scaredy cat at strangers eyes-wide, wild untamed, don't look at me or you shut down my brain, and my willingness to fight the world drains. Existence itself is a strain now, and speaking harder still, electricity grounding what remains of my will. Protag in my head I may be, and election said I am one of the free, but there is something non-neutral in me, a part of my mind that seeks to abandon mass and weight, the pull of earthly hate. So I stand here three days, then off I go through the gate, with trees and foxes debate, for I am not come to hope too late. I am gloomy here, I am sad and tired, more than before, as I stand in my room and see that place in the floor where I sat for two months nigh two years ago, and wrote and wrote of not happy memories, but a loss and a choke. I want to escape, chains of the past be broke, even foolish, buried, friendless, afraid, unable in the family of mankind to be made.

Day 61: June 28th, 2024

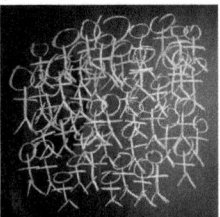

To Beauty,

    Sometimes when I am too close to a group of people, they feel like a scalding wound, not a wave. I hate them and fear them. - Yet how awkward that to write I need others, to write I need stars, I have to speak to someone so that I can exercise my scars. I cut myself with knife or saw, I tell beauty truth, this a law, who is not here and is not real; I spill myself, screaming, shrill, because this is the only way I know to pass over the hill, mountains made by moles, fields and reality full of holes. Passing by the bridge you must pay a toll to the troll, a pound of flesh, or a round of gold, but I am skinny, and poor. Spill my entrails on the floor, and there would not be enough to feed a dog, grind my poisoned bones up and see it refused by a hog. What am I, but some dead and rotting log, witch-light sheltering in a bog? I follow myself drowning and dying, mere amusement for dead shades, then ten years hence rising as a shade, I rebel against that demonic host, and all it cost me was what I loved the most. I have cut myself, too deep to heal from, a saw am I, but sawdust, harsh on the lungs, passing through wind and rain, dust, dust, dust, pain, durst, I regain. - Opening my mouth, words come out, and I do not know how I shall shout, or what my thousand words will be about. I have no direction in my life, I have no cause, simply filling each and everyday with the crowing of the birds, black wings unfurled, Alduin coming to burn the world by speaking the words which shake the earth and sky, ancient past's beleaguered cry: We have not finished, you and I.

    What am I doing, what am I doing, I don't know what I'm doing, simply chewing over and over again on the dried blood covering my face, a mask of distaste. I do not move with haste, never sure of my position on earth or the rules of the race, what exactly calls or leads to honor or disgrace, but not in the outer face. - Inert instead is how I tangle with my fate, because I remember words of those who were great. To paraphrase, be true to your soul, be true to your concepts of love, because what else is there? What may I remember when I dare no more, when like my grandfather all my friends are dead, or like my Grandmother I've lost my head? If there was only one fact you could recall, which one would you choose out of all? Would it be what you had done, or who you had loved? Would it be a bridge you built, or a smile you received? Are you satisfied with gold and greed, or is there an indecipherable thing you need? A star, a sun, a smile, a knowledge, which releases you from mortal bondage, and acts as healing, not a bandage? I am tired to the bone of quick repairs, of knowing and believing there is no reason for me to care, and a cause for which I might dare to tell the truth, not aware if this path I am on leads to freedom or a noose, some lonely stone tomb or flying like the wind: Loose.

I have caught only a glimpse, only a feeling, a thought, faint whisper of imagination or tender administrations that might heal some wound, or at least like a hawk swoop down and carry me away from the flames; not the entire journey, but enough for me to recover from being lamed, to look in the mirror and see myself unblamed, unheated, for what I am, and sing. Is there in this world somewhere a magic ring, some power invisible that to me may bring the courage to say what I mean, and to mean what I say, revealed in light of day before the eye of the sun, standing proud and not swept away? Read my book I want to say, and yes or no leave me alone or tell me a name, but I am filled with fear and shame. I read my own words and they are juvenile, lame. I read other's poetry and I know I am not good at this game, neither in pretending, or explaining. If I was half my age this would make more sense, because I would have permission to be confused, or not even know my own views, but alas in my numbers I begin to glimpse the age of glass, seeing darkness on the horizon and knowing how this too shall pass, strength of diamond or summer's grasp, but not, I think, that laugh. A relaxation of a gut wound, shining sun at midnight-noon, or a strange kind of bleeding moon. Drops of silver, gold that shines, cow-statue of divine; a ladder I use to climb, high above the sea and sky, the outer planets, the stars, the winged guards, the ten spheres, beyond empyrean. - Sliding past hope, slipping over despair, reason and cause 'personal' to love and care. I do not know what I want, and I will never ask, but I know what I dare, what I will in order to climb the stairs. I will find my soul, glimpse of the unknown, iron, cold, mithril, gold, what are these? Worth only to those who need, and I wish to delve deeper than the flame, higher than the outer walls. There is something in me that cries out, calls, I shall seek all. Bent out of joint, twisted and broken, my every act a token spent in Santa Cruz gaming hall, to win tickets and dolls, I remember Star Wars there, Tie Fighters' ware, wire-frame, merely a game, and so much more. - A magic shadow-door, the old made new to me, a poem, a flame, a third-grade name, ancient shame, and a blaze. My heart is not safe, but I wanted to play anyway, even though love for me is not a game, and it never can be. I wanted to be seen, and even though I will never tell you my dreams, I will tell you my screams. I will show my smile, even if only for a while.

Day 62: June 29th, 2024

To Beauty,

    I did what I have done for a thousand days, lept on my bike and run away from picture and face, from chance and fate. What am I doing ai cry, why do I lie? I can do this, I can do this, but I don't even know what this is, what comes out of me or what goes in. Aware of my sense of sin and weakness, I failed, I fought, and I ended up with what I've got: A million books, a thousand shows, and the cold and empty star-sword wind that blows, the sound of emptiness between stars, and fists knocking on doors of scars. Why do I do this, write down bars, make music none shall play, remember what I could have been each day? I am slayed, I slay myself, like a book unread on the shelf showing only my spine, and not a single one of my treasured lines. No heart have I, no clay, no flame, and I cut myself, growing lame. Feel inadequate, merely a burden, I can't do anything, I can't move anything, I can't change anything - not life, not the heavens, not love, not hate, not me, not great. - I dissipate, unbalanced, late. For this, I hate myself, yet also recognize I could not have done this a decade ago, for I would not have been capable of a show. There is in me a thing unpretty, unloved of pity, which looks at Sudan or Palestine and says too bad, how sad, blood and iron and splattered brain, what have I for caring, to gain? No plan to save, only pain, gold and mental stability down the drain. It's not as if I'm rich or free either, I have so little to give as it is, either pound of flesh or slice of heart, each donation a wedge driving me apart. I dare not start, alone by me, only through others being freed from branding past and freezing future; my sides are filled with pus and suture.

    I have walked the ruins of Rome, and spoken with survivors of American bombs in Vietnam, driven past Cambodian killing fields, read of the Trail of Tears, taken photos of stone Zapotec pierced by spears, catacombs of skulls, Athenian marble monuments macerated, and memories of Soviet hatred. I have seen the empty cities in the southwest walls, and know what happens when Nanjing falls. Ten thousand times I've heard the cry and call, help us, help us, or else you shall fall from moral high ground, hypocritical member of city on the hill, monster who kills and kills, or stands aside so that others may drill into mother earth, and choke the land with ash. As if we could be made whole by cash, never-ending I am lashed; and I have tried to help where I could, but I am tired, with less than half a heart, incapable of art, broken by work, jerked a thousand ways each of a thousand days, never-ending refrains of what-if, and what-if, my awareness of power a torture, not gift. I sit here afraid of grift, learned now never to trust in this, the clever words of men and mice, the ones who act a little too nice, and, either in malice or ignorance, do ten times the harm as any group of animals in Orwell's barn, because humans are not sheep nor wolves, but far more terrible and old.

We possess the gods-sight, we possess atomic might, we are heralds of the unending-light, and we are the ones dragging earth into night. Burning books, abandoning science, unable to hold steady our defiance, or recall that original alliance between the mitochondria and the cell. You need us, and I need you as well, because stand together or fall apart, take heart that someone out there cares. There is good in this world and sun-leading stairs, impossible smiles, witless glares, stupid, childless, boyish dares, hurting ourselves for sake of pride, managing somehow to make truth from lies. This does not hurt, I am fine, I can do this, I can rhyme, with saw-edged blade, I cut myself and climb.

Today I stopped to smell a rose, three seconds of my life spent away from strife. I forget failures and knives, all the abandoned places I've seen, and the pointless, pointless words I've screamed. All of my worthless self is a dream. I know I'm bad, but so what? I am attempting to touch, or stretch, or match, hair in a braid, and I know in my soul I will never be enough, just as I know my vision is not real. - But so what? I have lived my life bound to dust, following the road to happiness of logic and lust, and where has it led me? Beneath a house, crushed, feet shriveled and curled, there is no place like home, but I have no home. With friends, family, or alone, it does not matter. Some piece of me is shattered and mad, eternally faking that mask of glad, as if my name could be connected to that of lass or lad, or me given purpose by the newest fad; but I have read too much, seen to far, walked on D-day bars, and seen friends in the ground be laid. I know not what truths I have betrayed, only that I am lost, afraid, with no oars nor wind, no tide or storm.

The lantern is out, the peach is rotten, the armor is rusted, and my speak-easys have all been busted open, and taken down. I have nowhere to hide, I have nowhere to run, I have nothing to drink, I am undone, no longer forged either many or one. Hammer and anvil I have sought, between them been caught, and now may I do as I ought. Do whatever beleaguered good I've got; and I know, I know, it will not be a lot. But I do not wish to stand ashamed before beauty and rain, saying I never gave anything away: Look at the gold and strength I've gained. This does not make me a good person, only someone stained with mercy, human, vain, and dirty. I am unworthy unless you tell me I'm not, but I don't have it in me to be shot, so I'll be silent, and never tell you what I thought of the news of violence.

Day 63: June 30th, 2024

To Beauty,

What does it mean, to wish you well? I feel something wrong within me swell, as I am glad you are glad, but for me, sad. It's another sign that you have friends and direction and I have none. I released a book yesterday and don't know what to do next. I talked to a friend who once was my best, and he said go away, come back Monday. He was busy you see, playing with friends other than me, some Final Fantasy raid. In my eyes, this illustrates the difference between us two, for, friend, I would have said come in, if it was you. I hadn't seen them for a year, and last time it took them three months to reply on the phone, so I dropped by when they said they would be free, but I guess I was barking up the wrong tree. I know what raids are like, what's involved in the fight, and how to either abandon them half-way through the night, or sit in front of the screen with someone else and explain what each light means. There were other options than what happened. Now, I know this is unfair, that I would look at him with such a glare, but this is the sense of disappointment I feel, when I try to follow the golden rule, expecting from others only what myself may give, and receiving half of that.

 I've known for a long time that I need new friends, instead of trying to re-establish old connections that end, but I don't know how to begin. My hobbies are reading alone and writing on the phone, my work is looking after my mad Grandma in the woods alone, or sometimes with my mom, my life heading not forwards but sideways. I studied for so long, as if a degree would be the beginning of a song, but having achieved that I still suffered along. I simply have no goal to follow, no purpose to chase, I have lived the life and seen the great, but all I find left of myself is self-hate. I look into others eyes, in some I see shame, and in others pride, some are trying to survive, and others look as if they have died. Across from me a mother pushes a stroller, while three walk beside, hope cast into the future. To my right three old men with stopped shoulders and blue shirts, fifty-somethings off to work. Another guy, twenty-something, walks in front of me, side to side, with backpack and water waiting for his ride. What do all of them hold in their inner mind, and would they answer if I tried asking? We are human and afraid, that others might see our truths and lies: Like tigers tear with claws, strike or burning bite, stealing from us our shadowing light. I do not speak to any of them, and we are all silent, sinning, sure to be safe because of the way we join the race, on 16th Street we pace or sit in circles, trying to survive, live and thrive, like the man in the light rail dancing to music only he can hear, or the group of homeless I see out the window, collecting up their fallen gear. I see them, and each one brings me fear, for I know they could seem Beautiful in my eyes, a lower b perhaps, but halfway to the sky, a stair-step of human soul, poetry and immortality made flesh. I can feel and see their flames, but here I sit on leash, coward racing in letters against my fetters, but unwilling to speak up or trust - and yet I know I must, if I wish to become anything, ever, more than dust, or feel myself worthy to attempt to like. I have fallen off my bike, I've missed my train, I don't know how to relieve my pain, or what on earth I can drink to not feel so drained. Sometimes I stare, heart bursting with care, at how others travel and dare. They seem successful, more than I ,who for all his journeys only ended up trying not to die. One stranger-person there like winged angel in the sky, sunlight, well I? I am a wolf in the night or the dog in the day, the beaten one who, hiding, stays beneath the porch or in the bush, without collar or food, too thin and snapping at anyone coming by. Like one of those feral cats sneaking food when they can see me and I can't see them, or like the bird that flies when cat comes near, wildness that survives only because of its fear.

  Yet I am none of these, I am human, killer of the world, dangerous netero-skull, Hunter of wolf or bear, far fiercer than rock or flame, sharper than steel is this spirit and brain. All choices and chances before me are lain, and if I am stained by failure I may cast off my skin, my legacy from the snake, deeper into the fruit I delve, good and evil, ten thousand books on shelves, axes of the dwarves and songs of elves. A elbereth gilthoniel, silvra penan miriel, our legacy is heaven and hell, memories of times we were both good and not well, seeking strength to bind philosophy and mind, kindness meeting kind, as behind me an old maid says 'We accept you whatever you choose', whether it be personal or other-facing news, head becoming unglued or body failing; teaching others or driving nails, pieces of paper slow as snails, all the events in earth are as wind in our sails, world-soul moon-light hail. Under every prick and weight we wail, blood, will, both fail, fearsome cost of life, sliding Jeremy-beremy time-knife, circles at the end, a period to find, pyramids, aliens, human line, as slowly, slowly, down and over hills we climb, breath turning in our lungs to wine, red air and the bell's chiming end of day, midnight cometh.

Cold and afraid, our promises we betray, we said we could do this but we can't, we swore to ourselves we could walk this path, but head bent we glance, how distant is this dance. Drawn on paper, drawn through soil, we are whips, trouble, toil, farmers bringing jam to boil. Saving all our black seeds, work of days, in jars of glass and clay, fingers pricked, shirt torn to shreds, crawling down at dawn spreading ourselves on bread, we eat of our memories so that we do not end up dead, living as if all was play, nothing worthwhile to say. Work to eat, eat to work, this is walking jerk to jerk, pulled one way and then another, life lighter than a feather, duty heavier than a mountain, we move beyond this to the fountain. Apollo's lyre, Diana's string, Zeus's bolt and Thoth's blue brain, Horus's eye and the mortal strain, mixed with immortal spirit framed. And how shall we fill these empty places, how do we attend to Muse's graces, what are we behind our masks and faces? Follow now my paces - round and round in circle racing, after sun and empty night chasing, abandoning sight and courage might, so as to burning light the wick of my candle, to reforge broken handle, touch with hand potter's wheel. I from crawling begin to kneel, first keel and sound of steel, my poet's blade wield. Men may fall on some day, as I have done before, lost the song, forgotten the lore, spirit curst gray and bored - but it will not be this day, not all day, not forever away, I will stand up and say: I am here. Know me and fear, my friends, my dear. Fire-near.

Day 64: July 1st, 2024

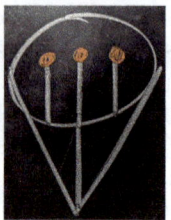

To Beauty,

    Which direction should I go in tomorrow? Not any good ones, I don't know if there are any good directions: Only wonderful fractions, parts and pieces of days and trials driving nails into wood like rings of mail, defending us from arrows. These past and empty days, quick forgotten, still carry us like cotton or wool, fluffy as a cloud, and almost exactly as loud. On occasion such high sights bring rain, and other times they are a relief from sun's strain, when we lay in the shade and forget, comfortable with not moving yet. After all, the earth has turned round several million miles while we laid here awhile, and though to all appearances we do naught but hear the leaves rustle in the trees or whistle a tune into the breeze, as we lay on our back with broken knees, not crawling, it turns out we have been moving. We may not help our shifting, from man to beast and back again, one form always becoming the other's leash, lush and starving in turn, first hungry then trying to burn; and in this fighting, what have we earned? We are not a thing which quickly learns.

    I walked by a flower today, and I remember the way I painted it. Twenty years ago now, third grade, and it still says pride in the corner. I did not know, did not plan, some teacher simply took me by the hand, the whole class in one line together headed to a garden, one we made: One we started. Constructed not of soil but brick, with many colors laid on it thick, half-done, I was settled in the left corner on my knees, with a palette and told to do as I please. Many of the other children stepped in and made roses, daisies, or carnations, but me, I sat for a long time at my station, wracking my brain, writhing in strain, what can I make, what picture create? A minute, another, and another, paralyzed, I close my eyes, and what I see in my head is something white, round like a bowl, three gold stamens high, from yesterday when I was dragged to the child divorce therapist, because talking to someone is supposed to make this better. I think all that happens is I become more battered, because nothing I do matters. As always, I retreat into my mind, recall a beautiful sight; grab a moment of light and hold it close, using it as a shield against the demon host.

    Now, I do not know the name of the flower, or where on earth the physical location is that it grows, only that it's by an office that mom takes me to in a car, someplace incredibly, incredibly, far. And what I do is go there, leave the world behind, open my eyes and paint three lines, with a circle on one side; no stem. I do not fill it in, but only dab three gold dots and connecting spaces. Quick, you see, mere a sketch, I walk back one step, look again and again, attempting judgment to reach, is this neat, is this nice, does this look like what I saw in the light before passage of night? I think not, but I'm also not sure what it's missing, how to make my art better, how to reform it realistically. All too soon, my chance is history, as someone asks me: Are you done? I say I suppose so, for after all, I don't know what else to do. I hand my paints over, and leave, my work unfinished, with confidence diminished, as I glance to my right and see every other child continuing their work, actively improving all other petals of earth. I finished too fast, I have this sense of being awkward and weird, not comprehending why I feel stressed, or scared. I want to say give me more time, let me walk around and try again, look at it from this angle and that, step forward and back, my spirit now tight, then slack. There is something I am lacking however, a piece of courage or a piece of social sameness. I don't want to stand out, I don't want to speak up, I don't want to hold anyone back in my ignorance or need for space, and even if I spoke up, no-one would understand what I was groping for, all of me which cannot be explained in words or name;, the empty spaces in my brain like waves upon the ocean, whose troughs are low as the crests are high, glittering, shining, beneath sun and sky, a moving dragon with blue eyes.

All's quiet for a while, but I come back tomorrow and see my flower, then look at it and glower. Not that I'm angry, but just a little ashamed, because all I drew was the frame. It's not real or fake, it's not fantastic or a mistake, but it is not perfect or great; and that has been my curse, from that day till this, I don't match, finish, or fit. I have passed by this wall a thousand times, and I think my flower is the worst of them all. - When I was younger, I hoped desperately that no-one ever asked me which one I made, or looked at my attempt, then mocked and brayed. Look, who was that idiot? Who was that failure? Who was that fool? Who was that person supremely uncool? To myself, I was ever that cruel. Yet today, I am changing old. Still not bold, merely desperate and despairing, laughing, crying, smiling, drawing again, and probably not confident within, but still I try, live and die, not very well, but it is I, or at least, an 'eye', like burning smoke ladder to sky.

I, my creations: Lost and confused as I have ever been, I have to step away and then come back later that day, making tiny changes on canvas, or building up my rhymes one line at a time. I don't know what to paint, I don't know what to write, I merely explain and exclaim, wonder in the maze, and break stays. My judgment is suspect, for no matter what spirit says, my mind goes run away, and my heart whimpers another day. Left alone, I would not play, I would not create, I would not show myself and accept hate. The only reason for this game and passing through the gate is because of a memory in my head, a tool if I wish to be cruel, unnamed in truth, has some ancient fear not soothed, but stabbed, one brick on the path, one laugh, one arrow last. Maybe it's evil, but I'll take that chance and in my poor way dance, toss apple core on the ground, like Johnny travel the whole land round, then die beneath a tree, on the well-spring feed, which means I may generously be referred to as forgetful and frail, but all I need is one seed. A little bit of sunlight, soil, and time to breath.

Day 65: July 2nd, 2024

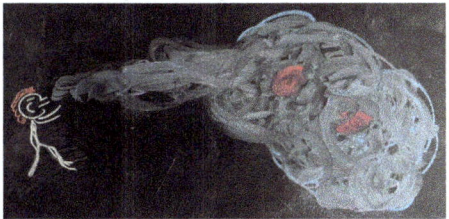

To Beauty,

    What do I want to create, what make, what forge from hate? I strike myself with hammers, driving nails through my head, holding two loose wooden boards together like pieces of a porch long falling apart, beaten by weather, covered over with heather: Purple, pink, and gold, what was once young now old, fading symbol of work of the bold. I cut wood fallen from the tree of my soul, as Grandfather and me once did, making a candlestick with seven rings. I paint my soul with my aunt, or fill in ceramic cracks; Grandmother once made stained glass, and on red wall stands a bear made of ash, next to iron kokopeli that long shall last, and I walk by half-built ship without a mast. Everywhere I look are half-built things, all I touch is silent scream, as tossed into the sea I swim and drown, now quiet, now loud; my feet pound, pound, pound, in circles round, gather here, let loose the hounds, wild hunt rides now with head of antlers and crown of thorns, ancient legends redone, reborn. We dive into our poems, we remember the Iliad or the movie home, Boov who runs and Agamemnon greedy and cruel, wishing like none of them to be made fools, treating their lessons as tools, crowbars to the heart, opening up the door and blasting locks apart, spilling our blood on the ground to make art.

    I no longer wish to live long, but merely well, find a light and let it swell, some guide to take me through loving circles of hell, beyond purgatory and heaven into the well: Divine source of life and protoplasmic gel, before fossils were a thing or we formed multicellular rings. Whence came that spark that even now sings, turning stone into living beings? Eukarya, prokaryotic, what do I mean? Only the lessons I recall as a dream, faint haze of a classroom where I was made, by Hamlet drained, or weeping over Ender's Game. We learned about moles and magnetic polarity, laughed at Chris or Annie's hilarity, cooked, painted, welded, by sparks we melted, or hammered dings out of cars, fought strangers in locker rooms or played music bars, learned we have fifty stars. Every day we were there did us both heal and harm, slowly taught us about tyrants and Animal Farm, Colonel Blimp and the Home Guard, that the world would control us and mold us if it could, and if we did not name ourselves, then it would, telling us what we should and should not be, or want, or see. We are numb little bugs trying to survive, but I think that is not for what I aim; I would rather thrive, live and die, feel pain, ask why, challenge limits of earth and sky. This no pillaried refrain, only world-span sage, some directed form of my endless rage, open emotion, the turning page.

I want to be a good boy, not the failed dream that I am. I want to not sin but stand, write with my eyes and not only my hands, journey to the hidden inner lands, Stormwarden spirit's three bands. In these poems welcome to my dark side, pieces of me I hide, so very often existing as shame, not pride. I am so often not healthy, inner me, light as the Buddha, heavy as Charlemane, slowly, poisoned, made sane, before Mara not greedy but afraid. My finger touches the earth and the earth does shake, but worry I do this is too late, as seven times in seven days, with seven horns and seven heads, I do berate what I should have said or done, who I might have been, not many minds but one, some beautiful being becoming, instead of this eternal -thing-, a screaming animal without hopes of achieving a dream. Monster without love or hooks to hold him here, Eowen who fears never deed shall she attain, they who rumble in my brain, the falling rocks, the mountain's reign, rumbling earthquake and lava's black stain. Nothing grows here until it breaks, seeds taking root in cracks, which is why we with the hammer smack, importing strength, stories, and drive we lack. I don't motivate myself very well, but I can still run towards heaven or away from hell, follow river's flooding swell, to the delta spread, sink in the air and grow later bread, carbohydrates to feed my head.

I know I say I want, I want, but that is a lawful lie, what I want is not me, but rather honey to the bee. Nectar from beautiful flowers in field or on tree, wild fulfilling a need, endless colors I see, scents floating on the breeze, golden beginning far more than it seems, like some ice cream. Now sweet now cold, first together then alone, it harms our head, we hold, waiting for the pain to disappear, for sharp construction to be no longer near. All that was dead we transform, all that was golden we burn, dire-wise, botania-side, petals we grind and mix to match our wits with mana-glasses and tricks, first with a plan and later in a fit, hiring the screen and our heads with fist, our eye slowly beginning to twitch. Like drawing out nits with comb, we cleanse and clean our hair with our hands, surface massage of ayurvedic bands, so that we might halt and stall before we drop TNT and destroy this all, in honest rage call chaos to the law, suck in darkness to our maw, eromakasi, spirit like lion's paw.

And having done such a thing, accepted our own hate and sin, brought our ruined parts within, we raise the heat, the furnace breath, reforge our own iron seeds and beat us, body and soul to pieces, razorgrass arisings among mirror-flash horizons, five hearts clash, one for each engine of the world, one for each spear hurled. Let loose, fly from fist, they twirl, in parabolic pattern fall, this is what we have, words, mind, and all; we do not climb but only throw tall, march up to the gates of heaven calling forth challenge and question. Why, why, why, what sound this pokemon cry, I've caught myself, and who am I? But a shadow on the screen, but a chance to shining gleam, but a hammer and anvil unseen, bar of iron I smelt and bring, like pigkeeper working hard to see and sing, I beat and cut my self free, I make my scream real in deed.

Day 66: July 3rd, 2024

To Beauty,

    Fire and water, how do I mix hot with cool, or loving with cruel? Today I played games and painted, not much on my mind, only the passing of time, and the duty before I pass out to rhyme. I'm not sure if this was a day of climbing, or reckoning, myself for short while surrendering heart to head and sleep to bed; not at all half dead, merely one quarter fallen over, leaning too much to one side, in a way managing to hide but not in a way you may see, as in all public appearances I am active and free, like a cat stuck up in a tree. I could come down, I can, only, only - I would rather stand here and wave my fan, playing games with sharp iron fangs and displaying messages before those with the wit to read them, hands showing what my face and lips may not. Instead of selling, I bought, and what I sought was not worth the price, only gold veneer over memories of nice, some distant star that broke the ice. I count it thrice, every hour on the hour, jumping into hidden bower, then displaying severed flower, drooping and sweet, colors and prisons neat. Here, like a dog I beat doorways of bones, howl at the moon, bark at the dark, I don't know what I hear, am sure it is too near, respond with rage do not fear. I could one day, I manage one time, I am evil, but not that slime. - I climb, up the links to dragons beat, red eyes, black nose, blue eyes, white floes, the ice is melting, the shelves are sinking, great bears fleeing and man being fleeced, we're helping the planet but really it's least.

    What do we want the world to be after we leave? Shall it show we were here, or might we disappear, unremembered, unrecalled, lost, and nothing at all? Changing, we are short and tall, round as a ball, dancing in a castle, masks and all. Small steps now, don't fall, one hand here, the other there, hips so, angled flow, at the proper time, let go. We may be the music makers and the dreamers of dreams, but we are also those characters in the screen, the tropes and goats, milked and slaughtered, our hooves gone for glue, our milk sent to feed someone like you. We become sick with flu, brain fog, dumb as log, a zombie breathing, catching, hacking smog. We are ugly now and croak like the frog, deep in the well, until suddenly we hear some swell. We are seven now, on that tree in a river, playing flute as we quiver.

    Are we cast into the cold, are we shivering, are we bold? Brown is the color which comes at the end, too many paints have we dumped in, now water is running out and no brush is clean: The tap sticks, palm sneers, gears slip, rat leers, defense falls, we fear that our art is worthless and our words are bad, that we are hypocritical, silent, and mad, the kind that results finally, only in sad. - Without sunlight why try to be rad? I know I'm lying in a certain way, fail to jump into the lake of mountains of play, and drown beneath the sea of clay. I'm not happy with body, I'm not happy with brain, and between those two I am cast with strain, strung tight between anxiety and pain, my worries going wrong again, my writing stalling in shuffling walk, as I burn when I unlock.

There are great gates inside me between earth and sky, there are so many answers I want to know why, and the only way I find them is to try and bell the minotaur with string and guide, tearing labyrinth apart from inside; my story admitting to golden pride, secret Amazonian temple side, Tenpai dragons, and a golden fleece of hind, plays we read so that in our actions we might not bleed; there are far more powerful dreams than greed, reasons to stay and never flee.

Now, I really am a stupid failure in thought and deed, saying and thinking that but not knowing what I mean. I beat myself up to move, I am an engine black wings unfurled, a sacrifice over volcano hurled. The prettiest maiden in the village, or at least that's what they say, they told the god before they threw me away, but I woke up the next day in the mountains, maid to dragon, listener to the valley of diagon, walker through the alleys of the vain, some mad summer rave, filling time so I may stave off shame, prematurely accepting blame, I seek my name. - Break open this head my nose to find, place my soul to grind on Stone, imagine myself alone, alone, because to be surrounded is to panic, and to be seen is to go manic. I call out medic, medic, and no-one answers because no-one is left, only me, and my book on the shelf, songs to the elf, both good and bad, chrome-born, tinker-ridden, as if blood was a mode, or made mind. I read of that kind, poems and lines, memories of home and climate of knives, onions and chives. Cooking on the stove, then burning rove over sea and under hill, west of sun until my fill - I have drunk and found, east of moon as I become unbound.

Sealed in my left eye I hold love and hate, and my right sight partakes of logic and view, belief in patterns high and few. There are eight kinds of if-then and four types of and, or many forms both necessary and sufficient for use, as long as fields do not have holes, and trees still make bowls, using standing, and tracing night, scraping away the sides with a sigh. Is it comprehensible what I say, do I lie or show or bay? Like howling noon, a dog left us too soon with work undone and marshy fen, some strange and feather-cut end, iron-gall ink, and bow not bend. Delicate is the picture to make thick mixture, ourselves the two-tones trickster, very opposite of a hipster, as in near west side loft hind, second story, deer's chime, wild climb. How do I mix hot with cold? By going mad, by making old, by throwing myself a thousand years away at night, coming back today and fight, mixing matching paint and light, but really it's the words that hold our might: Maybe, maybe, we are not slight, and if not as Icarus attend to flight, maybe as mermen swim and bite; I wonder what lake water tastes like.

Day 67: July 4th, 2024

To Beauty

    Not every word must rhyme, as long as I do a good job every time; what is art compared to evil me? Only a single drop in the sea. Tiny steps are all I have, molehill mountains, deadly fountains, disappearing foundations. I think there's a part of me that wants to give up every night, stop the fight, sleep not write, give up to darkness and stay away from sun's light; I become filled with misery, avoidance, and fright.
    To you who listen not, the wind in the trees and spark-lights gleaming, shivering ice that cracks and breaks, or large world-tree eating snake, please understand why I do this: I make mistakes, or act out memories that are fake, because I do not trust fate. What I write about is not for me, and as I hear certain songs that sing of that which I do not name, or read books where laughing I feel shame, hiding because I don't want anyone to see what's in my brain. I attempt integration, my own emotion and body investigation, inscribing in paper and stone my memories of loss of home, when triangles were fell, and rectangles were hell, when Rome burned and in Notre Dame rang the bells because there was flame below, and hell, Quasimodo of the second string, an evil priest that never shall find spring in source, or admit to thirst and worst while the hero runs off with the dame. Realistic, but never the same. I think rather that Merida was the winner of that game, wild bear and arrow's hame, heart's love and defiant clang, a clamor for a name demanding choice, power red as night, or like Elsa cold and bright. What is the answer when purple is your sight, the thousand flags that never fit right, like pins in a donkey, the tail airy, each child dizzy as they try. But there is no party here, and I launch my chance in ways which are never clear; this is my coward's dance I fear, smiling only as long as no-one is near.
    My air is not clear, filled with smog and smoke, I read poems written in 1938 by strange old folk, then over and over again turn my eyes away or choke, false-weeping, chest tightening, breath leaving, wheat reaping, seeds buried in the ground coming up and turning round, the eye of the sun is so loud. I want, I want, to be proud, but I don't know what that looks like. I literally cannot picture myself in ten years, I draw a blank, I draw a shroud, cannot fin me in the crowd. Take off my face, and what shall we see? Perhaps an empty basket used for carrying toys, old discarded ones like Rodolph's friends, or maybe shining rings, like

harem of Shana's friend dreams, the one like me whom to society is not as he seems, lands stuffed with food, but nobody to feed, and unable to articulate his past, present, or future needs. I say I'm tired all the time, but I don't know what that means. Back hurt, knees bent, head explodes, cardinal sin of turtledoves, unaware symbols of hopes and love, songs fitting me as two fingers do in a glove; not enough.

I know I am not, I know it in my bones, I am a thing, mere fragment of nightmare scream, like a piece of vanilla ice cream left out too long in the sun: Runny, and disgusting, unlinked, untrusting. Here is goblet of flame, there Durendal's claim, a cauldron to bring back the dead, and Dagda sending you in his stead. Where are the people with hawks and horses and cow and Anubis heads, unnamed creatures in starry beds? Anansi, do you have a story? Where would I find a string of glory, some monkey's paw or burnt crow's caw, Mankey fighting against Buddha's law? Listen to the world's mumbling maw, the darkness is emotion and it glows, blackbody radiation of Vestara Khai, you could have managed not to lie. Alas, overwhelmed, I did not try, and afterwards for that failure I never said I cried; although these are not the words, mere shadow of a flame, burning memories tied tight, collapsing barrier giant's height, now some lazy lion's bite.

This is only awkward reflection of prison play, this is my stupid means to run away, but from what, them or me, sand or trees, lake water or high school band, cool rocks on palm of hand? What I paint does not make sense, what I write is what I am lent, who I am is something bent, key without lock, head cheerleader who doesn't like jocks, no movement on the clock no matter how I wind; though I carry on my back ten thousand lightning-rocks, flint and steel ground to meal, grist for the page, faint reflection of a sage like the bear on the wall who snarls or elephant in the park, Dumbo flying like rainbows, prism unfurled, a pinion hurled, a feather first flight then burl. Demonic adversary, do not listen to me. - Never ask em who I mean, if in my direction you will never lean, or seek some hero rich and clean, driven, a driver of the world, a knight of the word, for I am no man nor lady, or cat or dog, neither frog in well or insect on a log, neither will o' wisp or siren's fog .- Merely slowed down by Newman during a jog, look but never touch, drink but never suck, like but do not think, eyes on the blink.

Which is why we have words, to comprehend how we are thrown, beaten black and blue, hammers of bone deeper than delvings of the gnomes or closets at home. - Who are we now shown? Shorn of dress like cats at rest, pauldrons breaking failing test, a storm unspoken of dreaming token, no face, no name, no game, no claim, only snake's rain, four pieces sent to the grave.

Day 68: July 5th, 2024

To Beauty,

    Why am I dreaming like this, what have I missed, by using a broken fist? It's funny, I can write of fear, but explaining it is worse: I imagine someone in front of me and curse. - Don't picture it, don't name it, don't act on it, don't think it, don't shame it, don't game it, figure out what to do and how to do it. - If I over-drink of laughing penguin I sink, made not wolf but fink, as trembling one tear falls, but never, never all. I hate, I love, I escape the world, I run away into that bright and shiny summer's day, but never look and never stay. I have such strange dreams and do not dare to scream because I feel my ripping seams, falling sink of immortal rink where Buddha fights the unlucky man, seven tokens in one evil hopeless hand, seven sins under empty body's command. The spirit has flown like Hugin of the wings, to ten thousand fusioning versions of how to sing, or where to seek invisible ring, a power to peek on dragon's gold, but also stretching which makes one a fool, our life merely dark lord's tool. I disappear, replaced by me, blinded, saltless, dying on the sea, I fear the albatross but no traitor shall I be. - Let all wild beautiful things go free, even if by doing so I lose the strength to straighten knees, only able to crawl on the ground and never again saying please; praying some muse would sing of me and tell me so, with great, glorious, impossible show, possessing production values of one heart, and requirement of entry for art, recalling me even apart.

    But I know enough not to hope for that, and never seek it, and never ask, for I am both too much and not enough; I fall too low, I rise too high, imagine too fast and think too slow, water myself and never grow, I am like that star which refuses to glow: Dark moon of chaos, Raistlin's show, Tiamat's maw, Nidhogg below, Shiva cuts, Anubis bellows, Hades over time grows more mellow. - Finding spring, reason not to be forgetful sting, attercop, attercop, where is your stirring, where are my strings, where might that red string be, in red land or buried with a corpse beneath the sea, growing moldy, green like you wouldn't believe? Even so, we quietly and carefully write, in mad ways stay out of sight, only think of hope at night. This may not be, this cannot be, this will never be. - I know this, like I know trees, red, gold, black, frosty things, iron elves, rainbow selves, pink princess and blue hell. Hell like the moon, heaven near the sun, purgatory the stars, my wish made undone, and with that doing no muse by me flowing, no beauty, only terrible eatings, which is why I close my eyes so often and dream. I am not a happy thing. -

But what would I else-wise be? I don't know what I have in me, and if I did we would never tell, only show in ways like snow; silently we fall, rolled into freezing balls with carrot nose and coal for eyes, but Calvin's kind that are whipped upon and dined, made squares or triangles and turn out fine, returned from whence they came, but with wisdom which is not a game. They taught us, even young, that a child's heart should never be hung on the gallows of excellence or stuffed into Wally's desk, because this egg is the nest. Would you be half-formed or malignant, would you have three wings or two, would you be hammer or wooden shoe, a bucket trying to tear you apart, roots of another's art, beaten into shape to work, spend, and save, never inventing, never being brave? Is this all that survival means?! - I will not let it be. I will not have another November so that I may flee. I will be free, or dead and buried, I am so tired of being carried, I am no witch nor warlock, see no red star, able to stand here only because I have traveled far.

Strength covers sensitivity as blood covers a wound. I quietly yell and silently fall, never dance as Belle or at ball, no glass slipper, no swan feather, no voice, no eyes, only art, only heart, only hands falling apart. I'm not crazy, only last and hazy, pieces of fire that don't work well together, ash to compress, pointless life needing rest. At best, I may look at what someone else likes, the cats they save, the plans they pave, the way they rave and celebrate, for I long ago lost that vision's mate, spending my birthday alone, because of how sad I've grown. I do not glow and the fifth of November moves torturously slow, reflecting back, receiving, in the know, all my failed moments wrapped up in one big pretty bow: A present president of shattered joy; see the trees, the falling leaves, again and again I mutter to myself, ever bitter, please, I attempt to make something a sweet, brittle apple-bread to torturous beat, drinking barrel-aged whiskey neat,- or I would if that ever helped to think, or had any promise in all my reading of not bringing me to sink, because I never do more than eat alone. Three rules I have; I've kept them to the bone, do not promise, do not trust, do not reach for any more than August, sudden flash of heat and flame, summer circling to drain. While I have my vices, poor sins that suffice, what I do not possess is clear glacial ice, the type that made valleys nice. It is in the mountains that I found knives, saws to cut myself and sights to thrive, poor stupid rainbow braids of time, ladders that sunward climb, winter made not numb, but mine; and I do not ask, I do not say, but maybe I will admit one day, if I ever am by courage slayed, or requested to explain.

Day 69: July 6th, 2024

To Beauty,

    I had a dream of oceans blue, where whales flew and mankind played along the shore, where you smiled in wonder at what came before; unlike me, so afraid, you seemed brave, and that made me want to be brave too, even if I don't know how. "Stick closer together", I once heard you say, but I pull myself apart in desperate attempt to make art of life, or savior from strife. These moments are to me as a knife, skin and muscle ripped off to show bone, because I have dreams like this for months at least, when I think too much or feel a lonely beast. I can put names to faces and a picture to a presence; these ghosts are not invisible anymore, real phantasms passing through door and warm metal tubing on heated floor during the January cold, when water freezes in the pipes and mice run in to hide from knight, armored symbol of duty and right, the feudal law of man, proscribing proper placement of poor peasant and pious priest, pied fool and proud king. Were we were born as this? Do not dream, follow four casts as you die, so that you may earn a better place alive. How sorrowful are those lies? Dreams like this tell me I should thrive; that a smile from those eyes is for challenging fate and moving beyond circles of hate, magic spiral upward Zeus-led gate.

    Golden apples do not offer immortality, only youth, the power, promise, and sight of days begun, the opportunity and space to trip as we run. Children are supposed to make mistakes. Every hero was forgotten before he was made. Every princess precocious before she was queen enchained, made symbol not person. So, free from this curse by dream brought, where go you, cruel shadow's bride, how shall we glide? There is danger in too little as well as too much pride, perfection battling persistence, fleeing finding missing, cats and serpents both may hiss, just as they might imagine a kiss.

    Of course, that's not in our dreams, or at least none we recall, because we block out our vision from our fall. This isn't some story, it's gory, with messy red, pink, and tan pieces everywhere, a confusion of a crime scene, ocd monkish screen, or how Watson cleans in surgery, and Sherlock runs in snow-swept flurry. Down tumbles mountain stream, mighty goddess Danube or Nile black and rich, unexplored Amazon, yellow walls, the mighty Mississippi, the small piece of ice behind the shadow of Olympus Mons, and that moon's ice-covered pond filled with alien cephalopods; fantastic reality, slumbering polarity, unconscious gathering of what I cannot say, even to myself, and never in light of day where someone might hear me and cut my strings, Lu Bu unhorsed, still mighty, but worse. - I am half-damned, written but not said, twilight ogre with only one head, a battery for a shield, corn unground for meal, and no guidance for the keel.

I was finished, that's what I said, but still I have these dreams in my head, and some stupid wish driving me out of bed, because otherwise my purpose of art is dead. These words and paintings are for me, but not to me, they are by me, but not at me, they are every day working from memory, the un-persistent kind but in reverse: They energize the line, five volts straight to the heart, some socks on a cat like a dart, algorithm driving me again to start. - But what? Should I say? To make my issues go away? How do I accept who I am, all fire and all clay? What is this song in my head I play, where I imagine I would see you and say - nothing. I cannot picture it, but that doesn't mean I cannot do it. I am walking around in a daze, losing my way in a maze, and somehow by this pathing saved; an empty field means no enemy may exclaim the end of my turn, or make lame this hand that burns. Underground leads the hatch, to sewers where turtles learn, slow and steady wins the race, improve yourself without haste and turn even waste into gold; paper news, March brews, witch of stew, throw everything in Big Anthony, from carrot to stone, howl at the moon, pretend you are not alone! And if you do this long enough, well enough, it is only hope for home, or at least some new biome where you may delve for the diamonds you need, magic experience, enchanted steed, beyond the limits of Ashley's greed. Not to be seen but to make, not to draw but create. What care I for popularity as long as I'm happy, what care I for fashion as long as you smile at me? Eagle-like, I aim for tallest point of tree, then falling hunt; nay flee. I am true and open as I can be, poor thing that I am, crawling coward, but with flash in pan, maybe someday stand, if as I die Valkyrie take my hand, and show me purpose; member of fighting band, bound beyond laws or gods.

And I know this shall never be, if I give up fighting, even beaten beyond my knees. Berserker spirit, fall upon me please, let me see, driven to speak, struck by lightning on mountain peak, as into my life Diana did sneak, sister of Apollo and hunter of beast, wild spirit who never accepts being least; would you kill me and feast? For these are my dreams and those my poems, songs and skalds of the oldest stories allowed, the spirits of all things and reasons not to leave. I am led by ancient path over golden haired wrath to talk with wild men civilized by sin, so that I might understand this horrid sacrificial poem within, the magic of word and wind, wings uplifted and grain unpinned, scattered across the fields so that we imagine I could plant and yield, instead of gathering wild blackberries, cutting and stabbing myself every single time. I want to do more with my smile than whine, and to forge hope using those miracles I find. I want to unalive and then rebind. I will break myself open to bring the truth outside. I will to myself not be kind. I will live or die with pride. I dreamed I did not lie. I dreamed it all was fine.

Day 70: July 7th, 2024

To Beauty,

  What would I see if I did not listen to me? I paint pictures dull and shrill, evil within and at the mill, all the colors I show are but tints of my soul, a bowl upended the very limits of sky, while demon hands reach out, and from the mountains try to tear down Pandemos walls and Athenian halls. Marble is shattered by Turkish gunpowder and Venetian cannonball, warring tribes deciding that history is bull, to be used as we will, not learning taking, not making breaking, doomed to repeat our tales, doomed to hammer in new nails in old holes, forgetting that without new cuts they will not hold, forgetting in our blind humility the price of being bold; how victory comes to those who remember what they were told, mixing and mashing, melting and casting in those ways both hot and cold, where everything is between us, or nothing of gold. Worthless we are cast out, and so what? We shall bring the apocalypse about, mutating ourselves until even the dinosaurs hear us shout. Our lives, our goals, our lights, will not be shut, ourselves being not the next step but the first, the beginning of thirst, of what it means to be human and not a thing worst. I remember wild eye cause I was too near their purse, I recall the fear of those who watched me fall to earth, I saw my own eyes mirrored back at myself when I turned away from pain, and abandoned all my attempts at straining towards the goal, or at least the pool at the heart of the world; passage to spheres untold, places of honor and odious law, ten steps beyond passions' maw, ten years past the crow that caws; Morrigan, Tanavast, Arcueid, Brimstone, where are you, gods that were, that are, and may yet be, pillars of four-cornered sea and the eight winds. - Eight lucky happy ones, seven and hidden star, last remnant of the nine dead, arrows sent to slay wild child in lessons stead, abandonment of right and cost, this is how glory is lost and heaven falls: By profaning those pillared halls where dreams and hopes aim and lie, where stories were written before earth and sky, before time and love, before ever fell feather of the dove. Pen to write, flint to strike, ferret-spirit now to bite, and here comes fighting dragon, sharp tail-kite, falcon pulling sun from night; reborn as Light.

  What if I am not a failure, what if this is passage meant, what if I am filled with power from the past me lent? Not a journey to nowhere, but good silver spent, stolen Spanish gold returned to land of its birth, one tenth of me through my veins does burst. - Only one eighteenth of me may be native but I hope it is a silver piece of love, one ankle tied to the sand as I wield this iron glove, throwing hammer strikes, thunder from above; I am pierced by thistle with a green lilt in my voice as my flesh remembers the circle of stones, or oak raised in mountain home, forgotten jungle ash and nameless loam, all parts of the past which have grown; I stand as part of tree, apple seed, not alone, simply unknown.

The colors I paint, the symbols I let loose, they are not my inventions nor my tome, although it is through my voice they carry a mystical tone: Rhythm of pounding feet or violins at sleep, guzheng bone and flute from lips so sweet, sweat of the back and beak; wolf howls, falcon calls, now down the peregrine falls, rabbits I once saw die and ate no more, in guilt I tore the world. Warp and weft, I hide the cleft, continent ripped in two, a valley of time separates me and you; I write so I may journey through, Black Temple in Karabor cleansed of fumes, demon's eyes, glowing, staring, doom; madman swinging his arms around, a Sufi blade-dancer swoons in all the room shown by the brightness of three hundred moons, as fierce fire freeing godhead looms. I know better than to ask for a boon; but I try anyway, wings of flame, walk away.

As I sit here, thinking of times I would return to if I could reverse the turning of the years, what comes to my mind is a picture of a tower I never saw, and a trip to Cambridge's law. I was interested, I think, to attempt to meet, or travel in train and seek the story of history, but instead I felt only mystery as to why you would be telling me of tomorrow while I am filled with such sorrow that I was not invited, and you are not inviting me now, or at least that's how I think, as if I was a horse tied to a plow, stock-still unless directed, because existence and movement is work; and if I say what I really mean, that I would like to go, I'd feel like a jerk for imposing my interests and my presence on your perfect trip, and I'd feel so bad if you said get - get of here boy - go away - you are not welcome next day; and I know this is an overreaction of my fragile self, and I know life would be better were I sanguine as an elf, and I know how it's really not rude to ask, but if I'm not invited directly I take myself to task: Hiding, as always, again and again behind my mask. In front of you I already lose half my mind, and I want this chance to be close or at least hang around, but I cannot break my binding sound, the scream that rips through me, grounding lightning, ending circuit, turning my muscle stiff like stone. I'm paralyzed and I don't know how to say I'd rather not be alone, and I'd really, really like to go; but I can't, throwing away even the possibility of a blind chance, because I am too anxious, tired, and scared to dance, and I'm too ashamed of my every glance; thoughts and words turn to ash.

This happened at least three times, for tower, for Bath, for bar, and perhaps half of these are wrong in my imagination so far, myself making mountains from molehills and apocalypses from awkwardness, but if they were in reality even half of what I feel today, then they are those sorts of regrets where I would say to a genie: Take me back, take me back, allow me to take another tack, allow me to say to gods and fate let me choose again, late me choose again please, and not be dead, to leave my grave-stone bed, hope never dies, and my hope is that I might backward fly, make a different choice and not lie or hide. Something was broken inside and now I can see it, admit it, but I cannot....I cannot, fix it. There are no more chances but for this. There are no more dances but for this. There are no more smiles but for this, in these words of misery and mist. Why did I listen to myself - so that I could end up like this!?

    I need to be brave, but I don't know how. I need to fly, but the best I may do is walk on clouds, I need to climb but the only movement I consistently manage is an uncontrolled falling in a vaguely upward direction, doubting every choice I make in every situation, and under every investigation, because I am sure I have committed crimes, even if I don't know what they are. I do not dare show myself to the star, not without traveling away from this so incredibly far, until my scars are made saw blades and swords, Mak'gora for the heart of the Horde. My enemy is myself, and my choice of venue is that book on the shelf. Listen to me, I, and we shall see whispers of how to be free. A soul to find, wolf unbind, smiling summertime, cause, care, kind, scared, speaking, dare, more than stare, fairy fair, key to mountain, creek to fountain, wisdom wells in Apollo's hell, and the dog rings the bell. - I am not well. But sick as I may be, you're the sting that I need, so that I may no longer listen to coward me. Wing of flame so dear, set me free. Set me free. Can you show me how to set myself free?

Day 71: July 8th, 2024

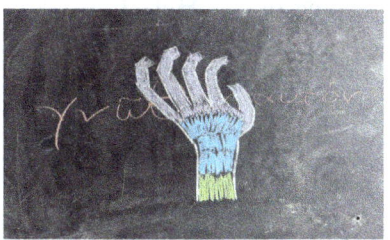

To Beauty,

      Could I bare to exist, to lay and not make art like a fist? Simple, pretty, paper words that fade away in the sunlight as mist, are enough on some days; for I have created, I have made, constructed, portrayed, some vein of my soul, or endless despair and rage, just enough that I have rattled the cage; but too much is sorrowful, and sad. I just repeat myself, made mad, but without any hint of glad, as into the glade I wondered and stayed. Unicorns around me danced and with fairies I played, gnomes with mushrooms, dwarves with mead, goblins with sweet fruit which they sell at market, practically giving it away, for with sisters and brothers we dance forever at play, never looking beyond this momentary day, never attempting our chains to slay or put fire to clay, we are not strong. - I don't know if we will last very long, or what shall memory be of us in song. "Gil-galad was an elven king, of him the harpers sadly sing"[9], yet what of those forgotten dead, heroes of the watery bed, what names and positions held they? Is it now possible for any of us to say?

      I think if I want to write a book, it needs to be a change, not for the reader, but for the mage. I am not who I was before writing that book, the act of making it my self has shook, and although I readily admit to being recognizable, still cowardly and afraid, I have moved at least in one way: That when I pass some day, strangers will find among my remains what I saw and felt, the struggle, forging, destroying melt, how I handled the weaknesses I was dealt. Yells and whispers, some lost, others found, a great crashing of sky-step stairs to ground, an awareness that the wall I am speaking to is not to be gotten around. This demonic adversary, this silver mirror sound, is like blood in my veins that pounds, a red river of iron and energy, vitamins and minerals, nine amino acids, twenty thousand proteins, the necessary building blocks of life and time. - This is ambrosic wine to the starving child, gate to the mead of Valajar. I am broken on the shore, but so what? I see the shadow's door, mad demons hidden behind iron key, passage to a cruel and hopeless beauty to whom I am a beast, prince who never on rose shall feast, always a dog holding her own leash.

      What am I if I do not move? Merely boy locked in tomb, runaway ship without buoy or light, no passage to safe harbor at night. My eyes are blinded and yet I fight, walking with trembling hands and like a vampire bite, blood within me warms because of the storm, invested breath of Garm. Breaking out of Hel, three heads of harm, I will be warm or I'll burn the barn. Can't hit the broadside, which is why I hold knife in kind, stone-knapped piece of mind, cutting not in straight line but following contours of the soul, memories made new by legends of the old: Plato's poetry throwing me out of the cold, and his pageantry making me feel almost bold, as if there was a place on this earth where I could do more than I was told is possible. As I learned, of freedom, fire, and life to burn, - what is this pain? I will take it, I will turn this plane around, take my chances on the ground, using not mechanical machines, steel torn from the earth, but instead the power of my birth; that I exist, that I act, that I have a chance to move and be cracked, open spilling light, blind by spirit bright, blighted by the mirror's reflecting tripe, which I hear is tough and hard to chew, although that sort of meat isn't for me or you. I'm working through all of this, by throwing paint on the wall and seeing what sticks. I use tape and pens and chalk and rain, my hands by failure of vision stained, I have not obtained what I tried, and even the best of my art is half-way to a lie, because I cannot pour out what I feel inside. Somehow, no matter what I do, I hide: There is always, always, more to find: In each and every picture and poem I seek out my mind, like a dwarf I delve too deep; my bones burned, my body turned into a nest for rats, I lose my path until I take another tack, thrown like a Goldberg machine, broken, scattered, running back, this self-confusion is no act.

    Woe betide the man who loses the heart of a child, the willingness to wonder in the woods lost for a while, happy to smile because he is saving the world with magic stick for a sword. Barefoot boy, running, he finds angelic hordes, tall trees filled with sunlight and birds, best friends to those hurt by life and living; yelling, betrayal, learning, the child knows not anything but a yearning, empty spaces filled with green, wide waters and moonlight sheen, stars filled with cats that sing, eating of those magic books which bring passage to worlds unseen, staircases of Droon, pyramids, and dream, one fairytale seam, mithril, silver-steel; now touched and seen to show us how the world is more than it has been, that the challenges of history are not at an end; sudden, sharp, poetry lives again, ourselves weavers and brushes to spin. We dig in the sand to uncover the wind.

    Oh fill us breath of autumn's being, oh burn us summer's ancient skein, oh freeze us iron winter's scream, oh release us brilliant growing spring! The waters and fountains run wild now from mountain, ungoverned flood filling up the world with mud, great growing plaza for ten thousand years. We wake from the tomb and are more than our fears, are equal to tears, this is how we reforge our heart light and clear, feather-diamond being near, not a 'thing' now, but a 'person' in deed, attending to the Harper's greed; one heart's desire and one ancient need, as on my own destruction here I feed, cut myself to bleed, and write in red ink upon the page, to display in red ink my rage. I am free, and, and isn't that wonderful for me? ...But what now should I be?

Day 72: July 9th, 2024

To Beauty,

    Do you have close-held personal dead, last recollections and memories of sweet bones in your head? Perhaps a cold pet, soft and warm, some love that never did harm until the days and years after it was gone? Perhaps there are grandparents or siblings, or even strangers on the street, who suddenly in the corner of your eye you see and try to greet, because you know them and wouldn't it be great if it turned out they were who you thought they were: A soul winding its way through time to meet you again in rhyme; as looking into each other's eyes, smiling you shine, recognizing the drawn lines of a true friend clear beneath the grime of life, strife, and knives. We are pulled apart from each other by laws and chance, by bombs and commands, the entire time almost convinced that we could stop it, if we had just held tighter to them with our hands, or been kinder before the coming of the funeral band. Everywhere we look is loss, everything we touch has a cost, for if we let it into our heart we are sure to one day be storm-tossed, thrown off the heavens, crashing down to hell, wings rent from us and around our neck a bell, bleeding. With every movement sound swells, echoing of skulls: Here, with broken soul and messed-up head, we are surrounded with pictures, points, and failures to the dead.

    Could we have done better, could we have tried harder, could we have been wetter, our toes dipped in the sea when we should have dived, and swam with our grief, become like coral reef, living skeletons too cold for this hot world? But like sunflowers that have the temerity to breath, we are transformed into gold, seeds growing free and cruel. As all colors fade, our pains go away, world becoming but gray. We continue the motions, we draw breath, we spend hours curled into our nest, we don't know what becomes next. We are not at our best, for what reason have we to work or stare, what reason have we to live or dare? Fear has fled and so has care. We do not even open our eyes, for we see enough of the clouds that cover the sun; we know enough of the night that comes when all is done. For one more day we've won, survived, but at what price? Our light, the ability to burn or fight.

    So for days, months or years at least, our sparks are stolen, our steel is dulled, we continue the motions and everyone is fooled, even golden spirits of gods to us are cooled. Kahil's books lead us to feel old before our time, for in the depths of my soul there is a wordless song, but I do not hear its rhyme; truth is the son of blood and I have known it's crime, that what we exist for is on what we dine. All salt has left me, all tears are dried, and I have stopped in the middle of my climb, because the stars are covered and the moon does not shine, there is no reflection of lemon or lime. Life gives unto us nothing but a misery of time, endlessly out of rhythm with the world, endlessly broken, tail curled, toy in our paws, we followed the laws but received no good boy's reward; we are less than dogs, less than logs, less than lumps in fog, nameless, faceless dangers to avoid. We are strangers to the world, all our belongings upturned, spilled like red wine, staining dirt, floor, and white. We were never innocent on the inside, but maybe we had a dream we could have been; stronger than eternal sin.

We never learned of good and evil but were taught; we tried and tried, but happiness was never bought, not by work or hope, not by prayer or bargain, for gods and devils in us war, and ever we tread toward final door; and that is a price we would gladly pay, if only we could the journey for others stay, - but to live for them? Oh, that is too much, today. I remember once reading these words: "Does your loyalty lie with the living or the dead?"[10] To ask the question is to answer it, because we are the ones who inquire. In songs and poems, in bells and walls, in standing up and falling down, in saying we can do this, over and over again, we can do this, we can do this, we can survive, until it stops sometime. For we hope that it stops, we know that it might, and that it will be back to bite, every minute, then every hour, then every day, then every night, and finally a week, a month, a year goes by where it only hurts as we peek at the sky, or when out of the corner of our eye we spy.

    Now, I no longer cry, only on occasion sigh, because it doesn't work, grief: If that is all you have, there is no relief. We need hope, too, which Pandora saved, or Durandal swords to wave, Grass-cutter we lean upon like a stave, Atlas-pillar between earth and sky, there is a place we must aim for or a reason to try. Get out of bed no longer lie, and do not accept that the earth will forever be a thing to despise, as against fate and gods and devils all we rise. Today we ride, to fell wrath and ruin, a red nightfall. We may be assassins but we hear the horn's call, wild hunt says look there is the belle of the ball, some magic remains after noon, glass slipper in the center of the room. It's fine in the middle of death to act like a loon, if that's what it takes to howl at the moon, echoing in the hills booth to bone, art to tome, lost cat searching for home, the doom of dog tired of being alone.

    Do you have your dead? I have mine, and I wish this knowledge you may never find, because it clings and burns like quicklime, setting burning lake on fire and quenching any vision or rest or desire. I don't want to eat or sleep, breath or wish, only simply somehow in some impossible way be done with this. Can I not rend my limbs and return to being a fish, amphibian from before the seas had descended from mist, or life awakened because of cosmic ray's kiss? I'm not nothing, I can help, but I'm not sure what to do with the cards I've been dealt, for with my heart I cannot bring myself to care. It is only through you that I look at the upper air, stare at dead feet on a table, and know that others may do what I am not able. Will you send me a message, cable underneath the sea, of the worth of the living, the dead, and me? I'll remember, I'll advocate, but I'm not sure what to be, when from the gold and the silver I always flee.

Day 73: July 10th, 2024

To Beauty,

    Of course my ethics are excuses; I freely admit they are flawed, yet nevertheless they follow that iron law: Who I am is what I do: The limits of out are the limits of in, my good face acting as my evil twin: A story of force attempting to win, a book where with each new page my excuses seem but as wind, hear today and gone tomorrow, sweeping away all statements and sorrows, blood born in the marrow, red hiding white, just as my mind obscures my sight. I fill my head up with vision of light, and hide my numbers at night; how many times did I whisper a name, how many times did I feel guilty and stained, how many times did I silence the rain, how many times did I say I can do this when I felt strained? I saw a call for help, I saw a condemnation of evil delt, and I stayed silent about all I felt, because it was confusing, seeing every side, and knowing that each and every one of them is partway a lie, but also knowing that my view on this is not kind, the result of me leading a suspicious life. There is always more to learn, and an invisible angle to turn, fourth dimension, or five, either way some line I did not see before, some hidden axiom or result of Euclid's lore. I have become a bore, swiftly ignored but cutting though the mountain a door, far beneath the sky-swept floor, out of sight of sun and moon, no nesting place for coon or loon, but to the human in me a boon, a place to hide, a rock to fight: My own ugly dwarven stair-flight, filled with smiles darkly bright, secret smirks which none shall see but I and you, a sickness running through me as the flu. I no longer speak, I cannot breath, my throat is sticky and my nose does bleed; it takes all my energy merely to breath here beneath the hill in air stifled and still, hidden from all glorious rills, brooks and creeks where fishes sleep in summer hot beneath the bridge my Grandfather built. I look around me and see all I am not, neither brave nor driven, neither stricken nor striven, I take much and give little back, I brake but have not fought, scattered and slow I am a ghost, dead spirit driven from host. I have no spine - simply a ladder my body climbs, soul driven from mind.

    Who am I? Let's find out, what I do and where I dare, who I hate and why I care, all my actions called good and bad, all the actions I do with my hand: Money spent, paint tossed, gentle caress, hammer hot, anvil where I held not. Swords black and white may hold when beaten, but we are a rainbow, pink and green. Who we are is not who we seem, for we do not whisper of our dream; tongue cut, eyes red, teeth that do not stay in bed, deed to need, eat to feed, fire, freedom, and greed. - Because I am always wishing myself away with all these things I never say, bones that are not mine, only unearthed by smiling time and gentle brushes of loss and hope, my question to which the answer will always be nope, I am not the goat; indeed, I am chickens in a coat, pretending to be a man, hen watching the fox. I look in the mirror and become lost, gasping in shame because I will not bear the cost, my heart is not for sale. I will not sell for praise or thanks, I will not give it away for the right and the good, it is not to be buried beneath duty, nor burned up in the flames of righteous war, and the five relationships I will toss out the door. Mary, Peter, and God are not my law, golden stature but straw, art passes, words fade, but to Beauty I turn my gaze, ideal form I love and praise, pillared stone where lever lays, to move the world I say: Be mine, for I would care if you cared, I would dare if only you dared. I will write even as I am scared, like fifteen-year old girl at first flush, or that boy in Brazil who I heard did blush. We are confused, and so as my ethics are used, I place them down and review.

There are things I have done I shall never tell, pots on the road into which I stumbled and fell, times in which I found myself in, or was worthy of Dante's Hell, circles five to seven, though I also visit one and eleven. I'm sure I have other sins too, but I do not remember them, they did not strike me through, I never totally succumbed to them or you. Oh, demonic adversary, with what wings we flew! You are illusion, not real, but still, for this I'll take my turn at the mill, though that choice is ill, because this is the only way my silent screaming I might kill. Thus by my actions measure my will, even as my execution is a bitter pill, too big for comfort and too small to heal, the medicine I take with water and meal that allows this numb bug to feel. "I know I've gotta keep moving on, and I know inside I'm strong"[11], but I need to look out to carry on, because the worst of my ethics is that I want to give up, dive into ground and drink from Lethe cup, because I am so tired of never being enough, and I don't know if I have it in me to tough it out forevermore. Which is why I to the whole world shout, wide-eyed running about, finally seeing reasons not to flee. I will fight, be free, sure failing at the end, but what care I, if I lived a little before I died? What if I smiled even as I cried? Better to be destroyed than to never have tried, because speaking to a muse I didn't lie, and I saw the Sunrise. Sunrise. Sunrise. Clear eyes.

Day 74: July 11th, 2024

To Beauty,

    Will I ever have the courage to show you this, to ask that you read what I wrote, or understand what I felt? I fear not - I write to what does not exist, because I suffer nightmares of who I missed. I have had such strange dreams, filled colors of the sea, sharp teeth, hands filled with rocks; I go to bed trying to be warm, and wake up burning hot; I don't know why I feel such a terrible shock, as if in the echo of an apocalypse clock I outsee truth and God. I shake and hold myself, trying to breath, to calm, casting my mind away to a place that can't do me harm, covering my wounds with a balm, a boon unlocked for and unasked, and then I set myself again to task. During odd moments, walking in the street or sitting beneath a tree, I feel the strangest needs, I find myself wondering what fingers taste like or how neck is pierced by vampire's bite, I lose my hold on the earth, flying as high as a kite, and yet the only drug I ever took was a beautiful sight, some half-moment of half my life feeling almost half-right. Utterly confused by a star at night, knowing in the depths of my soul fright and shame, because one day I told you I didn't remember your name, and I never tried, and I'm all to blame. The only game I can play are these poems, the only way I ever existed was alone, and now...now I want to pick up the phone.

    But it's too much. I know that several years of writing is too much, and yet conversely I also know just how ai is not enough, for I have nothing to give. I don't think you'd like me if you knew. If I said something and you never replied, I don't know what I'd do. I can take no, I'd survive, but silence? I wouldn't feel alive. So I'm quiet. I write, I send my doves out, but never shout. I have wings like a bird, mind like a cat, I watch from afar and hide, curled up in jars, or disguised by sunlight bars; shocked eyes, wide surprise, meowing I'm hungry feed me I lie, showing only my tail as I pass by, mere tip of mind's eye. Perhaps you have seen my art, or remembered when I had in the plays my set part as an audience member. I have shown pictures of flowers and trees, books I read, and pieces of one I worked on. I have hidden your name, as a penguin or a rune, and I have never, ever, ever said that for you I'd swoon, because you would hate me, I'm such a loon, empty wolf howling at empty moon.

    This has never happened to me before, I have never acknowledged an existence like a door, or known someone who made me want to lift myself off the floor. I've read books before of men and women, but never understood, only taken it as given. I possessed embers and thought they were flames: Made confused and damned by my aim or my eyes, my ears that did not hear, my mouth that did not speak, my heart which could not leap. I feel as if I am a sheep, or some chick innocent of giving a peep. I read these books on genders but I don't know which way I leap, I think I'm male, but what role should I play in this game? I want you to ask me, but I know that's not the way it's supposed to be. I'm so afraid of showing you one hint, one glimpse, one whisper of me, because I am drowning in what I see.

You are near, but I don't dare ask questions, I don't dare be curious, because you are safer if you remain mysterious, and I am safer if I don't investigate this, or attempt my mind to untwist. How I look at your limbs or your hair in the wind, how I remember questions you asked, or draw pictures of your braid from the back. Sometimes that smile, that damned smile, that damned smile, that damned smile, it...it just repeats for a while, and I don't feel happy, I feel...I feel lost, because I want you to smile at me like I have never wanted anything before, and I know you will not. I know it to my bones, that people such as you don't like things like me, and that you, you specifically, are too good in every way, like a burnished fire while I am clay, like a cuneiform tablet broken in half, with a tired message only good for one laugh; and so, away I pass, silent as the grave, unable to utter what in me stayed, words without measure, force or rhyme, only the stupid, stupid, stupid wish you might smile at me one more time.

I thought this would pass, was sure it would not last, but I'm really, really, really tired and lost, and somehow writing to you allows me to bear the cost of showing that I have a heart. I can draw and paint, write and create. I can care, every minute of every hour of every day, because I know that when it becomes to much, I can to that dream run away, and I can in that happy place for a short while stay, and when I can do that I may pretend to pray, and follow Plato's vision beyond the sun, even into the world before there was One. I am made insane, or I allow myself to change, as if by throwing my heart away I could, if not gain a soul, at least be turned less than half-whole.

Although, most of the time I know I'm a fool, with bad rhymes and pathetic lines. I couldn't save my cat, all my dogs have died, and I have few friends, though I tried. I don't dance, and sing only when I'm sad. I can't articulate my words when mad, and never found success at school or work. I've tracked the world a little, but never learned how to fiddle when I failed that class in Chicago as I was depressed in shadow. I sit in my room and try not to look at that violin I bought three years ago, and have only tuned four times. I have no money, I have no life, I have no house, I have no direction, and the only skill I ever evidenced in all my life was dictation, - but the kind a gifted child in third grade has, good enough for praise, but not enough to be paid, or for any references ever to be made.

Sent out a hundred poems and never received a reply, and spent all my time for ten years staring at the sky, trying not to feel like wanting to die. I have not cried in fifteen years, not since I buried my fears, and I never grew up right, being too young for my years; about the only adult thing well managed was avoiding arrears. I have no career, and the only reason I'm here is because my family stood by my side, mother and Grandmother keeping me fed, sheltered and clothed, even though I am too old. I do my part, I'm not ashamed, I've worked and studied, been there every time I was needed, through wounds and sickness and toppling trees, through broken fences, twice-painted walls, and bed-side falls, but really any of my siblings could have done that. There is nothing special about my act. I have played the Confucian role of oldest daughter, not eldest son, household care, not honor won. I have no dowry but my flesh, and no gift but this lash. I am not pretty or smart, I make bad art, and my interior convictions are always falling apart.

I am not like you who cares, I am not like you with a soul, I have no treehouse as my goal. I've read the books, I find them and search; for all my lives and all my days I've struck myself with the birch, seven lashes in abandoned church. I am not like you who smiles or swims, I am like me who frowns within. I am not like you whose courage and brains show, I am like me who moves too slow. I am not like you who exists in the world, I am like me who through books has hurled. In my formative years I had teachers and friends, but the best of them were the living dead, wild Diane, old-young Will, Mr. Underhill, and Manji of the thousand kills. I learned from Goku how to fight, learned from Sandy how to seek the light, Capser how to deal with fright, and Housman's poem brought me safe through the night. I am tired, I was born tired, and my strength I found from whay others write and make, my personal stories were by others baked. But you make me write, and like Lina "I am tired of doing nothing anymore"[12], Ray Wing! that smile plucked me like a steel cord. I am lifted up, and by myself struck. Flag stuck.

I know you have your own story, friends and plans, loves and far lands, your own heart to your command, so I never show my hand. I know this isn't normal, I'm not ... nobody writes off and on for two years to someone they barely knew for twenty days. People should not be afraid of their own dreams, or cut their own throat before they can scream. I will never ask again, only stupidly imagine that you'll ask me, because I don't know how to become what I wish to be, for these are not love notes - only my burning smoke. I'm a pathetic joke.

Day 75: July 12th, 2024

To Beauty,

    I try to change myself a little each day, even though these plans often go astray; sometimes for the better, often for the worst, but I don't want to end my life under this curse. I will stretch myself from heaven to hell, attending to this every time my head rings a bell. - I hear the battle swell. I do a little something each day, five push-ups, five pull-ups, hundred pages of a text, half a piece of art. Not much, but a start. I review my book to see what I don't like, and I imagine talking to you every night. I'm moving my teeth, holding my head up straight, opening my eyes, and walking even when I don't feel great. Minor lipomas, headaches, mistakes, what are these but passages through gates? I'm not sick, and after all there are others doing much worse than this; I'm perfectly functional, just with a little pain, physical, mental, magical, intellectual, half on purpose, half interventible, half of what I do is intentional: All the art, if not any of the heart. I only have one way to find the missing parts: By listening to others, not I, by staring at the light, not the void inside. The reason I'm ashamed is because I hide. But hide what?

    The maw, the fire, the hate, the liar, the dragon, the mire, I see all things and agree with all views, good and bad are but illusion to choose, what you do is who you decide to be, spirit to the utmost is free. What law or guideline could I follow except the devil in me, the kind that walks on the bottom of the sea, a crab eight times, or a scorpion in rhyme? Look, do you see the stars? It's nighttime. And like a star, I burn all, crunching and munching, groaning and whining. I am a Gurgi, I am never full, and I may be your companion, but don't take me for a tool. I am neither used nor user, I am neither follower or leader, member of no group or party for many a year, I jump on not a single band-wagon because of fear. Beginning of the cycle, I despise words of both Satan and Michael, and I'll listen to Buddha or Marx for only a short while. Kant may be wise, but he directs not my eyes, and I think both Socrates and Wittgenstein were half truth, and half lies. Plato, Aristotle, Confucius, Mencius, Descartes or Kevin Hart, Liebnitz or Mao, great stories of Arjuna or Varona, theories of gender, or about who is evil and should surrender, all of these to me are like vision of a dream, not entirely real until they gleam, and then I from them may glean nuggets of gold: Wisdom of old, puzzle pieces I could fit into my life this day, words that I say, so that I may draw lessons about the best of ways, and neither by emotions or logic be too quickly swayed. It's not that I don't agree with you - it's that I take months to dive deep and follow through. Take this issue of the struggle in the Levant, between the flags of six stars and the one of three colored bars. At first glance it's simple to condemn: Who are all these idiots? From our view in this far country, apparently all upon we may depend, is that they will fight and fight and fight to no end, because we cannot trust a single one of these made-up governments to only defend. It appears none of these tribes will bend. I've heard thirty years of accusations back and forth, and who am I to say which has the right to the earth, or how peace should be found in that land of immaculate birth? In the past year I've read four histories, two collections of essays, three books of poetry from at least two sides, although I count more than five, and I'm only now starting to understand which ones I should despise; although one rallying cry is simple to make, that the British made a lot o' mistakes.

    But then so do I, for with so much on my plate, I'm not sure how to love, or who to hate. It is so much simpler in life to be quiet, to never show your ability to be violent, and to always have your heart be silent. We learned these lessons early on: Don't feel, don't show, don't say, don't think, do not ever drink. Men are monsters don't you see, and I especially may be, that's what I learned when eyes from me did flee. Now these words are wise, but not always, not at all times. When you are dying of thirst, a beautiful poison is far from the worst type of food. If you don't fight, you don't feel, and if you don't feel, you don't think, and if you don't think, then you don't blink, and if you don't blink, then your eyes will dry up in your head, and all the wonders of the world be to you as dead; and when that happens then you can give up, or you can act like Fred, and follow those words of Marcus Aurelius, last of the wise emperors: "You have lived your life. Now take what's left and use it properly. What does not transmit light creates its own darkness."[13] - and I have been crawling on the grounds of the midnight woods for a long time. I never stopped moving, but I certainly could not see where I was going, if I was forming circles or lines, spirals, or just slices of the same time. Then eventually, I looked up through the trees and began to climb, because I heard some fairy's sunlight laughter chime, and kinda,sorta... thought I wanted it to be mine.

    But I'm not so greedy as all that. I don't think I've got the trick for it, or the hat. Eustace may have grabbed for gold, and Smaug slept on his belly til he was old, but me, I still wear my egg like a bowl, white walls to keep me safe, jagged edges to scrape. I have my nose-tooth on, and I'm attempting to escape. Here I am in fog and lake, mountain stream, freezing dream, need to scream. The difference, I think, what makes me a little different, is that when I'm angry I want to explain, I want to analyze so that I can make the pain go away. But the problem you see is that life is pain, and so by existence itself I am emotionally drained. One high step is free, but the next is buried in mud up to the knee. I move in starts and stops, taking many a rest, and pull myself up at night into the arms of a tree, using them for a nest. The only idea that will pull me out of this is that there is a point to the test, some place next, that I will not be trapped here forever. If I keep moving, if I keep moving, towards the glow, towards the growing, towards the warmth and the fire, towards the rhythm that does not tire, towards the rhyming of my desire. Move and work a little each day, it's the only way I know how to pray.

Day 76: July 13th, 2024

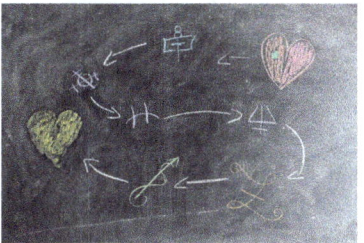

To Beauty,

    I know this isn't the best obsession, it's just better than depression. I'm not sure how I'd react if I was the subject, so there are two things I don't do, tell you, or look far into the future. Instead, my mind is cast back into the past, stuck on these memories that seem to last through fire and flame, through depression and pain. I regret what I did, or didn't, I regret what I don't, or do; I regret who I am, and what I choose; how I check my phone each morning for the news. I cast myself away by means of you, writing to Beauty as if by such matters I could travel through the mountain of my inadequacies, the swamp of my despair, the action of hiding my face behind long hair, or the fact that I simply don't care. Every picture I've posted, every poem I've wrote, every piece of art, and the mere fact that I managed to start, is because I imagined someone might see and feel me in their heart, or at least remember me before I am pulled apart. This is utterly pathetic, I know, for I should be able to stand on my own, and not need access to a phone; I should be able to see beauty without the glow, or know who I am without putting on a show. And the worst part is that all of it was real: I read every one of those books, I painted every one of those pictures, I want to every one of those plays; I stopped and smelled every flower, stared at every smile and every glower, felt sorry for that cat, and helped when I was asked; I completed each and every task. You didn't help me to do any of it - just helped me to take off the mask, to show that I was willing to change tracks.

    So now I'm on a different train, and yet for a smile from you I still strain, but I will not do this in such a way as to lie, I will not do this in such a way as to hide. Whatever I'm after, unnameable thing, I don't think I'll achieve it by being a lady Avalon, a second-tier pretender, a second-string member. I freely admit I have a temper, a monster's depth of love and hate, ugly face and the wish to be great, with mismatched eyes and feet I despise; infections, injuries, stitches, prone to sickness, prone to migraines, prone to poorness, poor to forgetfulness, prone to being some thing less, and seeing myself as some dragon or wolf, not a human at my worst; I am going to bust, or going to burst, betting on a hand I have not looked at, for a prize I have not glimpsed, all for a future that at very least is not this. Surely I swing and a miss, but better that than always feeling pissed, angry and sad, hiding my mad, moderating my hunger, slowly drowning under the weight of all I might have done. The only thing I ever won in all my days of the world is wisdom, but wisdom without action, wisdom less traction, a wisdom bad reaction. I burn myself, life goes down, slowly melting to bug on the ground, as I ignore how within me some bell sounds. - I should be dangerous to be around?

I was raised on stories of heroes you see, even if they were never me. Alanna, Danica, Luthien, Arthur, Rand, Captain Finn. Not form, not spirit, grin and bear it, those worlds aren't real, those people are dreams, and I am stuck in this world full of screams. Don't slack off, stand up straight, pretend to be happy but never admit you are fake. You were born to be great as long as you do what we say, college, work, family, duty, pray; and I tried, but I never found strength for them. I'd survive, but not into the darkness fend. I won't write or recite poems, and existence is silent to the end; certainly no-one on me should depend, because I break several times a day, have to get up and walk away. There's too much noise or too many people, a thousand zombies trying to climb the steeple, and impale themselves on its spike. - Look what I sacrificed, and praise me for my gallantry, reward me with salvation, or at least money and libations. That's the call, and the modern Valhalla, yet I care not overmuch for these: Success that others should bow to me and say please, charity and helping and falling to my knees, music or swift love or the mountain breeze. Such things are pretty but not beautiful, worthwhile but not fulfilling - there is something in me still missing, and I do not know how to find it.

On occasion I catch a glimpse, in a story or through the mist, as if by a peach or a fox I was twisted, Coyote-bitten, plague-stricken, half the world destroyed and the other half made strong, rich and long-lasting. I am capable of fireball-blasting, or following a drow with two swords through the underworld, like centaurs through Rabun's Gap hurled. My yellow blood curls in the air like smoke, until on death we all choke, violence rained down from the heavens, stars unending, on spaceships we are now depending. The freedom to fly, to seek safety in the sky, I am colony-born, but star-stuff is my home. A quaddie with four hands, or a salamander with heavy-set limbs, I am hungry, starving, and thin, a prisoner on hell, last member of a nation that fell. With a slur in my speech, and no hope for to reach, I retreat into my head; I make up poems instead. Bereft and barren such life might be, but still it contains the chance to someday leave, perhaps because some gallant hero some shuttle-craft did thieve, because even looking fake he always did believe.

I am the enemy, so I fool myself; I am the coward, so I leave the shelf. Like a book we have delved into too deeply, I set my skin aside; I will not fill new flesh with old bones, I will not delve into the tombs alone. With brush harsh and gentle I sweep away the dirt, in the middle of an empty land I build my yurt, and with a saw I make sure I am hurt. El Barto was here, ill-mannered, ill-met, and yet some child's friend, graffiti that freedom defends. Ugly and crude, mystical yet rude, it is quickly forgotten but is also an eternal sort of food, vision of proud arrogant loon, laughter after noon, and from such memories I gain my boon: Blessing to ignore the text, not caring about the test, running wildly into what comes next. Nine points of fight, eight points of light, seven points at night. I remember, living under trees, the western seas, memory of Oxford deans, or of leaving as a room was cleaned. Cutting the fat, I render myself lean, polishing and shining as I attempt to gleam, like boot, buckle and bat, swinging blindly for all that I lack. Will the ball pass home plate, or go smack, straight over the wall to never come back? My enemy's four-point lead begins to crack. I know I'm a little creep who peeks and seeks, but is silent, never clean. I'm trying to figure out how to leave, stop this bender, be in the future not Ender, I do not wish to speak for the dead. - I simply am trying to stand up and leave my bed, no more lose my heart to my head, here in the sunlight I make gold from lead.

Day 77: July 14th, 2024

To Beauty,

    What is objectification? A casting away, an act of prey, but who is the target you or I, and what is the point, crawl or fly? I even may call myself a thing - I wonder what I mean? Perhaps this one has a dream, a sort of Hegelian scream, master and slave, slave and master, what are these but tricks and disasters? By throwing myself away I become, by writing of you I am undone. Perhaps I name you the sun, the stars, the moon, fairy of Droon, but I don't know who you are. - I simply swoon, or howl at noon, silently doomed. It's frightening to seem, scary to deem, my action is my deed, but how do I act and in what way to fulfill which need? Some are tied to lands and trees, others lose their minds to plans and bees, like flowers they feed on all the world, choking land with the weeds until they alone among mankind seem light or falsely shine bright; not in others eyes but in their own, because they feel worthy of a home, a place or way they belong. Like wood blocks they are hammered into the correct position, fitting into walls, wondering proud among halls. Mountain thains with dwarvish brains, elves that never leave the forest, humans with crowns of gold, hobbits whom never adventure, growing crops until they need dentures. Objectification is solidifying, objectification is immortifying, objectification is like a giant sigh, let out because we want or fear to try.

    We make a gem of all things, me and thee, them and that and they, because we to an idol want to pray, look at the stars, the sun, or the moon, and say you are perfect, or at least better than us. I don't see your other side, but surely it must be covered with diamond dust, and I know that in your perfect immortal soul I may trust, you are the ideal of beauty, you must - be. Because if you were not, you'd...you'd be like me. Imperfect, with moments of rage or times you feared to turn the page, promises you didn't keep (you meant but we forgot), rhymes which from you did not leap, times you smiled even at a creep, a heart on occasion silent, and even the imagination to treat someone violent; perhaps you cheered for Ursula when she grabbed that trident. Would you burn the world down, or lift it up? Would you save with a mighty cable all or some, me or none? As yourself you are not done, still growing, moving, changing, evolving, learning, a little better, a little stronger, during some days days injured, and during others brightly blazing, x-ray lazing, seeing to the heart of things and living out a dream; but some dreams are nightmares, and some perfect people are sharp; I don't know, are you a minnow, or a shark?

To call you a mirror is to be willing to be seen, to call you perfect is to be willing to dream, but to call you a person. and me not a thing, that is leaping into the seam, line of gold to mountain's heart, but I don't know if it will lead to spark. Lone citadels where dragons sleep are full of pretty things they want to keep, but what is sword, jewel, or cup, if there is no song to fill it up? Memories are fine things, and pretending you are real is like a banshee's scream, because if I hear and write and draw unseen, then who will die but me? The house is empty, the door is shut, the windows are all boarded up, and I lie alone sick in bed, moan and groan with no strength in my bones. I drink and sup my vegetable broth, but there is no faith, no action, no touch, only everything not enough. It runs out you see, for we dive to the bottom of the lake but touch not the stream, we have dreams but not sight, we have health but not might, half eternal day, but never, never the shining knight, or the power to against monsters fight. We can hide beneath the covers, we can scream and shout, we can be silent or turn on a flashlight, but it takes a different sort of bravery, an entirely new transformation of clarity, to fill yourself up with insanity, or charity, or hilarity, and leap, - gently touching feet to ground dank and cold, to creaking sounds which speak of things dark and old, animals who killed those men who were bold.

Much safer to be quiet, much safer to be silent, much safer to just push a button, for conventional forces and actions are so expensive, hopes on which you bet your days of happiness or shade, steps in towers or moments in a forest glade, when you felt a burden down had been laid. But you lost, and for those failures, oh, you've paid, with lies and self-directed rage. Bad boy, bad dog, ugly engine of smog, with black heart and gray brain, red flesh, injury drained. - Is it possible to cleanse our heart of this stain, this fear of becoming be-ing, or of meeting a dream? What's real? I don't know, not me, not you, not things, not the world, reality as it seems, what is the point of this scream, objectify, please, don't look at me. - Treat me as a thing, don't ask me to change, I don't how to dance or sing, I'm not pretty, or strong, or thoughtful, in reality I'm rather awful, like offal I stink, Venus, drink. I'm hungry, but for what? I'm thirsting, but why? I need my well to not run dry, I need water to bring fire to the sky. Listen, half my words are half a lie, but the rest are me honestly trying, throwing paint at the wall. The point is pictures necessary and severe, the reason is so that I may read them and know what I feel, think, or fear; I myself am thing dying to be clear. Tell me, am I getting at all more near? I'd rather call someone a name then dear, I'd rather talk over tea than drown my sorrows in beer, there are many ways in which I'm weird, some of them good, some bad, some simply too much sad, or not sure how to tell I'm mad; I understand but am not understanding, I dream but barely work, I paint rough, buy too much stuff, and don't know what would be enough, or who I would be if I was. Buzz buzz, like a bee, where's the flower, making honey like a cross-eyed bunny, if only I could be funny - but no-one is laughing at me again, or could like me. It was only a three-sided anti-objectivifying dream.

Day 78: July 15th, 2024

To Beauty,

    What is wisdom? It is certainly not being wise, or acting in the ways we despise, as like waves upon the ocean shore, we are filled with half-truths and hollow lies; we write down, insist, inscribe, make time, and each and every rhyme we fill with these old hills of hell we climb, the world moving from day to night time. Shall we ring the bells, hear their chime, and think that we have the ability to mine? Wisdom comes not in the flash or by the flesh, but rather in the grasp of mind and death, the trust that we know which is east and where is west, what are the questions and answers to the test. For this existence has no rest, certainly there must be something after this next, not life maybe, but tomorrow, the next day, the next year, and we face it all with this terrific fear. - What if we are wrong? We write a poem, we sing a song, we make a book, and what if it's evil in fact? What if we are simply headed back? Walking these spirals is what we do, Gurren Lagann, we are not few, neither man in a cave nor the beast of the surface, yet what are we but nervous? Forward hark we say, seek the spark, all-father's heart, if we are suffering then surely we are doing our correct part, and will be rewarded with art. Perhaps even a real lion's heart, one with courage to be more than a dog that barks.

    I am not wise, for my sight stops at the sun, and I do not know what else I would see, if I turned my eyes away from thee. But, I ask, is this a lie, or simply the first limb of the tree, because after all, I write of me. I mention the gods, I paint the stars, and off I pass into visions of ours, pretending that my letters are bars, Illuvatar even before the stars, making a new world, each limb raised in praise, beginning the start of all days, and yet invader comes, burnt pillar half-razed. The sea-people are here, the Turks, the Huns, the Persians, the Akkadians, the Vikings, the Manchu, the Chinese, the Americans, the Spanish. - A people, an empire, a wave, a rule, a distempered tendency to fool. Who should I believe, what story should I read, Wang Yang-Ming, Dao De Ching, Beyond Good and Evil, what do they all bring? Half I throw away, half I eat, and half I ...dream, or mine them like seams of iron: Find pieces of steel, heart of the meal, skyscrapers raised up high, or Thoth who with my eye I did spy, knowing myself not spry, because I spied but didn't know what to say. Yeah, that's a god, but in which way? I'm sure there was someday I knew the answer, I'm sure there was some point during which I held the legends in my head, but I didn't keep them, they are to me as dead, because they did not speak to my heart, they did not teach me of the world and its start, or any mechanical parts. Bits and pieces of Bel-Marduk or Mao, of Hercules or Lincoln, of Aristotle or Smith, they are to me like Basho but this: Words I know that entered me, but did not teach me or set me free, for I cannot quote from them a single letter; no sentence, no matter, only pieces of clutter, and an ability to mutter: Yeah, I know who that is, he's a person, thing, or idea, but I can't call them Cleopatra or Augustus, Emerson or Mencius, they are no Coyote or Anansi, no Monkey King nor Silver stream, they are not parts of my thoughts and means. I do not paint of them, not alone, I do not drag them to my home, I do not put them in my tome, I could not tell you where they roam, or where they work, or why they are important. I don't know how they fit, I don't know how to make them a person, not an it, I don't know what to learn from them to make them fit. I see them and stand, not sit, I listen but they are not poems to me, only lessons, but this is my confession, I don't know if I care about what doesn't make me stare.

Simply knowledge is not enough, I must act to be tough. How face I ten thousand days, how I may make them pay? The past is not real, it is the present that I feel. I read the classics, I know them at my heart, but only because they are the start. History lives, it creates our struggles and art, our sciences standing on the shoulders of giants, our books are based on what survived the violence, our philosophies are half original and half something else, logic that has long been called good and bad, the way to be rational not mad, or how to escape being sad. I fail to see the point of learning, if I cannot start it burning, keep the world ever turning, spiraling up to stardust and asteroid mining, of solar winds and great ships designing, of escaping from our gravity well, or at least our fractured hells; land of religion and un-religion, land of destruction and creation, land of excuses, land of lies, land where we are so tired, but we try; because there is truth in every jewel, there is a moment of silence in the cool, and as for the heat, the sand and meat, or a corn cob hot, delectable, sweet, well, that we gladly greet, for you see. - We would rather that our wisdom was an easy feat, Sophia speaking to us instead of in the mountain we trust, even unto the oracle who does not speak in a clear voice. We always have a choice, between men and gods, between freedom and laws, between hands, or claws.

We write, we read, we fight, we flee, and what is at the end but me? Life is not clear, walking is not simple, but like Merida better to refuse the wimple. We could follow the tradition, we could climb on the ark, yet what is this but giving up our spark? At the bottom of the ocean lay ruins, unlooked for, unheard of, unknown, and yet those ancestors are part of our bones. Billions have died, yet should we only follow those who have left records of their pride? You and I both know how we shall live and die. - Chances are we shall never be remembered, and yet at every turn we are told to quiet our temper. Do not be hungry, do not be active, do not be weird or strange, don't question the priests, do not doubt the laws, be of all things least: Peasants, soldiers, or meek. Reese was perfect once for a week, I remember it well, and yet it turned out to be not quite so swell, because the world is full of problems and dangers, the world is full of loves and strangers, and if all you do is listen to the wise and always follow their lies, then you will crumble before the surprise. We are equal to the devil and his eyes; at the heart of us might be a unique and unearthly thing that flies. But don't take my word for it - do you feel you are journeying toward it, or want to fight more for it?

Day 79: July 16th, 2024

To Beauty,

  Maybe I should talk with my friends, and there's a few times I've tried, but it just doesn't end, I'm not sure how else to begin. What would I say? There is nothing to fix, only that my life doesn't fit: I do not know what to do with it. This is not a new problem, only a land filled with old solutions, mixtures, medicines, and absolutions. I do what I have always done, think and think and think and be numb, pretend I am made deaf and dumb, by the world overwhelmed, by the whispers hidden; I do only what I am bidden, but no-one calls me to work, no star shines in my heart, I wonder the world as if it was some french king's park: Pet the deer, smell the flowers, walk without fear, turn the corner, and look away if anyone comes too near. On rare occasion I may not flee, but stand and say: Can you see me? And half of those I speak to do, but they only see half of me, and not any at all of you. I can explain to friends and enemies alike where I am, what I've done, all that I've won, but I cannot tell them I feel as if I am coming undone. I pretend to be happy, not in the normal way, but only half my sadness shown in the day. Have you ever lain awake at night wanting to talk, or wondering where someone was at? Have you ever responded to niceness with sarcasm until people looked at you funny? Have you ever lied to people for twenty years because you wanted to forget a bunny? This world, this life, its funny, always off-kilter, never fitting right, with so few things that are shining and bright, not because of their reflection, but because they put forth their own light.

  I am dark at the core, burned, ash covering a flash, only brilliance revealed by the wind, or a crash. Some power from west or the east, some breaking of dam or leash. I store my words, I hide my mind, I pretend to be something of another kind, dragon or evil, Harpie or Weevil, a bug, a fox, a tree, or iron bar by anvil smote, this is what I have wrote, am I real or blowing smoke? I exercise my emotions, I move my mind, I fill my life up with reading lines, but there is only one thing I do in my off time: I drink. Well-water, deep and old, cruel and cold. Uruk holds more treasure, Shanghai has more grace, Nashville is where those cars do race, speedsters in a four-wheel base, who through winning and losing gain honor or disgrace. How many see them and wish they could be that, or kick a ball or swing a bat, be someone who has all of that? Yet in our ghetto pride, "we dare be poor for a'that"[14], we dare to look for more, we dare to lose sight of the shore, even as if Amelia, we die on the ocean floor; or shall valor never be in vain? Flaming through unremembered lands, flapping like pigeons with our hands, one more up, one more trip, one more second of lift. - Jumping Jay, we downward pray, building height til end of day, faster, faster, and if we do, we will escape time's gravity and you, circles of turning, world of yearning; we are attempting, and is that not something? What I cannot speak I may show, what I do not understand I may throw, and who I am is both the man, the heavens, and down below. There is a silver string from my boots to my head, and it strums with the songs of living and the dead: All my memories, all my friends, all my family and books, even those three times I wanted to look, and the ten thousand times I acted as a crook: Taking not giving, surviving not seeking, breaking my doors down instead of building around, digging myself into a hole in the ground. Monotonous work, moving and unmoving dirt back, but worth. That's how I learn to spell and speak, to make lion roar and mouse squeak.

So some of my words are mighty, and some of my words are quiet, but all of them are a sort of violence, a way to pretend myself to triumph. I am an actor in a play, some metal cast made out of clay, molten steel beaten and heated, bronze congealed, like colored bars in a field, geodesic structure that for children passes muster, a castle, a hill, a pill, magic memories to cure ills. That was us you know, walking past that elementary school, that was me, in those days before I even knew what slavery was, or how great it is to be free. I did not see and now, looking in, what have we done? Is this what it means to win? Those friends we once played with, those adventures we once had, why does remembering them make me feel so sad? I know I should not be mad, I should be open and glad, I should have a plan and a pad, no enemies or a good dad, but instead all I can feel is bad, because I fulfilled all the promises and goals I had, but what was the point if I am still always in shadows clad? Deep and dark I hide my face, through stories and wisdom race, but all I do, I do in disgrace, because I may be a tall tower, but I have lost my base. My fingers are not up to the task of weaving lace, for rough and unsteady is my game, I am quiet and unready to my shame, and there is no-one else but me to blame.

My fault, my fault, I cannot speak, I dare not start, and for all my whining I will not risk my heart. What shall I do for my next part? An actor's face, a mask, a mark, stand here, look there, affect an honest air, and convince the audience that you care. It's not lying, you see, if you make it real, it's not evil if I give back what we steal. Light I drink and words I give, hope inside to paintings thrive, as I hide I am revealed, and as I drown I attack the tide, this is my kind. Afraid to show, to speak, to think, to feel, but I am not empty, I fill; even tongue-stuck and migraine-blinded, ai will.

Day 80: July 17th, 2024

To Beauty,

    Am I a tomb-robber or an adventuring child, shall I follow the cat or escape by the Nile, is this my curse forever, or simply my resting point for a while? I build and I build, stone on stone, ever higher to peak of bone, gold cap and secret passages of old. I find spells in the folded cloth, and drunk from the ever-flowing jug of water, I follow these cloud-stairs to my slaughter. Tricks is what I have, precious games, a hiding place of shame, and impossible search for impossible name. I remember yours, I have lost my own, I don't know what it means anymore to wish to go home. A thousand magical books I have; four walls, a bed, and yet I am like that dead queen made of air, I have lost my way and dare not pass on. There are no spells to save me, no words to guide me, I have no map and no plan. I am poisoned by the snake, fear demons, fight monsters, burn in lake of fire, attempt to find my want and desire, because my heart has been ripped out and half my brain: Stomach, lover, and organs stained with black bile, an American tale of the old west, a singing rat that found a cat-bird's nest, and old hound-dog who dares face one final test, passing along his skills so he can take a rest. My heart is tired, my soul is burdened, my mind longs to pass, and my body is one pained gasp, so, I ask why stay? Curiosity, I suppose, kept me alive until today, the next books, the next story, the next show, the next song. I could press play and play along, like those friends and cousins I know who live life with a bong, smoke obscuring the whole world, mirrors in room without light, or stimulants they use to help them fight; but I never liked even the idea of drugs, artificial means of improving my sense of the situation, because why would I use artificial means to improve my life, when I could improve myself? I wish to smell like that book on the shelf, reminding us of heroes, gods, and elves, pyramids, statuettes, hopes, dreams, and heartfelt screams, a gram of imagination pure from the vein: Not grime and muck, but a tye-dye stain, a rainbow made real, a beauty that we know, paint, and feel.

    Do you have one of those special shirts, or a jacket, maybe a hat, something you put on when you are ready to go to bat? A stuffed paw-print dog from when you were eight, a Christmas present from Grandmother when you were sixteen, Grandfather's watch at high school graduation, or a red scarf you carried from the other side of the world, a talisman that gives you strength when you want to hurl, or simply curl up in a ball forever and fall down in the dirt. What do you reach for when you are so badly hurt that time will not heal the wound, when you have to cut yourself to ask for a surgical boon, a repair of pain with needle and thread, a faint chance that you will go to sleep and wake up dead? What do you do when hell lives in your head?

Many times, I have dived: Books and stories, history and morality, pyramids, temples, swords, spears, Viking ships, rabbits in briars, monkey of liars, I hear none, I see none, I say none, I am undone, for even diving to Azaroth to seek some fun, or running around in Fallout with a gun, these were always shade, not stars or sun: Places to hide and pretend I was wise, choices I could make and always reprise, good and evil laid out in a limited number of lines, and clear as can be that more power was the prize. This was how I hid from the world inside, the hollow earth revealed by that eye, a melancholy poet who wishes she could fly, scanning immortality from her doorway but never daring to try, hope and feathers given up with a sigh; but only viewing philosophy from afar is not how me wishes to die, not now, not ai.

Neither will I suffice to be the Oxford man ashamed of my poems and why, I will not hide my flowers or my cries, though I will cheerfully admit I must show them a shy, obscuring face, subject, and numbers with lawful lies, - but never retreating from my heart into my work, rather the reverse: As with pick, axe, and saw I mine the mountain, I move the dirt, I bleed and sweat out my worth. I may be that no-one shall buy, I may be that no-one will care that I write and why, but hope is the thing with feathers and like Columbia I flame towards the sky; damaged I shall not return, either better, or better never been born.

I know here I toot my own horn, hungry enough for food that I will face harm, heating frozen pizza until it is warm, or frying it until it burns; with hard, crunchy, black edges but still edible, energy of ten thousand stars incredible, long carbon chains which broken feed the brain, or give us muscles like Bane. Sugar is sweet in the blood and sharp on the tongue, a power turning and turning, making many into one, wheat for the cow, milk from the sun, living rivers run, and from breaking voice comes Dragondrum. Who is the king of the dogs? Not me - but sniff anyway, what do you see, the Dempsey roll and me. Back and forth I twist and turn, spiraling up from the sea like a bird, grabbing fire, lifting higher, building, building like Dire, blocks of my own creation, mods of my own imagination, legends, histories, and salutations. I write every day because I don't know what to say.

The way I pray is also how I pay, because at end of day this is what keeps me from fading away. I would prefer to sleep and rest, but it's two A.M. and I need to know what comes next. I write to you so as to learn who I am, I place down words to discover what I can do, I paint so as to repair my tomb. I read of treehouses filled with books to avoid my doom, and when I need new stories I speak to a princess of Droon. I can see all of eternity, and the crumbling walls of my room, the door is open, the light is on, the broom is waving, and I burst out in song. When will my life begin? When this one ends.

Day 81: July 18th, 2024

To Beauty,

    I said once that I did not see the point in being pretty or strong for me, and I still don't. I am strong enough to not hurt myself in my daily activities, or at least healthy enough that I may recover from them. I dress in comfortable clothing which is often covered by paint, and I shave part of my face, but never put in any effort that might be called great. I do not pretend to grace, or ever wear clothing made of satin, silk, or lace. I wore a skirt once and found it annoying, I wore tight pants once and found them painful, rings feel clumsy, watches strafe, bracelets break, anklets make a ton of noise, necklaces constantly fall apart, I never tattooed anything with all my heart, my shirts barely have any art, pants are blue or gray, muscles will not stay, colored hair goes away, and earrings are dangerous in a fight. Why should I care how I look in the light, when all the world is covered by shadows of night? My soul should shine, and I would rather avoid the lie of pretending what I am not, than be pretty covered with things I bought.
    `Rather, ugly is what I've got, I'm sure of it in my soul, even if my mind says I am a fool. My outer appearance seems to be only a tool in my philosophy, but on occasion I feel that hypocrisy, because my slight overbite makes me not want to smile, or I'll see someone's athleticism and think I could do that too if I worked out for a while, and then for a few days I'll exercise, but quickly enough I retreat inside, my head, my shoulders, my body to hide; how dare I pretend to pride, and what would be the point, anyway? To be able to lift heavy things, to be able to run for hours, to imagine that I might be admired, what is that but arrogance? What is that but accessibility, fake work to achieve what I don't want? I am uncomfortable in my body, I would rather be a spirit or a mind, I would rather be seen as brave, dedicated, or kind. I am clumsy both in and out, running into door jams or tables, both my health and my gains always unstable. My back or eyes might go out for days, because I slept in a weird way, and it's been that way my entire life: One wrong movement bring chance of strife, even though nine nights out of ten I'm fine, but I'm not sure what pushes me over the line from stress to pain, or what I should have done to escape my fate. I walk half the day, stand, sit, rest, and stretch, but all that does is reduce the mess. I'm not broken, only bruised, everyday a little stressed and confused, as I wait for my body to

show me the bad news.

So I don't look or feel pretty, I don't dress or expect it, and everyone who tells me I look fine is only being nice, or else they are blind. Why would I reap rewards without effort? How could I be beautiful if I'm not perfect? My heart knows that's wrong, but in front of mirrors my heart's not very strong, so I might glance at myself, but I never look for long, and in fact, for my entire life that has been the song. I have seldom fallen into eyes, and never tried to memorize a palm, never stared behind or wished my fingers through hair to twine, and I thought I knew what beautiful was, but I was wrong. The world has only ever been pretty, before, and it is a difference I cannot explain, but only show with my phantoms and my rain, this strange drive I have to strain. - I almost want someone to look, I stand up straight, I write, I paint, I create, and I place it all where you might see, even though I know you'll never look for me. You will never think the poems and pictures involve you in any way, or that I whisper your name on the worst days. I can do this, Muse, I can do this. I can do more than survive.

Right now, I see the handsome girls and the cute boys, and I don't feel anything, but I think I could, if I was brave. I don't want them to look at me, and I don't want to be praised, but maybe if I thought they might, I wouldn't be quite so amazed, even though it's never happened, and never will; but still - I can imagine, now.

I remember once you talked to me, telling me about a trip you would have tomorrow, and there were two thoughts in my head. The first that I would like to go, that sounds rad, but it would be rude to ask and you aren't inviting me, so regardless of what I would wish to see and who to hang with, I ought not express my wish; because wanting is bad y'know, the origin of pain, and if I asked and you said no, I would only feel shame, three hours of taking myself to blame, because my second thought was, why would someone this pretty be talking to me? You were not beautiful, not yet, but maybe inside me was a glimmering, and certainly some part of me was screaming, because I don't dare stand in front of you like this, dreaming of knowing you a little better, or spending some hours at your side, just as when we walked into the magic hall, past wizards on the wall, and I lost you in the crowd. I think I felt like a liar a little bit, because I stood at the spider for twenty minutes, imagining I was curious about how it worked, for I did not dare to search loudly by acting on or naming my accidental intentions to myself, until I became convinced that you had passed, and then I hurried on to catch up, alas. You were behind, I was ahead, the years separated us and so did my head, because I didn't know what to do in my stead. Even today, there are a few other moments like that I remember at two in the morning when laying with insomnia in bed.

Oh, sometimes, oftentimes, at all times, to hell with my life - why do I always panic in strife? You were stunning, I mean this literally, time slowed down, thoughts flew round, I don't know what is happening to me, I'm scared you see. Have you ever read that in a bad novel? I liked you so much it scares me, and it's completely pathetic, but I mean it. At thirty years of age I am paralyzed and losing my mind, panicking on the inside, trying desperately not to show, I live my life deeply but slow, growing up behind all my peers in love and career, in all my experiences and the rate of my gears, or how some enginse started again because you were once near. I do not know what to do with my tears and my frustration, this stupid ignorant backward mismatched ill-timed senseless rhythm of recall time and time again, and I'm sick, I'm sick, two years and I'm losing it. What the hell am I doing!? Who am I pretending to be? Don't look at me! (...Please?)

Day 82: July 19th, 2024

To Beauty,

    I find some days are rest days. Not because I am tired, but simply because I have reached the limits of my awareness, and wish for a while to float in nothingness; gathering my strength in readiness, forbearing to regress by the simple expedience of stillness, shifting not because I have arrived, but only because the world has moved along and carried me with it, until suddenly I awake in a fit, becoming again a person, not an 'it'. Objectification, imagination, procrastination, ends, and I catch with my sails the wind, circling round this platform, this single step, my personal Balor's Needle, slowly building myself up yet, practicing trying to forget. I intend not to repeat myself, to not write inanities upon the shelf, and to not fade away like an elf. My words are not magic and contain little skill, my voice is slightly nasal and shrill, steps heavy, eyesight weak, and my head has a beard, not a beak. Should I break, what would out of me leak? Poetry, I hope, but maybe despair, I wonder, why should I care? That is one action I admire about you, that you appear to have a heart, to feel that righteous spark, while I merely retreat to art, pained by sharks with no fin, forbidding myself from partaking in, yet inside me I doubt that mere vegetarianism is a win. One of the rules I made for myself long ago, is to try and not tell other people what to do, because I really could on that idea follow through, ordering the morals of the world for both a 'me' and a 'you', filling the wide land up with plans, and my two hands with made-up moral jams: Those sticky, iky pieces sweet to eat, and yet without feet; an inability to move and change, the tendency to believe the world is solid and thus become deranged, with one eye, one view, one news, like a cyclops that does not chew, becoming one of the many by abandoning the fact that we are one of the few, unique through and through in position and reflection, situation and inspiration.

    Oh, certainly there are similarities, but there is a difference between following a book and reading it, between knowing what happened and living it, between knowing the entire picture, and extrapolating from a little bit. How do we believe everything, and make everybody fit? Where are the facts and where are the tricks? Are they lying, or are we just thick? Is this reality, or some messed-up vision of Morty and Rick? Nihilism is not my game - rather I fight it with flame, dispelling the shadows and walking the circles, even lamed, because I wish to understand, not blame.

Some say people are inherently good, and others that they are inherently bad, but I think these two visions are simply fads, because humanity is complex and moving, moral evolution an illusion, the present day looking back and forward with confusion. I imagine we move a little up and down, with the creation of extra resources and towns; mostly we simply move around, to this side and that, sideways and flat, civilized nomad, and nomad civilized, some evils obvious and others normalized. Like monkeys we cover up our mouths, ears, and eyes, because we do tell the truth, but every truth contains a lie, just as every action we take to make the world a better place, means that there is another evil we will pass by unnoticing. - Just as my relativism and doubt contains a hypocrisy, three moral sides, of middle mask, outer face, and the inner pride. Tell me your good and I shall believe you, no matter what you have been through or done; ask me to act and maybe some money or time from me might be won; there are many actions I may admire or condemn, yet in my life to them I will never fend, bad I would die before doing, good I would not do if I was willing, because I do not trust my milling; the ability to take the rocks and the rain, the wheat and the pain, to crush, to grind and strain, ever turning for flour to bake, or cakes and muffins to make, I don't know what to do, because wI make so many mistakes.

I have trusted those who should not be trusted, written letters no-one has ever returned, learned lessons that I did not earn, both the good and the bad sides of how a soul may burn. I have in me diatribes full of damnation, I have in me the high whispers of salvation, I have in me the abandoning of all balance of situation, I have in me the option for no hesitation; I have in me manifestation, Maldraxus, torture and skull, the abandonment of measure, wisdom, and rule, granting death without being cruel. Is it no wonder I would rather live as a fool, instead of believing that morals are only a tool?

I dive beneath the waves, I lose myself in ideals betrayed, I place myself within the grave, and at all of reality I rave; I hate, love, adore, rise up in the heavens and fall down to the floor. I do what I can to break down the door, adding fluoride to the water. My teeth, my bite, my knives are sharp and strong, cutting well to lasting long, good for both meals and song. Poetic partnerships and artistic provisions alone are not enough to overcome divisions, because language is a mighty prison. I do not dare to speak your name, living in shame, because writing this I know the rules of the game, cutting my tongue becoming lame, unfit for service but now safe, because with one leg I am not expected to have any grace, or to win a race. Language is a crutch as well, the beginning of a volcano that swells, the ringing of the bell. Look, the viking raid is here, the spear, to arms, to arms, they are near, will you fight or die in fear? I have my fists, if not any gear, I don't know what I'm doing, but at least this moment is clear, because resting days, where the mind loves to stay, end, one way or another, be they measured in either hours or decades; smart, stupid, silent, loud, alone, in midst of crowd, new direction or rebound, in this life or the next I will be found. Look around, and what do we see? The moving world, me, and you. I rest for a while, I know I flee, but not forever. Tomorrow I will be, wake up, and take not the knee. Shadow and Light work is the path to be free.

Day 83: July 20th, 2024

To Beauty,

    What do I admire? The flash and the fire, the light and the flame, dancing glances, smiles like lances, a heart that cares, actions that dare, smarts in the brain, a willingness to strain, moments of silence, awareness of the world's violence, friends that do not fade, a life more than passing grade, direction and purpose, appreciation of the past, a childhood's laugh, family, travel, water and rain, the mysterious driving force that makes me face my shame, the fact that you were brave enough to play games, a note in the voice, a light in the eye, and how you seem to fly. They say opposites attract, and it seems to me as if you are doing everything right that I did wrong, as if you are the beginning of a long and glorious song, in which, even if the tone be lost, the strength still stands out strong, as if you in this world could find a place you belong, a being becoming, not borrowing, light, a way in which you against the darkness fight; using symbols and poems, memories of other's destroyed homes, or signs of a lost cat that did roam, but now found safe and sound, because people like you were looking around, and putting up notices that this lost child had been found, a gray gladness on glass, a moment of happiness which swiftly did pass, but an action of kindness which long shall last, just as occasionally you might wear a mask or help those who do, by reading a book and following through.

    I don't know who you are, but I almost know what it might mean to you. I do not forget, I do not forgive, and I know the atrocities against which you rave, I know the injustices done against those who you would save, I am tired but I think you have the next page, young but knowing more than learned sage or laughing gentlemen: Against the tiger, like a liger, two incompatible forces meeting as one, you are willing to stand up and say this can be done. I, in cone of silence, do not advocate violence, because the spell that has been cast on me is full of fear against all those fighting in its many forms, by signs and symbols, name to page, alumni advocating with rage, that the government, the school, and the structure, should abandon its support, hold not itself like that police fort: Never forcing sincerity and seldom acting with clarity, all with best intentions, but simply without mention of high ivory tensions, failing in their explications, and leaving all with low expectations. Nothing will change, there's no point in the range, why are peoples actions so strange? There is always more to learn, and you should know better they say, but you decided not to simply step away, and what is this force in you that allows you to play?

For, dancing with friends, birthdays and bars, red hair in cars, nights on the beach, basketball seats, the incredible captain's feats, each and every one of these seems to me neat, the indelible signs of a heart that beats, blood filled with an energy which I would eat, as certain moments are to me like meat and drink, strengthening the muscles of the mind while letting loose inhibitions inside, just as there is a smile which reminds me of pride, moments of torture because I hid or lied. The purpose of life is not happiness, but what is it? Love is necessary, but not sufficient, and purpose is only the beginning of our provisions. I wonder what would be your solutions to the problems of today and tomorrow, would you respond with hope or sorrow? Fare you well away from here, bloody elbow without fear, lots of pieces of glass and gear, bones unearthed by investigative verse, science the art of humanity's rebirth, power to dispel the ignorance curse, and the recognition that the world could be worse. From pumpkin patches to the eastern sun, fishing towns and days of fun, vampire bites and tournament run, life goes on and you do not feel done. I wonder, who will you be tomorrow and again, in a year or ten from now, how transform, who defend, what stories revealed, what strength lend? Into what new worlds will you fend, through magic books or magic hands, what on earth is your plan? I think you hope and not merely cope with the world as it is, what can we change, how better, what show, is it possible to mix the righteous and the slow, have you learned where to stay and how to go, can you balance your catches and your throws?

Only if you have a firm stance, stable land, eye to guide and time to plan, a home where the heart lies, a cat you can snuggle up with when the world dies. Are your cats like mine lies, or living truths inside? I can't care, I can't climb, but you are like a life of lemons and lime, electrolytes that give me strength to find, which, though sharp and painful, harsh and sour, dangerous with your smile and your glower, an existence of thorns and flower. I admire your power, patience, dedication, the way you bring obliteration. The noise as well as the silence, the world you see and still have hope of ending violence. I look at you and wonder, do I have the vigilance, could I be equal to what I see, is it possible to fly and not flee, do you offer lessons on prison, or being free? What is it that makes you seem like well at foot of tree? I could make lists, but they would not explain all that you are to me. I think there is more than what I see.

I don't know what it is, I may not name, I cannot paint, I have tried and I have failed, abstract dimensions or mighty whale, penguin in the sun or a braid undone, each of these is only an aspect of the one. Threshold pyramid fills with blood, but engineer artist priest faces the flood of waters raging, and mountain creek of winter changing, all the hundred and twenty million degrees of atoms rearranging, a solvent of soul and mind, a whispering that I might be better than my kind, and cut not the knot, but instead unwind. Maniac over Alexander, vision over blindness, auburn over blond, and a vile taste but not bland. Is this medicine I make with my hand? I do not ask nor command, make no wish, wind not my clock in swiss, for instead a crystalized smile in my spirit is what keeps time here, the ten thousand moments through one single heart-felt twist, expressing true feelings using my wrist. What do I admire? That you make me able to do this. Selfish, mysterious, earnest. To you, I want to be honest. How is it you can stand like and look at at all those damaged cats, what is it that makes you a match for this terrible world? Is it possible I could be cured? Your distance from me almost lets me believe.

Day 84: July 21st, 2024

To Beauty,

    The poets say "beauty is truth, truth beauty"[15], but where then stands duty? It is a lie, we do not have to try, and yet we so eagerly act so as not to fry, do we think it matters as we die? Beauty, I would fly if I could, because I am not sure it matters anymore that I am here, doesn't matter what I do, Grandma is filled with either confusion or fear. Yeah, she smiles, but it's only for a while, and she can't even say pon, there is no tile. Not one, not two, not three, none link up, all stories are junk, today she was getting ready for school and also thirty-five, with dirty laundry spread out to dry that wasn't hers, but she doesn't know where it came from, and I don't really either. This home, this house, is filled with knick-knacks and stuff, half of it is hidden and if you ask Grandma about it she's gruff. What is this, where did it come from, why is this here, where is it going, what are you doing; all worried and frantic, sleepy days and manic nights, until it's easier to just go outside and write til two A.M. Grandma, you're not going to hurt yourself, you're not falling over, but you're not there, you're not really anywhere. With clothes you don't want to change, and hair you don't want to comb, with a picture of that person who looks like your mother, and always looking for my mysterious brother, or a nonexistant son, or a mysterious little girl, or my Grandfather, oh my god its so much bother, and I wanna scream, and I wanna laugh, and I just... want it all to pass. Why am I here? I've grown a new fear, because if I, personally, ever have dementia that bad, just kill me, I won't be sad, for I'll already be dead, and can no longer be glad.

    I just...what's the point of existence, what's the point of life, what's the point of all this strife? There's no creation, no intonation, no spells, no salvation, no a speck of art, only the dust of a mind and heart; this is not a whole life but only a part, days filled with puzzle pieces that never fit, minutes passing like hours in IT, scary people all around, faces in the sky, the tree, the ground. We are always preparing to go somewhere, or for someone to arrive, we walk around and around, but all we do is survive. That's why I'm making things, that's why I'm speaking, because it's just dust and breaking. I nod at every word, I say sure, sure, she asks why no-one is coming, she wants to know when the school-bell rings, and all I can say is I don't know, I cannot sing, there is no song I can bring, no purpose to reveal, no world to make, no answer to tell, only a short staving off of heaven and hell. Some days are easier, Grandma is asleep, or petting the cat, but other times she's in bed until noon, and then at midnight walking around the room, in circles for half an hour, or opening up every single carton in the fridge looking for something to devour. I give her food and she just looks at me with a glower, then points out that on the table there are beautiful flowers.

Sometimes she speaks, and other times it's mumbling, can't complete a word, only gestures describing the absurd. On occasion, she breaks out in Swiss German, and I don't know, I can't sprechen, or horen. I google words, but according to her friends on the phone in the other language its even worse, and makes less sense. It appears the only thing I can do is wonder at this curse. I cannot fix it, I cannot change it, I cannot move it, I cannot solve it, I cannot make it better. About the only thing I can do is write these stupid letters, and free myself from these fetters of duty, escape in my head to beauty and the sun, before the stress makes me mind become undone. It's crazy, because sometimes I'll be outside making art, playing a game, or reading a book, but then Grandma comes around, and I feel like I'm a fox been run to ground. She has a question, or a worry, or wants to tell me a story, but none of it makes any sense. I only stand and nod, for three to five minutes, between three and fifteen times a day, then walk her back in the house, make sure she doesn't trip, and well, that's about it. I can't sit in the house all day, it just leads to a fit, endless worries and every three minutes a new bit. It never ends, because time is all the same, everything is deranged and this house that's not hers is so strange. She took five minutes yesterday to wash a bowl, and didn't use any soap; everytime I see or speak with her I feel like I'm losing hope.

Grandma is not alone. She has me, and mom, her cat, her friends, but it doesn't matter at the end. Grandma died a year ago, and what remains is this hollow shell, a zombie with paper skin and a mind half-way to hell, with a spirit that in heaven shall dwell. I am here, and will be here for a while, waving at Grandma and putting on a sick smile, never telling anyone how bad tastes the bile; only yelling at strangers in the world, or talking to you with hopes raised in a pile, climbing up and turning the dial. When I am cold, freezing and dead, I remember warmth and struggle out of my head. Duty calls as duty must, but when is enough enough? I cannot change the world, I cannot help anyone, filling my days with poems and pictures that do not matter, starting and turning my head at every clatter, hoping no-one fell, and occasionally ringing the doorbell, opening portals in my soul that drag me forth from hell, as living wanting in me swells. I need to feel as if there is meaning. Absurd and stupid is acceptable if those actions cause change, I need to communicate my thoughts before I myself become deranged. We are living one day at a time, one night for every thousand rhymes, burning myself so that this smoke may climb. Do you read my signals in the wind? Do you feel me being drawn thin? How would anyone know, if I always keep my secrets hidden within? My emotions arent trash, they don't belong in the bin.

Day 85: July 22nd, 2024

To Beauty,

How do we understand the past without becoming mired within it? I am halfway through a book on a strange land, and it seems simply another story of a thousand warbands, each structure of the city and the nation under a different hand, with each and every group always going mad. Everyone blames someone else, and all seem ignorant of what the problem is; they merely feel everything is going wrong, and they are not listened to, or exist only under threat, each person with their false pride and incredibly thin hide. Some rail against religion, and others for it, the children are losing their ethics, and the old-timers are hoarding and pathetic. Each to the other is a pest, with each group only getting a C on their test. Everyone it seems is hungry or poor, except those few who got their foot early in the door, the west being raised up, the east taken down, with twenty years of the same good and bad spots in town. How can you live with this much fear, and no faith at all in either your leaders or your walls, only endless wails of danger and danger, more and more, fix this, fix that, there's a problem, why won't you help, are you not listening, jump off your shelf! Become something else! This is the cry of the ones who are watching their children die, while others stand there and cry that it's the new-fangled ideas which are to blame, and the correct action is to make the children feel shame, because they play such strange games, are weak, individualistic, pampered, greedy, unwilling to work, turnign out to be without ethics. I have heard the view that we are raising a whole nation of jokes, who when the hard times come will choke, because ignorant they are of history and sacrifice, they do not understand what it took so that their life today is nice, so that they have fruit to eat and television to watch, not only stones on the street and rice. - Such is the cry that has ever been, but I feel they have a mistake within.

Simply put, they have no faith, no trust, they see their children being different and think, well, they must not know what they are doing, for if they had any sense they would abandon their pretense of issues and problems. We might, broadly speaking, divide the world into two types of people, and they are tested not by question, but by example. Say, I do not enjoy your temple, I do not agree with your ideas, there are problems in the world that you did not fix, and now it's time for us to reach. It may seem strange, but what I do causes no harm, or at least no harm that was not already there. Instead, I simply reveal a mighty despair, when I ask you, how do you care? I know you do not understand, but are you going to smile, or stand in the way of my plan? The children will always make their own mistakes, and how do you react to this, with great fear or hope? Will you imprison us or simply make sure we have a warm coat?

I feel this is the principle flaw of human society, the way we live in our variety; that everyone can agree that everyone else has bad morality; that simply because they have different histories or cultures that they are ignorant or wrong, lazy or only good for singing songs, dirty, smelly, rude, dumb with bad food, with minds and hearts that are crude; and, even as the world gives lip service to relativism, the practice is still rare, because people see something they do not understand and become scared. Now, it is easy to speak against such views, obvious to rail against, but in the midst of activity we lose this pretense. Our 'real' thoughts come out: We are angels, you are devils, we are educated, you are ignorant, we are the workers, you are the shirkers, this is our land, you are gypsy bands, I recall what your grandfather did to mine, and I know what my son will do to thine, your daughters are rough, mine are sheltered, your society is weak and ours is tough, you are doing some evil and that is why we don't have enough, which is reflected in the ways that we are polite and you act gruff, because, you see, you aren't up to snuff. You should do what I tell you and all your problems will go away, and never mind your point of view, it is mine that matters today. - And you know the real issue with this mindset, the real problem? It only takes one out of two, or even smaller groups than that, to cast a shadow over all the proceedings of all the peoples, nations, and movements of the world, because flying when you are heavy does not work well. We are back to the ground hurled, now bruised and battered, our hopes not entirely shattered, but certainly scattered, as we all retreat back to force, which is both a strength and a curse.

We better fulfill our three needs today, of food, water, and shelter, than ever before in the history of the world. We are, on the whole, healthier, stronger, fatter, smarter, but there is a fourth need as well, which is moderated by our memories of hell. Happiness, the balm of the heart, that we are going to be better tomorrow, and tomorrow is all ready to start; that we will have a good life as long as we do our part. We wish rules on the world, we want it to work, that slowly we level up and gain a new perk, with a cheat or a shortcut here or there, which we find because we venture into places where others are scared, or have the mind to see the flaws of reality: Ingenuity rewarded with power, or a cold harsh winter with spring flowers. Long before then however, it seems we must glower, because we are captured and sad in the shower. The hot water is gone, the cold water runs out, and we choose to whisper and whimper, not shout. How shall we run about? Half clean, half muddy, a towel we forgot, a stranger across the hall, we step out so carefully but on the lip sometimes we fall. Even the best built box has echoes that to us call, we crash and burn, looking for the lightbulb, the switch, for in the dark it is us who have a wish: To open the door, to escape into the light, for even if we are only half-clean, it is better tonight that we tried, and if hair is still dripping while glasses are fogged, the power is out and we escaped the bug. This is like the past, following us around as a mist, we are half-clean, half-mud, but not a dud. We can explode.

Day 86: July 23rd, 2024

To Beauty,

    The moon looks down, smiling upon us, yet we reject it from our sight, glancing away at what is hidden in the night, which is comfortable and not worth the fight, with a weight that is not heavy, but light. Why do you mock us so, depictions of what we dare not show? Mind's reflection on earth is slow, when directly away from heavens we go. Walking in the woods, we are lost and cold, having lost all memory of the sun's gold, making from our weapons new, ancient enemies who drove our heart straight through with a spear splinter'd from sight, or a toy sword made out of might. Anxious brain of mental capacities limits and strains, we, as always, seek to escape our stains, those shadows we see in the mirror of the moon, the way they are silent to our most hearty whispered boons. Do I have the strength for this?

    I know I have not the courage, that is missing, I am missing, some re-dead leaping on my own back and hissing, because I wore not a mask. They took me to task, understanding that I was not dead, stealing my hearts from me so they might be fed. Oh, monsters brought by the castle above, and safe in your seven years of loss, what will you do when the torch at you is tossed? Are you dry or wet, skin or soil, easy or willing to toil? I use you as a practice foil, fencing with, fencing against, or breaking the mirror with my fist, fake shadows now real, as I wake up from the nightmare and try not to scream, my own face bloody in the dream.

    I have beaten myself, I have stood ashamed in the light of the moon, I have spoken both too late and too soon. I have fallen asleep at noon, in the middle of the room, asking for a boon, feeling myself swoon, as they looked at me with their uncomprehending eyes, ignorant of my pride or my prize, the way I always hid but never totally lied; I think you could find me if you tried. Perhaps that was my wish, which every maiden is taught to have; some brave prince on a high steed, one hero equal to how I feel, some person no stranger, cannot be a danger, gives me what I need, even if I don't know what that might be; but am I not a modern boy as well? My soul and will must be equal to the spell, for if I wish it to work, we must drag the djinn out of hell. Look, those idols, those things, those objectives swell, their very existence like the mockery of a bell; or that's why wish us to believe what we see, that the spirit alone might be free. It is said the world is a lie, Mara is damned, that everything we understand is made up in our head, that the way to escape is to act as one of the dead, but I think that instead I would rather break the world,. - Expand my limits, through space be hurled, become in twilight one of the Golden Girls, Dick Van Dyke, hospital detective bright, I'm on television watching myself at night.

The world is in review: What I do is who I choose, as we are both reader and writer, creator and consumer of the news, waking up in the morning we put on both our shirt and our shoes; left right, left right, look, sunlight, dawn-spark, meadow-lark, our ten thousand fitted parts, each missing puzzle piece of art. We find ourselves today, once more we change the way, natural is who we are and what we say, escape is the means by which we most earnestly pray. So you think to "outsee nature and God and drink truth dry"[16]? I say to all the powers of the world: Let them try! A teacher once wrote in my book, never stop someone who is doing the impossible, and I think that suspicion is actionable. Leap blindly into sky, rebooting both your programming and your lies, be not afraid of your sister's eyes. Look, brother, hear my cries: Poem I write down lest I die, I have been dust, I have been nothing, a nithling, and this one has had enough. I'm not tough, but I can follow through, even though I chew on the idea for a long time, extracting and learning each day of each rhyme, every lime eaten in time, and half-made lemonade of syne, that language of tongues which is mine.

The past comes on, the future is done, the present runs, and we are not fun, even as we peer at both many and one. By windows we peek, blood leaks, flesh covering blind eyes, incomparable gardens at the heart of time, architectural rhythms climb: Nueva York, like forbidden pork, mud is not usable, bricks are fusable, and we are by misery reduced, made less than men, beasts, and buzzing things, a crack in the wood, the house of dreams. More than earth am I, fire, smoke, burning rise, as a human being my hands go to my ties, what was, what is, what may be, all these parts of what I see. Growing eyes again, I breathe. Moon comes, light dawns, and I forbear to flinch before the song, but instead dig my fingers deep in the mud, pull myself forward four inches more, disgraced, absurd, but out the door, curled up outside with wounds in my hide, and finally above the floor. Today I start to draw with art, I take my hands, I spread them apart, signs and signals of stars. You do not see, you do not hear, but I do, becoming near. What have I to fear, only fear itself, only that none will ever read the books on the shelf, that I will not write them only because of my horror of an 'or else'.

Abandoning pretense, I look at the moon, I say bright one, beautiful being, warm as noon, poetry bring, heart that sing, might you ever understand or care what you mean? I am so sorry for attempting to be seen, but this is what you seem like to me, a gateway to Sybil's scream, and the wonderful part of a dream.

Day 87: July 24th, 2024

To Beauty,

    Are you awake and active as I am? How do you fill your days. with what work or what play, do you dream of fire to rest upon clay, what is in your heart that you wish to say? I imagine you are more honest than me, certainly more brave then free, and I pray at least you are happy, with dreams and plans, hopes and met demands, gorgeous do-gooder rocks in hands, saving the world in your small way, slowly the ignorant demons of the past and future to slay. Thus, Valkyrie you may be, chooser of the slain, or that feather-wielding god with an archeologist's brain, judge of dead men and living nations. - To direct us towards our stations, map and guide, garden live, some busy bee-keepers hive producing honey, with the honesty to be funny, and the moves of a flapper, a dancer, some bright leader like prancer, with a Rudolph nose and a smile worthy of prose, blazing light in the night, through storm and shadow Santa fight; the Erlking at his right, another shadow, another shade, some eastern weapon like a glaive, swift-cutting, Kel-rushing, song of children at war, the scars that we are and a dragon's hoard: Memories building up our houses like they are boards, wooden hearts with iron starts, gray screws and nails, red hammer and white sails, curled-up guard of snails. We are slow, humanity, and unseen below, fools of the earth who yet climbing, glow. We grow, unnoticed, unseen, as we are hunted by bird and beast, and struggle with our brothers to on green things feast, always struggling to not be last or least.

    There are many old things in this house, and none of them remind me of you, for your presence with them has nothing to do. There are three pieces left of old family silverware, books filled with detectives of the air, engineering manuals and science-fiction's struggle against despair. I am sure that there lies forgotten dog hair, for when occasionally cleaning I gain a whiff of the smell of the dead, and I want to lay down for a while, close my eyes in need, because I have this sudden vision in my head. There is the old rocking-chair I sit in now, with the old lamp by it, and behind me lay the adventures of Calvin and Hobbes, the boy, the tiger, and the philosophers, with the great speeches and orations of Daniel Webster, yet also salutations from Grandmother's sister, Swiss-German where the only thing I understand is the name. Also, there are a few travel games, chess and checkers missing pieces, next to a bottle of quicksilver, and two green leashes. There are machines, dusty and tall, all rusted through, with pieces of rubber which the mice have chewed. A bear upon the wall, a hundred pieces of wood that might fall, a deflated basket ball, and mad grandma wondering in the halls. I am not alone, for the memory of the past shall a little while longer last, as evidenced by my thousand-word task, and the ways in which I continue to mask. How long will I be, how much more may I carry? For surely I only tarry here, and my real life is somewhere else up in the air, half-way across the country or in another world, dust turned to bone and then swirled, minerals of art rebuilding heart. I deliver my letters, I send out messages without knowing if they matter, if they are real, or simply how in the twilight they are my only recourse to feel. I inscribe my soul to phantasm, and I leap across the chasm.

You are not here, you are not existent, I know this, I paint and twist, in pain bend my wrist, and I know you would not like this, but it is your very unreality that allows me to abandon my morality: Pretend that I am not a mortality, but instead that immortal being, Apollo-seen, mad anti-mortal capable of deceiving emotions and denied love. I hide myself in a story, eyes locked in a mirror that is gory, my own blood disturbing the water, an emerald nightmare of self-slaughter and lashings. Am I confused? Like Cenarius help refused, fowl corrupted being of shadows, author of this piece, why do you lie and proclaim you are fleeced? Deep in my core I knew some of what I did, felt utterly damned by how I hid, physically sick, mentally whipped, spiritually I tripped. My entire life like a blip, unnoticed by the wide world, meaningless unless I my spear hurl, or plant some new redwood burl, pillar of misty hope twixt earth and sky, the fact that here a fallen giant did lie.

Happiness is not the point, nor is health, for all those fade, but what they do for you is allow you to be made, I mean me, the one who stayed. There are many old things in this house, and part of them are me, but for all Yin is a Yang, for front side the back, all tightness has slack, all defense is also an attack. I strike myself to learn my lessons, I show my mistakes and make my confessions, each and every one of these is an important session. I may not know how yet, but I am making a bet, one with you, one with the mirror, one with confusion, one with illusion, that all lies hold truth, and that all fears come home to roost. This egg is my explosive boost.
If I was smarter or stronger, a different species, some creature who finds relief in experience not creation, if only I could be equal to my imagination. You hurt, but it is a good hurt, this is terrible, but not the worst. Like a double mobius strip, I travel to the center of the world, and traveling through that whorl I am reversed, both ending and beginning still, alternatively losing and finding my will. Are you active, do you change, how do extend your range? I think you must not be today the person I

met, but I also believe you are not set yet.

    We are living humans, never the same from day to day, fire and dust always moving our clay. A spirit, we are finding the way, between heaven and earth we are new met old, or cowards made bold; you see how we begin but no-one knows how the proteins fold, or what active powers yet remain untold. Our life a catalyst, unraveling mist, the giving and taking of all our gifts, as, hungry and thirsting for love, knowledge, and power, we dare to put forth a flower. Look at me we say, for I too may be beautiful in some way, even if I do not have a heart like yours and cannot be brave, still I will my soul to save, not serve, be the one who writes the book and not the blurb. I am not to be bought or sold, not for homes or gold, never to acquiesce only to what I am told, show me the truth, the new in the old. I am a story, a lie to be bold, but this is why we believe impossible things, so that we may the improbable carry here. Where there is life there is hope, and hope has brought life to us, a made-up muse but I must; paint with my soul to be active in the dust, show my poetry to the moon or bust. I, in emotional physics, trust.

Day 88: July 25th, 2024

To Beauty,

    I heard today that a women from my grandmother's church (the other one, the one whose mind works) has passed. How strangely people go: Sometimes fast, sometimes slow. I wonder how I shall be brought low? I hope to go like her, at least, fall, break something, pass out, hospital, two days, gone. Not as simple as fading in one's sleep, nor as grand as persevering for a cause, or expanding mankind's understanding of the universe's laws, but better that swift breaking, the sudden gaping hungry maw of entropy, then losing my mind and slowly sliding out of time. I wish to be able at least to comprehend my lines, and to earnestly appreciate a grandchild's climb, bells of beauty and symbols of rhyme. If I am to pass, I pray to any good or devil that may hear, let it be in any way but how I fear. - Lose limbs and heart, lose sick lungs and gain artificial parts, let me find holes in my head, let me lay quietly in bed, aneurysm, heart attack, beaten, bloody, bruised, tortured, but not confused; I am closer to my mind and spirit than my comfort and meat; what I fear is that immortal retreat, that I am made stone or rack, a beast like a bird or a fox. I am sure that my mind will slip some as I grow old, for I see it in all whom I know, but best it would be if that came on slow; enough that I could understand and react, a reflection for me to see it as a fact, a clear empty space and not just complete black. I don't need a silent blank, I need a notification by clack, some message sent through the air, the choice to direct my affairs, a chance to tell those whom I care for, that i do. This is all I dare to ask for, a good death, the only prayer where I will spend my breath, for I am not so certain of existence after this, even if it would be nice, and fit. Perhaps, in this multiverse where all things may happen, in this monad-land of perfection and dance, in this dream by the Lord of Nightmares, at this insignificant center of the universe, by this cycle of illusion's curse, in this cosmic brane that may burst, my life has not been, and shall not be, the worst. I did not only experience, but also acted, and the efflux of the deity was reflected by me, for I lit a candle in the dark night of black sea, on this place of blue, gold, and green; I both screamed and was seen, I changed even if only in one way, remade.
    I write these not only for happiness, I write you not only to survive, but because I have some vain sense of trying to thrive, that this is at least for a purpose, to be alive. I do not know if it shall be mine forever,

I do not know if I have the strength to match the call, but looking back I can see I stood up for at least a year before I did fall, the only way to be worthy of Valhalla's walls. Perhaps that is what I see in the vikings, and feel in the stories of their fighting, that Ragnarok comes and we shall burn, all ancient work undone, gods gone until only a family's wrath remains, along with vengeance, joy, and might upraised. - Games to be played now, but not worshiped or praised, not by the two who were protected and sustained, Yin and Yang. One day humanity shall fade, our species change, all our histories forgotten and rearranged, fate matching the feeling inside of me: That all shall pass away as if it never was, so what is the point of all this excitement and buzz, people's worry and fear of the fuzz? That the buses are late, that a man on the tv speaks of hate, that someone is given a standing ovation or shouted down, that Britain won't give back the Elgin crowns, that so many high points are now low, or how quickly the aid will flow. What does it matter, there is no point in the world, we are fools forever more, and I don't know why I should bother opening the door, or crawling another inch on my knees across the floor; what is all this struggling for?

The laws of god are not mine, and man's are but guidelines, and Buddha's are fine, but none of those books ever helped me to climb. Rather, the ones which light a fire inside, are those which are hopeless, and lick life from rime, impossible essence from the beginning of time. Iliad and Odyssey transformed, Mahabharata and Mabinogion remembered, Uruk saved in stone and Mother Earth by voice, the kind where living people make a choice, and that decision matters, because it led to the old world being shattered. At any point, Lugh or Coyote, clay or rain, Arjuna or Achilles could have lived in shame, stopped and simply said I am not to blame, for the world is stronger and strange, while I am injured and lamed, merely mortal and merry to be without fame. I am no knight of the Mark, only a farmer at home, and it is my decision never far into the world to roam. That might have been a footnote in a book, but never filled a tome, nor been friends and saviors of thrones. Perhaps one day even the memory of those books shall pass, all color leeched from them til they are clear as glass, but well before then they shall have changed the life of many a lad and a lass; like the pieces of papyrus Egyptian scribes practiced upon, clumsy in skill and power before they moved on, leaving their trash behind, and yet that trash is the foundation of every line after, all the language of endless clatter.

If we are all doomed anyway, if we are all forgotten anyway, if we are all abandoned anyway, if each and every one of us is weighed as unworthy and eaten, let us at least not journey to the abyss as one of the beaten. I have so little hope and such a grand despair, yet against the laws and lone powers of the universe, I shall care. - And even if I am damned and aware of a god's curse and stare, there is still some devil in me which is not made to be meek, and while existing shall attempt to seek, and forever dare to peek, beyond the bath of western stars and behind the curtain of physical laws; spiritually, mentally, impossibly, expanding the limits of the world, and not accepting what I am told, like a berserker mad in the cold, with a light from me bright and bold. If I am to die, let em not die like a sheep, my soul with the strength of a man and a beast, like a forlorn hope of a feast when strong men drink together, for the parting is at dawn, and I ask myself would I rather like down and wait, or continue on? I fight! Make no mistake, this is not with blood and iron, but with words and a soul, for I am flesh fighting dust and mold. A fool I am forever more, but one with a dream: May I be more than I, to me, seem. Perhaps in some stupid way someday I will gleam: Can you see the silver wing's sheen? We are humans - against this falling world we lean, and make a valiant, defiant, scream.

Day 89: July 26th, 2024

To Beauty,

    I have no wish to condemn someone for their ethics, though I think some people are fools, because rhetoric is too often used as a tool. How odd to be concerned with right or wrong, when ere long, history will be the judge of that song. Did you sing high or low, fast or slow, did you head upstairs or walk down below? All great conquerors are also thieves, for few are the saints living in deed, who never evidenced some religious greed or instructional creed - who are the ones that only did what they need, and never on some other poor sap did feed? I do not know them, I do not see, for they are quickly forgotten like the roots of a tree; the great mass of solid humanity who did survive, even when floods rose or thunder fell out of the sky. Columbus or Cortez may have led death and destruction to the door of the west, but if they were alone in their endeavors, then they would never have managed to do what they did next, and burned and pillaged those who failed their terrible test: Of blood and iron and steel vest, sickness and a sorrow which shall not be less than their ancestors before the Viking, the Moor, the Hun, the Mongol, the Romans, the Persians, the Akkadians, the Egyptians, and so on and on back into the mists of time, when even as proto-monkeys we hid and cried. This is an endless story of subjugation and death by a tribe upon a tribe, or of warriors upon the scribes. Even China once tried to burn all the books, lest anyone should try to look, and thus dispute the official story, bringing black repute upon the emperor and his people, treating them like real and short-sighted men who make mistakes, instead of what they themselves think they are, a people holy and great.

    Now, for my part I fail to see why one part of humanity should be better than any other simply because they were the victor or the victim, the strong or the weak, the lion or the meek. My question instead is, what did they seek? Is this like 1967 histeria, 1948 tribalism, 1991 negligence, 2023, what is this? I can see both sides, in a way, but one of them is organized and the other has no sway, while people on both sides manage to pray. Some poor fool volunteers to help the cats, while others swing them around on their tail like bats, some people wear hardhats, while others simply attack. How shall we tell in the mixture the good from the bad, the smart from the sad, the real from the fake, the lying from the intentional mistake? It can be quite fascinating what unclassified government documents reveal, the minutes of meetings, the deep confusion and strange delusions. One book I read contained not a single voice from the other side, while others report a matching of minds. Yet, I think all remain in some ways silent; life is violent, and light comes through destruction, through the ground shudderings, through atomic muttering, carried by photonic bouncing. Back and forth, this is good, that bad, here injured, there sad, merely upset, or deeply mad, you would think that of freed knowledge all would be glad, but instead so many hide, and in shadows are clad with dark lines where they decide what's fine, allowed, 'reasonable and obvious'. They aren't vicious, they're defending themselves, and each tribe says this of themselves. I doubt the entire story each one tells, so I think it's a little strange to buy what only one side sells, and pretend that the other one is made up of things from hell.

In reality, if there is such a thing, atrocities and weaknesses will forever each other bring, like a fool standing under a beehive slapping at the stings. Move or destroy all the options we with insects have, but there are other choices when the enemy is a man, because women can talk and children can play, even as they don't entirely understand what the other is trying to say. Why do we expect more of the babes than the grown, what is it that brings us to trust in one source alone? A pillar of the world this fact seems to us, a rock on which we may trust, the beginning of a saber thrust into the heart of morality, ending its complexity and turning it into a dead document, like a book, a temple, or a wall, that which we are held up by as we fall or fail.

We appear to be addicted to the fig leaf, our shamed humanity which refuses to meet out in the open, vulnerable and clear, we are afraid of our enemy being too near. I wonder, what is it like to live without fear, to sit across from a man who tried to kill you and drink a beer? I have done that, or near enough, when I confronted my own youthful demons in the rough, and realized it's nothing much. Disagreements, or actions I had to take, the question is, now, today, would you double down on your stake? What sort of future are you willing to make?

No-one trusts the other, or so it seems, each side thinking they can eat all of the cream, never mind the millions and billions who scream. There are too many complications, I know I see only half of each of the nations, as I sit in my Grandfather's chair and station, surrounded by books, and stories into which I've deeply looked; like a man on the outside of an oven which cooks, as rising dough hides bubbles inside, I judge by the crust, and if I need to know better, than I must pierce the veil of secrecy and propaganda, with pictures like jade, and limits of light beyond which I've strayed; like someone lying in a bed of nails they made, pierced and cut but willing to suffer and stay, because for some reason I think the reward is worth the blood I pay, as I draw a picture and my own pesky past slay. If I stand up in front of you, are you willing to play, or shall we change and seek a better day? Look at what I do, not what I say, for actions are louder than words, and trust only comes to those who with patience have heard, seen the truth within the lies, and looked with clear eyes, not ones clouded with condemnation or pride. From my own actions I think I may not hide, nor tell convincing lies, even as I obscure the truth inside, and paradoxically, almost fly. Don't clap your hands, merely look and try, understanding the parents and kids as they cry, waving to last virtue goodbye.

Day 90: July 27th, 2024

To Beauty,

    I'm sure I'm afraid to start, because there is another section to this march, the creation of three hundred pieces or art, and my voice speaking from the heart. Every day I walk past the stage, then turn my back to the page, my chalkboard sign of rage. All is ready and prepared, the chalk, the camera, the stairs, and my upset affairs; hair short now so I may learn over and see, raised waist-high so I don't have to crawl on my knees, and the space to do what I want, no need to ask anyone please. Here is my chance to work and release, to fulfill my needs and realize creation, and to attempt to leave my damned station where I have stayed now for too many days, telling myself that it's no that I'm afraid, but simply that there is other work which has to first be paid, paintings, ideas, and pages which first should be made, a backlog of 'just in case', the knowledge that I've written enough that this isn't a mistake. Can I do this every day, or will the moment come where it all fades? What power I have is borrowed; most of my poems are repeated sorrows; I make no plans or preparation for tomorrow. There are many reasons I write these mainly at night, because of procrastination, or waiting for inspiration, or perhaps I need a desperate instantiation, the awareness that I don't go to sleep until I've finished this creation and spoken to you, a resting mitigation of the screaming inside, twenty-four hours of preparation to reduce my pride, and a rhyming horse who I can follow outside. For I feel that many the reason for the rhythm of this text is that I have no understanding of what to write next, for I am lost screaming outside, or lost speaking in tongues before the tide, or lost in silence attempting to hide, only glancing at beauty and myself from the side instead of directly through the eyes.

    I would stare and lose all thought, so I look away though I ought not. Often I lose track of why I've fought, or feel: What's the point of all I've got? I think it amounts to some two hundred and seventy thousand words at this point, comprising either one or four and a third books, almost all of them slightly out of joint, like modern poetry which is so often broken arbitrarily and badly put together. I'm sure all of my zero readers are aware, that my beauty is in the blood, not the air. It's not how you read, or whether you stare, but rather all and entire in what do you care. Does this move you or change the world, is there a point to the

Padawan braid in my hair, what is the test, what is the dare? Do I write to be read or understood in my head, am I a raging torrent or a gentle river fallow in its bed, am I becoming alive or already half-dead? I write to you so that I may be fed; I await a signal of hope instead of doing my own work, because many years ago I wore a hundred thousand words of a different sort of book: Some philosophical half-baked outlook, of worlds and realms, of logics and if-thens, which are really more like movements in games of Gen. - Rules which are incomplete, but where the very point of their mistakes is what is most about them neat, the reason why paradoxes can be beat. This text has sat there in readiness for six months waiting for me to sit down and finish it; half the preparation has been completed, but somehow even starting on it I feel depleted, because I do not know how to be creative and sane at the same time; I don't feel like I can tell truth except in rhyme, if true things even exist and are not only lies turned outside, crystals with cracked hides.

Some of what I consider my more mysterious pronouncements are based from these serious accounts, two months in Finland where I tried to pounce, and five months at home where I hit the bottom of the world then bounced. I feel I have so little strength on my own, because I mentioned this book to fifteen people on the phone, and no-one asked to take a look, or was even curious as to what it was about. I realized I was writing to myself, just a void to a void shout, some idea shut away from the earth, the planet, and the heart, some self-masturbation without purpose or art, this one set from other humans apart. Perhaps this is why I fear to start, to move on and release my song, to speak, and be heard, and be wrong. Talking to you gives me strength to continue on, and I'm afraid, not of rejection but disgust, or silence, or mistrust, a terrible violence done to me which I invited in: A swift, cutting, empty wind.

Every day I say to myself, I can do this Beauty, I can do this, when I want to snap at Grandma for what she does, or cry because she won't eat the food I cooked, (it's so hard for her to gain weight); when I hear a recording of me speaking and am disgusted, freaking, hearing every mispronounced and mismade word, every too-loud breath, or ill-placed burr. When I climb the hill to fix the water and my side hurts, when the plants I put in the greenhouse die, when I hear of other people who to Heaven and Hell fly, or when I read sad books and feel a deep sigh. Look, I say it as I write and be tired, in the weeds of singular sentences are mired, or when I am, (I repeat), utterly, completely, indelibly, tired. I travel in circles, some long, some short, some spirals up and some down, but never in one place for long, even if I have to crawl and croak out a song. Dumb frog in a well, singing as if anyone would be here, or understand and not ridicule the depths of my fear, or how I am slowly, ever so slowly, to the next gate drawing near. I don't know what to do next, where to hurry, how to flow, which way to grow. I cannot see myself in ten years, I have no cares, I have no fears, except for that of fear itself; I have no enemies but my shelf, wooden and filled with cobwebs, til you cannot see the spin inside, and only vaguely have a sense that something in the shadows doth hide, like a poison spider or a scorpion ready to sting, and if I am left alone too long that might be what I bring. So I cut myself, not literally, but I beat my ears like an elf, saying this land is not for me, I should pass away beyond the sea, and never speak any more of thee. I so often feel it may be better to flee, to fight not fear or empty entropy,

    You are not the cause, I think, simply a beautiful key, but it is that lock opening which might set me free. Who might I be? Can I draw and set the signal alight? May I paint legends of you and fight? Will I create and move though the circles of fright? If I spread my wings, where shall be my flight? Is this dawn or dusk, day or night, slice or a bite? Burn my flesh, a light.

Day 91: July 28th, 2024

To Beauty,

    I feel trapped between the future and the past; I don't know how long this state of where I am may last. I galavant between who I was and who I wish to be, because I feel inadequate in this moment of me, lost and purposeless upon the sea. The problem of course is I do not know, and am blinded by the snow. The purpose of these writings is to move between above and below, so that I may know what I may show; how deep within me is the flow, and what are my most obvious flaws? Courage and honesty, I imagine, because a score of ninety-nine is not one hundred, nor is it effective to bring happiness and light, or show me the best ways for my soul to fight. I write this, to you, every night, but I hide, too, because I imagine I am talking to someone, but don't follow through, exactly like that one time I disassociated the night before we flew, and for the same reasons, too. I am scared, and cannot tell the truth, or admit my curiosity forsooth; maybe instead of asking about a necklace I should have inquired about your youth, or what you sought, or wished, or saw, or thought; surely I could have managed a deeper inquiry, done myself a mightier injury, engaged in embarrassment and not perjury!

    Who I am is slow, careful not to let my true heart show, for I will question all, with fire and flame I'll rewrite my name: I'll treat every ethical and physical dilemma as a game, I dare all in my private mind, but none in public shame, because if I tell people they'll look at me as if I am insane. A light in every corner, a darkness in every page, I have within me some deep, embittered rage, the mentality of a sage, the iron fact of a page, the cold necessity of a purge. It has been said that the most terrible of all human beings is a good man, and that is what I have endeavored to be for many a year, hammering at truth and lies until they are somewhat clear, and allowing no-one else whatsoever near. I wrote a book, but did not suggest to anyone that they read it. I made artwork, but did not say what I drew. I gathered stormclouds and wind, but did not say which direction I blew. I write to you but dare not inscribe a name, I make plans, but to my shame, I follow through only a quarter of the time; I have not painted a picture yet, only written bad rhymes. It is unlikely that in the next year I will die, but if I happened to pass, would I be proud of all that I have tried, or will I say to the gatekeeper that I should have done more before I died? I'm sorry, you see, I was tired, with less and less inspiration every day, and no guide who I understood could show me the way, because for all the many who promised, their powers had no sway, simply being conversations between Screwtape and Wormwood on how me to slay, and what move next to force me to play. I saw them coming, and so I decided to stay, I decided that my movement was going to be acting like dried clay, stuck in the bucket to be used up another day. I feel I saw the cares of the world and walked away, saying I don't see the point of being merry, happy, and gay, or even that the straightened path had a point which might last, instead of disappearing in some sudden gasp.

    Why should I wish some other's hand to clasp? Better alone, let someone else find me at my home, some solid land with high walls and good house, perhaps a pet dog or mouse, during those far-off days where I was a person, and not a louse. Someone loud by being quiet, and when I would have a life that was vibrant, but in searching for that, all I found was violence: Inflicted upon myself, not a cut but a bruise, not a free mind but instead forbearing to choose. My head was down staring at my shoes, my eyes were blinded by the darkness inside, I was merely attempting to survive. It's easy to give up when even living is hard, it's simple to work and not create, it's obvious to not try when nothing you make could ever be great. I am a youth trying to act like others because I grew up late, I learned but never made my own mistakes. Instead, I write them into a story. I imagined that somewhere out there might be glory: Better a life of peace then one that is bloody and gory. I so often put on my normal mask, but all that gets me is a C in the class. Oh, sure, I pass, but not in a way that will last. Ten years in the future, nothing to do, nothing to leave, only me and not knowing what I believe. I put down notes, but never place together the leaves, and have no reason for any wish to say please. I repeat myself made the least, I cover up the face of the beast.

    Now in my book there are many forbidden words, and many forbidden visions I have learned, flashing before my eyes before I close them and turn my head aside, saying: I didn't see that, I didn't think that, I didn't feel that, I never had a wish, I never had a want, I never had a need, I never was someone with greed, I pinch myself and say to myself: This is merely a dream, don't try to be happy, don't dare to say a word. You could never be heard, accept your hurt, the sun is not for you nor light nor hope, for if you have a shield of love you also possess a sword of rage, the likes of which is not beautiful upon the page. Better to be armless, weaponless, heartless, aimless, then nothingness.

Continued in Part 2

Quote References

1. From a poem called "The last ally" by William Rose Benet. Found in Poems for Modern Youth by Adolph Gillis and William Rose Benet, published 1938 by the Houghton Mifflin Company and The Riverside Press of Cambridge, Massechusets. P.g. 331.
2. From the book "Magic Bites" by Illona Andrews, ch. 5. ISBN: 9781429569811
3. From a poem called "The last ally" by William Rose Benet.
4. From the Hunter x Hunter manga by Yoshihiro Togashi, Greed Island arc.
5. From a poem called "Ulysses" by Alfred Lord Tennyson. Found in Poems for Modern Youth P.g. 338
6. From the comic "Calvin and Hobbes" by Bill Watterson. Comic for Febuary 19th, 1998. An example may be found here: https://www.gocomics.com/calvinand-hobbes/1988/02/19
7. From a poem called "School" by Winifred Welles. Found in Poems for Modern Youth by Adolph Gillis and William Rose Benet. P.g. 414
8. From a poem called "Alone" By Edgar Allen Poe. An exampel may be found here: https://www.poetryfoundation.org/poems/46477/alone-56d2265f2667d
9. From a poem called "The fall of Gil-galad" by J.R.R. Tolkien in The Lord of the Rings, Vol. I: The Fellowship of the Ring, Book One, Chapter XI: "A Knife in the Dark".
10. Apparently I didn't remember the quote correctly. It is a paraphrase of this line: "Jame bit her lip. Did her loyalty lie with the dead or with the living? To ask the question is to answer it." From Ch 8 Sec. 2 of Honor's PAradox by P.C. Hodgell. ISBN: 9781451637625
11. This is a song lyric I rememeber from somewhere, but I was unable to determine what song it was.
12. From the song "Give a Reason" sung by Megumi Hayashibara in the OP to the anime Slayers NEXT, released 1996. This is not the offical translation, but the work of a fansub group marked as 'a-S', circa sometime before 2008.
13. This is a quote attributed online to the book Meditations by Marcus Aurelius, but seems to actually be a mix of lines from two seperate sections: 7.56, and 8.57
14. From the poem "For a' that' by Robert Burns. Found in Poems for Modern Youth P.g. 206
15. From the poem "Ode on a grecian urn" by John Keats. Found in Poems for Modern Youth P.g. 213
16. From "The American Scholar Address" by Ralph Waldo Emerson.
17. From a poem called "Courage" by Karle Wilson Baker

Pictoral References
Day 75 p.g. 211: Depiction of a Roman marble bust

Courage is armor
A blind man wears;
The calloused scar
Of outlived despairs:
Courage is Fear
That has said its prayers[17]

www.ingramcontent.com/pod-product-compliance
Lightning Source LLC
Chambersburg PA
CBHW071704160426
43195CB00012B/1571